MEETINGS WITH MALLARMÉ
in contemporary French culture

Michael Temple is a lecturer in French at Birkbeck College, London. His previous book, *The Name of the Poet: Onomastics and Anonymity in the Work of Stéphane Mallarmé*, was published by University of Exeter Press 1995.

From reviews of *The Name of the Poet:*

'. . . a solid hermeneutic theory from within which we are enabled the better to contemplate the manifold mysteries of Mallarmé.'
Times Literary Supplement

'Much of the pleasure of this book lies in Temple's convivial imitation of Mallarmé's theoretical teasing . . .'
Modern Language Review

MEETINGS
WITH
MALLARMÉ

in contemporary French culture

edited by Michael Temple

UNIVERSITY
of
EXETER
PRESS

First published in 1998 by
University of Exeter Press
Reed Hall, Streatham Drive
Exeter, Devon EX4 4QR
UK

Cover photograph © Shigeko Kubota,
courtesy of the John Cage Trust.

British Library Cataloguing in Publication Data
A catalogue record of this book is available from the British Library

Paperback ISBN 0 85989 562 9
Hardback ISBN 0 85989 561 0

Typeset in Caslon by Kestrel Data, Exeter

Printed and bound in Great Britain by
Short Run Press Ltd, Exeter

Contents

et on a cru à quelqu'influence tentée par moi, là où il n'y a eu que des rencontres

[and people believed in some influence on my part where in fact there were merely encounters]

Notes on contributors

Geoffrey Bennington is Professor of French and Director of the Centre for Modern French Thought at the University of Sussex. His publications include *Jacques Derrida* (Éditions du Seuil, 1991) with Jacques Derrida, and *Legislations* (Verso, 1994).

Malcom Bowie is Marshal Foch Professor of French Literature at the University of Oxford. He is the author of *Mallarmé and the Art of Being Difficult* (Cambridge University Press, 1978) and *Lacan* (Fontana/Harvard University Press, 1991).

Patrick ffrench is Lecturer in French at University College London. He is the author of *The Time of Theory: A History of Tel Quel* (Oxford University Press, 1995) and the co-editor of *The Tel Quel Reader* (Routledge, 1998).

Michael Holland is Lecturer in French at St Hugh's College, Oxford, and a founding editor of the journal *Paragraph*. He is the editor of *The Blanchot Reader* (Blackwell, 1995).

Rachel Killick is Senior Lecturer and Head of French at the University of Leeds. She has published widely on nineteenth-century poetry and fiction and is French editor of the *Modern Language Review*.

Charles D. Minahen is Professor of French at Ohio State University. He is the co-editor of *Situating Sartre in Twentieth-Century Thought and Culture* (1997).

Clive Scott is Professor of European Literature at the University of East Anglia. His most recent book is *The Poetics of French Verse: Studies in Reading* (Oxford University Press, 1998).

Michael Temple is Lecturer in French at Birkbeck College, London, and the author of *The Name of the Poet: Onomastics and Anonymity in the Works of Stéphane Mallarmé* (University of Exeter Press, 1995).

Rei Terada is Associate Professor of English at the University of Michigan, and the author of *Derek Walcott's Poetry* (Northwestern University Press, 1992).

Burhan Tufail is a founding editor of the journal *Interstice* and has published on contemporary French and American literature.

Kate van Orden is an Assistant Professor in the Music Department at the University of California, Berkeley, who specializes in French lyric poetry and music. She also performs and records early music on period instruments.

Acknowledgements

I should like to extend my thanks to Roland-François Lack, James Williams, Burhan Tufail and Patrick Pollard for their help in preparing this text, and to participants in the Mallarmé Study Group for their advice and encouragement.

1

'M'introduire dans ton histoire'

Michael Temple

> et quant à lui, je pense qu'il considérait mon étonnement, sans
> étonnement[1]

There are many good reasons for producing in 1998 a volume entitled *Meetings with Mallarmé in contemporary French culture*. Most obvious of these is a simple matter of timing, for the year will have marked the centenary of the first and most authentic of the poet's many disappearances, which we have ceaselessly re-enacted and inexhaustibly interpreted ever since that violent surprise at Valvins, in 1898, when Mallarmé was still only fifty-six years old:

> C'est notre plus grand poète. Un passionné, un furieux. Et maître
> de lui jusqu'à pouvoir se tuer par un simple mouvement de la
> glotte![2]

> (He is our greatest poet. A fanatic, a madman. And master of
> his destiny to the point of being able to kill himself by a simple
> movement of the glottis!)

The rehearsal of that moment signifies today that, with patience and passion, we have been reading Mallarmé for more than a century now. Nor is there much indication that our curiosity has begun to wane. In fact, one could reasonably argue that Mallarmé's power to attract and retain our attention has steadily grown over these past one hundred years.

It is true that during the three or four decades immediately following his death there seems to have been a respectful pause in those attentions, as if as readers we were afraid to acknowledge that there had actually existed a man called Stéphane Mallarmé, who had performed certain irrevocable acts on the sacred and ancient practice we call Letters, and then quite treacherously had disappeared in an act of sharp brutality that seemed to contradict his benignly enigmatic presence. The signature he made and the signs he left behind suddenly took on such a vertiginous aspect that, timidly, we preferred to look down or away, consoled by the sure knowledge that, soon enough, some new meteoric figure would appear to thrill and guide us in our symbolic vagaries, be they decadent, modernist, futurist . . . be they, for the purposes of our historical argument, surrealist or neoclassical. Thus it is that circa 1920, despite (or, more probably, because of) Paul Valéry's proud advocacy of a certain *méthode Mallarmé* that he exemplified in his critical discourse and poetic practice, one scarcely gets the impression that masses of young versifiers were eagerly signing up for lessons. Especially when the *cours Rimbaud* was offering crash courses in automatic genius and sensory deregulation at heavily discounted prices (i.e. painless, artless, and largely interest-free). This is perhaps why, in retrospect, we are pleasantly struck by Francis Ponge's statement in 'Notes d'un poème (sur Mallarmé)' that 'en 1926 [Mallarmé] n'a pas encore beaucoup servi, sinon beaucoup aux poètes, pour se parler à eux-mêmes'[3] ('in 1926 Mallarmé hasn't yet much been used, except a lot by poets, to speak to themselves'). A solitary reader in the company of an absent friend, Ponge portrays himself listening to Mallarmé as if the poet were his mysterious other half virtually speaking the words he, Ponge, might have spoken himself:

> Il [Mallarmé] a créé un outil antilogique. Pour vivre, pour lire et écrire. Contre le gouvernement, les philosophes, les poètes-penseurs. Avec la dureté de leur matière logique . . . Plus tard on en viendra à faire servir Mallarmé comme proverbes.[4]

> (He [Mallarmé] created an antilogical instrument. To live with, to read and write with. Against government, philosophers, and poet-philosophers. With the hardness of their logical matter . . . In the future, people will use Mallarmé as material for proverbs.)

Later, in a future we still occupy, Mallarmé was indeed to lend his proverbial powers to all sorts of poetic tasks and intellectual causes, his spidery network spreading steadily after 1945, from which significant point we can date the replacement of Valéry (a deep thinker but easily circumscribed) by Maurice Blanchot (a scatter-shot intellectual, like Georges Bataille) as the key symbolic purveyor of Mallarmé's influence.

It is not the ambition of the current collection to write an exhaustive, and fatally exhausting, history of Mallarmean critique or inspiration. We have tried in these exploratory essays to represent some of the more suggestive intellectual and cultural paths that Mallarmé's posthumous glory has illuminated, as well as to identify some of the great minds, artistic and philosophical, who have met him en route. However, in terms of Mallarmean topology, this book is certainly more of an *herbier* than an *atlas*, and much territory will remain unrepresented, if not wilfully ignored. Our aim will be to focus on a group of ten crucial 'meetings with Mallarmé in contemporary French culture', with a view to saying something original and exciting both about Mallarmé's diverse range of inheritors and about the curious process of cultural influence itself. For intellectual history to exist, as someone once said, we would first need some intelligent historians. The spirit presiding over this collection will therefore be open to contradiction as much as to coherence (great minds do not always think alike), and to error as much as to truth (missing is often more productive than meeting). The neatest illustration of a Mallarmean 'missing', which contains nonetheless an important methodological lesson, must be the following anecdote recounted by Henri de Régnier:

> Assidu aux concerts du dimanche, il m'arrivait souvent d'être assis auprès d'un auditeur qui ressemblait trait pour trait à l'effigie que Manet avait peint de Mallarmé et, trompé par cette ressemblance, j'étais persuadé qu'un hasard merveilleux me donnait pour voisin le poète que j'admirais. Ah! ce Mallarmé imaginaire, avec quelle curiosité, avec quel respect je le regardais à la dérobée! Que j'eusse désiré lui parler, lui dire ma ferveur de jeune rimeur, mais j'en étais empêché par ma timidité, et, à la sortie du concert, je me contentais de le suivre dans la rue pour l'apercevoir un moment encore![5]

3

(As a regular at the Sunday concerts, I often found myself seated next to a spectator who looked just like the image of Mallarmé painted by Manet, and, fooled by this resemblance, I was persuaded that a marvellous chance had given me for a neighbour the poet I admired. Oh! that imaginary Mallarmé, I discreetly watched him with such curiosity and respect! How I would have loved to speak to him, and tell him about my young poet's enthusiasm, but I was prevented from doing so by my timidity, and, as I left the concert, I contented myself with following him in the street just to see him a little longer!)

What makes this story both beautiful and true is the sequence and interplay of will and illusion. I fall for a picture of Mallarmé, and fall so profoundly that I project his image onto my unsuspecting partner, but this illusion I create is in turn so powerful that I am too scared to enjoy it, and in the end prefer, erotically and knowingly, to watch it fade away. My pleasure, deferred, will come in the later renegotiation of this failure. Little matter, in other words, whether Maurice Blanchot and Julia Kristeva (or our contributors Michael Holland and Patrick ffrench) ultimately get Mallarmé right. It is *how* they got or get him that is of interest, and *what* they get, expectedly or unexpectedly, in the process of exchange. Perhaps the most extreme illustration of such an exchange occurs in Malcolm Bowie's 'Lacan and Mallarmé: Theory as Word-Play'. In no conventional sense was the psychoanalyst a Mallarmean critic (he does not write texts about his reading of the poet), and yet Bowie demonstrates most persuasively that there is something going on—an affair, a deal—between the two figures. It is a process wherein Mallarmé appears interstitially in momentary flashes—semantic, syntactic, symbolic—as if in advance to illuminate our textual experience of the *Écrits*, and at the same time to imprint upon our blinking eyes an after-image of Lacan, which, when we return to the Mallarmean text, will insist and endure. Our observer, Bowie, watches over this slightly murky encounter, between the poet and the analyst, with a sharp eye for detail and, gradually and ultimately, no little sense of principled anxiety: is Lacan getting Mallarmé to execute a job that even his reputation for scandal could not contain, or is Mallarmé taking Lacan for a ride by passing on some distinctly unreliable linguistic information? So this critical position, in which we all must find ourselves, threatens also to expose us, rather as if a two-way mirror were suddenly to disappear and reveal us as fantasizers as well as observers of meetings which, after all, never really took place.

This basic structure, which obtains in each of the chapters you are about to read, may effectively be illustrated by the photograph on the following page:[6]

> Cette photographie m'a été donnée par Degas, dont on voit l'appareil et le fantôme dans le miroir. Mallarmé est debout auprès de Renoir sur le divan. Degas leur a infligé une pose de 15 minutes à la lumière de neuf lampes à pétrole.

> (This photograph was given to me by Degas, whose camera and ghost one can see in the mirror. Mallarmé is standing next to Renoir, who is on the couch. Degas subjected them to a fifteen minute pose under the glare of nine paraffin-lamps.)

The phantom and the instrument. This is as close as we shall get to catching Mallarmé in a natural pose. He is photographed in the company of Auguste Renoir by a third significant player, Edgar Degas, who is perceptible behind the flash of his instrument, which in turn is captured intentionally or accidentally in the salon mirror. Two other faces, two further gazes, may also just be identified in the reflection. They are Madame and Mademoiselle Mallarmé, who might be seen, I suggest, as occupying the critical position proposed to you, the reader of this collection. This suggestion is confirmed by the revelation that this whole scene or set-up had already been sketched out for us, by Mallarmé himself, in the *éventail* poems he addressed, precisely, to Geneviève, his daughter, and his wife, Marie:

> Rien qu'un battement aux cieux
> Le futur vers se dégage
> . . .
> Cet éventail si c'est lui
> Le même par qui derrière
> Toi quelque miroir a lui[7]

(Nought but a flapping in the air / Will the future verse now emerge / . . . / This fan if indeed it is he / Whose reflection in the mirror / Behind you flickering we see)

Stéphane Mallarmé and Auguste Renoir photographed by Edgar Degas
(courtesy of Bibliothèque de France).

Why is it that whatever precautions we adopt, and however carefully we prepare the terrain, Mallarmé is always one step ahead? The future instrument and the passive ghost will always conspire to hoist me by what I had thought was my own petard. So am I, then, a mere plodder? Am I some sweaty Chief Inspector, panting behind the impervious Dupin?

*   *   *

Clearly emerging from such confusion and uncertainty, two questions will now concern me more personally in this introductory essay. What is a *meeting with Mallarmé*? And in what sense can I be Mallarmé's *contemporary*? In order to discuss these issues, let us focus on a sonnet written by Mallarmé in the late 1880s. Since it only comprises one hundred and twelve syllables, I shall quote them in all their blazing, crepuscular glory:

> M'introduire dans ton histoire
> C'est en héros effarouché
> S'il a du talon nu touché
> Quelque gazon de territoire
>
> A des glaciers attentatoire
> Je ne sais le naïf péché
> Que tu n'auras pas empêché
> De rire très haut sa victoire
>
> Dis si je ne suis pas joyeux
> Tonnerre et rubis aux moyeux
> De voir en l'air que ce feu troue
>
> Avec des royaumes épars
> Comme mourir pourpre la roue
> Du seul vespéral de mes chars[8]

(Entering into your story / It's as a hero who's afraid / Of prints with bare heels he has made / On some verdant territory // I don't know what innocent sin / To melt the most frigid coward / You will not have disempowered / From singing its victory hymn // O say am I not overjoyed / With thunder and rubies

7

bejewelled / To see that this red burning void // Its royal realms
scattered afar / By the dead purple wheels was fuelled / Of my
unique vesperal car)

If we put together the photograph and the poem, what sort of a
meeting, what sort of a co-presence or simultaneity is taking place
here? As spokesperson for the various contributors to *Meetings with
Mallarmé in contemporary French culture*, I should first say that most
of us met Mallarmé a long time ago. For my own part, I remember
reading 'Brise marine' in a suburban gutter in 1981. It was my
eighteenth birthday. A concerned stranger came up to me and
enquired if I was all right. I said I was then, and I still am now. In
the intervening years, I have grown used to such interruptions of my
concentrated efforts. Whether your name is Paul Valéry or Michael
Temple, you first met Mallarmé what seems already like a lifetime
ago. It may have been in 1842 or 1942, it may have been in 1898 or
1998. It may have been no more than an instant, at any time during
those fifty-six or one hundred and fifty-six unreal years. And whether
your name is Maurice Blanchot or Michael Holland, Rei Terada or
Paul de Man, you will have sometimes wondered if you ever met
Mallarmé at all. One thing most of us know for sure is that we have
all recited to his absent corpse the very words he chose for Théophile
Gautier in similarly mortal circumstances:

> Ton apparition ne va pas me suffire:
> Car je t'ai mis, moi-même, en un lieu de porphyre[9]

(Your apparition to me will not suffice / For I put you, myself,
in a porphyrous place)

We know, therefore, that we've been dealing mainly with a ghost.
And we've learnt that, whatever your science or your patience, you
cannot tell a ghost when to enter, or when to exit. If you see him
now you're happy, but you're hardly surprised if you don't.

So how, in 1998, can reading 'M'introduire dans ton histoire'
prepare me for this fresh encounter? For another necessarily un-
predictable meeting? And how, in these introductory pages, can it
help me prepare the ground for the series of intellectual summits
to follow? For instance: Mallarmé/Derrida/(and Bennington);

Mallarmé/Sartre/(and Minahen); Mallarmé/Boulez/(and van Orden)? And so on. Structurally, this will always look a little like the same encounter. But equally, the one figure common to every encounter will precisely be the one who isn't quite there. So the common denominator is more like an *x*, marking the treasure-spot. For Mallarmé, of course, that *x* takes the form of an *M*. As we discover in the cited instance:

> *M*'introduire dans ton histoire
> C'est en héros effarouché
> S'il a du talon nu touché
> Quelque gazon de territoire

Most of my actual difficulties may be perceived in these four lines. It may be the case that by translating them into something that looks like English and sounds like verse (as above), I have done the best I can in the circumstances. But the present occasion demands something more substantial than verse, it requires a more scholarly gesture, a more grounded tone. As we can see in the quatrain, however, touching down in this fashion is often an uneasy matter and a scary moment, even for a literary hero such as Stéphane Mallarmé. Without making immodest comparisons, I must in some measure identify or confuse myself with that *M* of the opening line:

> *M*'introduire dans ton histoire

If Mallarmé is somewhat startled at the idea of entering into an amorous relation, I might feel similar alarm at the prospect of introducing myself into Mallarmé, or introducing him into some kind of critical relation or literary history. Nor would I be the first to wonder at the implausibility of such an introduction:

> Y a-t-il une *place* pour Mallarmé dans une 'histoire de la littérature'? Et d'abord, autrement: son texte a-t-il lieu, son lieu, dans quelque tableau de la littérature française? dans un tableau? de la littérature? française?[10]

> (Is there a *place* for Mallarmé in a 'history of literature'? And firstly, in other words: does his text take place, its place, in some tableau of French literature? in a tableau? of French? literature?)

9

It is comforting to see a big thinker such as Derrida disingenuously exposing himself in this fashion. Like the philosopher, I am startled by the double prospect of a certain implausibility and a certain responsibility, a certain frivolity and a certain gravity. I am troubled by a certain demand for certainty, when frankly I'd rather show a clean pair of heels. Suddenly, however, that *M* of the opening line looks like a good place to be. It is *M* for 'me' and it is *M* for 'Mallarmé'! Yes, the mere name of the poet still holds for me this powerful magnetic fascination, its empire extending back into infinity —an infinity of study, patience, and doubt—starting with what appears, on paper at least, to be the simplest signpost of all.[11] So when Stéphane Mallarmé thus introduces himself into my story, I always have to look twice, and then once more. In the present circumstances, this double-take of mine vacillates between the gravity of the scholarly task I face and the humble fan's confusion when faced with the poet's renown. But as I look in this way at Mallarmé today, with a brief both to introduce him to a world of new readers and to reintroduce him to a host of star names—de Man, Kristeva, Lacan, to cite just three of the brightest—I hear the poet speak these avuncular words of advice: 'Think, when you see the initials *S.M.*, of *smith* and *smile*, of hard work and humour. Think, by all means, of *le sourire*, but also of the *forgeron*, whose craft and graft will always outwit your average æsthete or exegete.'[12] Following this counsel, then, to conduct ourselves both seriously and modestly, let us look hard again at 'M'introduire dans ton histoire' and ask ourselves how the Mallarmean presence floating there might help this matter of introduction.

I should firstly remark that there have always been a number of specifically readerly issues which both trouble and excite me in this poem, not least because I demand of their fragile stature that they support much vaster questions of textuality, interpretation, and intellectual speculation. When I noted, for instance, in *The Name of the Poet*, that the poem appears to contain two striking examples of what I had come to call 'signatures' encrypted within the texture of the sonnet, I found I was concerned as much as I was comforted by yet another impressive proof of my onomastic thesis:

> That first *M*, [I wrote], its apostrophe marking an absence,
> demands of the reader the rest of the name, which is duly

supplied at the end of line 2, thanks to the synonym of
'effarouché': <M' (alarmé)>. In the context of the poem,
Mallarmé feigns a display of alarm and unconvincing resistance
(either before the advances of a lover or faced with the
approaching interpretive ardour of the critic) both of which will
soon yield, as the conceit unfolds, to the easy victory of the
pretended opponent and the spectacular joy of the closing sunset
or sonnet. (89–90)

To this I appended a note that 'there is also an embracing or framing
signature from the first to the last line, since the initial *M* is met in
the bottom right corner by the other constituent parts of the
signature: "Du seul vespér*al* de *mes* ch*ars*" revealing "*al . . . ar . . .
mé . . .*" ' (169). But why should they scare me, these harmless
onomastic observations, why should they cause me to stumble? Might
they not smile approvingly at my tentative approaches, or indeed
solicit curiously my closer attentions? At the time I advanced
hestitatingly, yet fearless, and ultimately the doubt thus lodged in my
mind proved itself both instructive and admonitory, since it served
to check my nascent hermeneutic urge with warnings of future
ridicule (the signatory flourish as flash rather than system) whilst also
helping me to reflect more keenly on a set of problems vital both to
this particular poem and to the critical domain I was generally
exploring: authoriality, naming, impersonality. The sonnet was effectively and pragmatically staging the same intellectual drama in which
I found myself intimately engaged, entangled, embarrassed. It was
an erotic encounter. But also a crepuscular sublime. It communicated,
therefore, an invitation to readerly circumspection, a warning to look
both ways before crossing into the terrible territory of the beautiful
text. This ambiguity, this fear, begins with the 'me' and the 'you' of
the first eight syllables. They impersonally remove us to a prior
position where neither one nor the other pronoun looks terribly
personal or even definite: introduce *whom*, exactly, into *whose* story?
For enlightenment we may well look towards 'introduce *myself* into
your story', as this seems the most linguistically plausible reading.
Then again, we should likewise look towards 'introduce *me* into your
story', in other words reading 'me' as direct object pronoun rather
than reflexive pronoun. The agency of this introduction is reversible.
We find ourselves at both one and the other pole, in a state of

neutrality which is duly confirmed by the infinitive of 'introduire' and the impersonality of 'c'est'. This little local difficulty foreshadows the complexity of the pronominal identification at work in any critical encounter. Thus 'M'introduire dans ton histoire' merely poses more accurately and acutely the question we always encounter as readers when first coming upon (or approaching for the nth occasion) the critical matter of 'me' and 'you'. I want to speak in your place, but you have artfully prepared that place for me. Are you introducing yourself into my story or am I entering into yours? If it is the latter case, I must recognize, in my amorous and enquiring role, the responsibility I bear as trespasser, as guest; but also as a kind of host, a territory occupied (albeit with some collaboration) by the victoriously seductive enemy, who laughs long and hard at my feeble resistance. In the silent comedy of Mallarmean readership, the *arroseur* will systematically get *arrosé*, every time.

* * *

Running through these issues of positionality and identification, there are a number of temporal problems, which must also concern me in my task of reintroducing Mallarmé to the year 1998. Just as it will always be tricky to say when or in what time the critical encounter takes place (as 'M'introduire' makes perfectly palpable), so one would have to think long and hard about the kind or kinds of time in which to represent the story of Mallarmé's first century. One would need to focus on the notion of the contemporary (as in the phrase 'contemporary French culture') not least because it is so often the focus of much foolishness and haste. We want the contemporary to be right here, right now; but this very desire for immediate fixity sends the concept flying all over the place. Paul de Man makes a similar point regarding the notion of 'modernity' in his essay on Mallarmé, 'Lyric and Modernity':

> The term 'modernity' is not used in a simple chronological sense as an approximate synonym for 'recent' or 'contemporary' . . . It designates more generally the problematical possibility of all literature's existence in the present, of being considered, or read, from a point of view that claims to share with it its own sense of a temporal present. In theory, the question of modernity could

therefore be asked of any literature at any time, contemporaneous or not.[13]

In some simple sense, according to de Man, it's hard for me to be anything other than Mallarmé's contemporary. It's as easy as reading one of his texts. There are, in fact, a number of similarly simple ways in which Mallarmé seems to be our contemporary. Firstly, his verse appears totally modern, insofar as it would not look out of place in a contemporary poetry journal and most young poets would be surprised and proud to write anything nearly as sharp. Secondly, the prose of *Divagations* not only sounds perfectly right for today, it also preempts so much of what we might call 'the theory of our times'.[14] If tomorrow you were going to write a serious book about television or film, you'd first have to read 'Crayonné au théâtre'. If you were going to undertake a cultural study of consumer or spectacular culture, you'd have to read 'Grands faits divers' or the notes for the 'Livre'. Certainly you couldn't begin to think about twentieth-century poetry without reading 'Crise de vers' or 'La musique et les lettres'. The poet in society? 'Conflit'. The cultural marketplace? 'Étalages'. The fetishization of cultural artefacts? 'Arthur Rimbaud'. It's not that Mallarmé would provide you with all the answers, but he'd definitely put you in the right frame of mind. So much so that if there were one author, and one only, that you would wish every fresh French postgraduate to study today as part of an intellectual formation, you would ultimately have to go for Mallarmé. More specifically, in the context of these *Meetings with Mallarmé in contemporary French culture*, you would prefer your doctoral candidate to read Mallarmé before he or she encountered Valéry, Blanchot, Lacan, and company. The irony, of course, is that Mallarmé remains relatively unread in comparison with most of the stars lined up in this collection. No doubt this is why one often gets the impression that Mallarmé is ubiquitous, yet universally unread; terribly important, yet terribly unknown; mysterious, but ignored. Partly, of course, this may be ascribed to the debilitating tag of 'difficulty'. On this matter, let it be said here once and for all: Mallarmé is as difficult as you want to make him. If you start with the presumption of difficulty then it's hardly surprising if you encounter . . . difficulty. If you start out looking for obscurity, it's hardly surprising if you don't find . . . enlightenment. But if, on the contrary, you have some curiosity and desire for words, for syntax, for rhythm, then it is hard to think of a writer whose texts will simply do more to facilitate your knowledge and pleasure. As Mallarmé himself replied to a difficult Edmund Gosse in 1893:

> Je ne vous chicane que sur l'obscurité; non, cher poëte, je ne suis pas obscur, du moment qu'on me lit pour y chercher . . . la manifestation d'un art qui se sert . . . du langage: et le deviens, bien sûr! si l'on se trompe et croit ouvrir le journal.[15]

> (I only disagree with you on the question of obscurity; no, dear poet, I am not obscure, as long as you read me in search of . . . the manifestation of an art which makes use . . . of language: I do become obscure, of course, if you make the mistake of thinking you're opening a newspaper.)

If we discard this false problem of obscurity, how can we best allow Mallarmé into our complex modern lives? How can I best make a *contemporary portrait* of him? How can I best represent him as a *man of today*? Or indeed of the *next century*? One should certainly take heed of Mallarmé's warnings on this issue of contemporaneity: 'mal informé celui qui s'écrierait son propre contemporain' ('ill-informed the person who would declare himself his own contemporary').[16] In 'Derrida's Mallarmé', Geoffrey Bennington analyses what he terms the poet's 'exemplarity' as a practical deconstructor of 'une apparence fausse de présent' ('a false appearance of the present') as well as from a series of related demonstrations that 'il n'est pas de Présent, non—un présent n'existe pas' ('there is no Present, no—a present doesn't exist').[17] In a more conventionally historical sense, Mallarmé had considerable doubts regarding his contemporaries, both sympathetic and antipathetic. For the latter, 'je préfère rétorquer devant l'agression que des contemporains ne savent pas lire' ('in the face of aggression I prefer to respond that some contemporaries don't know how to read').[18] But even his young enthusiasts were often met with a no less corrosive scepticism, as we can see in Mallarmé's comments to Verlaine concerning his public recognition in later life:

> Vos *Poëtes maudits*, cher Verlaine, *A rebours* de Huysmans, ont intéressé à mes Mardis longtemps vacants les jeunes poètes qui

nous aiment (mallarmistes à part) et on a cru à quelqu'influence tentée par moi, là où il n'y a eu que des rencontres. Très affiné, j'ai été dix ans d'avance du côté où de jeunes esprits devaient tourner aujourd'hui.[19]

(At my Tuesday gatherings, which for a long time were unattended, your *Poëtes maudits*, dear Verlaine, and *A rebours* by Huysmans intrigued the young poets who are fond of us (Marllarmeans apart), and people believed in some influence on my part where there were merely encounters. Being very sharp, I was ten years ahead of the game that the young intellectuals are just discovering today.)

Not influence but meetings, a series of encounters. The text I have just cited (the so-called 'autobiography' or letter to Verlaine) is perhaps the tool most frequently used by my fellow commentators when attempting, precisely, to situate our poet, to work out his position, to determine what Mallarmé himself might have called his 'inutile gisement' ('futile bearings') in contemporary French culture. The term we have tended to fix upon most keenly is the *interregnum*, as in the following passage:

Au fond je considère l'époque contemporaine comme un in-terrègne pour le poëte, qui n'a point à s'y mêler: elle est trop en désuétude et en effervescence préparatoire, pour qu'il ait autre chose à faire qu'à travailler avec mystère en vue de plus tard ou de jamais et de temps en temps à envoyer aux vivants sa carte de visite, stances ou sonnets, pour n'être point lapidé d'eux, s'ils le soupçonnaient de savoir qu'ils n'ont pas lieu.[20]

(Basically I consider the contemporary period as an interregnum for the poet, who has no business getting involved: it's too worn out and too much in preparatory effervescence for him to do anything else but labour mysteriously with a view to some ulterior or unrealizable point, and send from time to time his visiting card, stances or sonnets, to the living, so as not to be stoned by them, if they suspected him of knowing that they don't really exist.)

This kind of reflection has sometimes incited socio-historical specula-tion on the poet's largely negative presence in a rapidly maturing capitalist consumer society. Julia Kristeva, for example, has articulated Mallarmé's position in terms of a 'future anterior':

> Aussi dirons-nous qu'un texte est toujours *avant* ou *après* son époque par le mouvement de la négativité qui le traverse et lui fait rejeter les thèses éventuelles (d'ordre 'linguistique' ou 'idéologique') du procès de la signifiance; mais qu'il est par ailleurs *de son temps* au point qu'il le *représente* dans la phase thétique du rejet, c'est-à-dire par sa disposition linguistique et idéologique. Par sa négativité, le texte est toujours un 'futur antérieur': écho et précurseur, hors-temps, téléscopage d'"avant" et d'"après", brisure de la succession, de la téléologie, du devenir, instant du saut. Mais par sa disposition et seulement par elle, le texte est un contemporain: il est présent, subordonné à son époque dont il épouse les limites pénibles.[21]

> (Thus we would say that a text is always either *before* or *after* its time, by the movement of negativity which traverses it and causes it to reject whatever are the 'linguistic' or 'ideological' theses of the process of signification; but it also is *of its time* insofar as it *represents* that period in the thetic phase of rejection, i.e. by its linguistic and ideological disposition. By its negativity, the text is always a 'future anterior': echo and precursor, eternity, collapsing of 'before' and 'after', rupture of succession, of teleology, of becoming, a moment of reaction. But by its disposition, and only by that, the text is a contemporary: it is present, subjected to its time, whose painful limits it touches.)

In a similar vein, Maurice Blanchot has described for us the futile if tempting project of writing Mallarmé's 'life':

> Mallarmé a très bien résisté à cette tentation. Ses contemporains n'ont su que l'admirer ou le méconnaître. Même pour eux, il était un homme vivant dans un temps très éloigné, sur lequel on ne pouvait songer à recueillir de témoignages historiques.[22]
> (Mallarmé has resisted this temptation very effectively. His contemporaries could only admire him or misrepresent him. Even for them, he was a man living in a remotely distant time, about whom one could not imagine collecting historical testimony.)

When ploughing through the tedium of Mallarmé's biographies, I have often thought that between 'vie de Mallarmé' and 'vide Mallarmé' there's barely the width of a mute E. In the absence of a meaningful life, in the absence of an author, how well have Mallarmé's 'future scholiasts' generally responded ? I'm afraid to say we have all been guilty of applying the unhappy principle that 'les absents ont toujours tort' ('the absent are always in the wrong'). At some point or another in our exegetical careers, we have all fallen into the trap of thinking that our duty as commentators must be to fill that unseemly vacuum with personality, authoriality, intentionality, systematicity—even with German philosophy (for the love of Wagner!), whose heavy artillery Mallarmé firmly if politely distanced from his own 'imaginative art':

> L'invasion je la guette
> Avec le vierge courroux
> Tout juste de la baguette
> Au gant blanc des tourlourous
> . . .
> Pas pour battre le Teuton
> . . .
> A la fin que me veut-on?[23]

(I watch for the invasion / With the virgin stick of wrath / Awaiting the occasion / In my pristine sapper's glove / . . . / It's not to beat Germany / . . . / But what do you want of me?)

What we all want—a little too much—is too much *vouloir-dire*, at the expense of *savoir-faire*. This is not the place for a collective confession, but some distribution of responsibility is nonetheless required. The worst of us have fallen for the humanistic scientificity (a deadly combination) of bio-hermeneutics. In other words: let the life supply the meaning (and, as Rousseau would say, if there's anything missing I'll just make it up). Although this approach may be irremediably dull, its nefarious effects have sometimes touched the finest of minds. Whilst the typology of its symptoms is sometimes quite dark and disturbing, one may safely trace its causality back to the coupling of Paul Valéry and Henri Mondor. The Mallarmé that Valéry established in his various writings on the poet is almost a pure product of bio-hermeneutics, even though this profoundly contradicts Valéry's neo-classicism and cold systematicity. In his general poetics, the life of the pathetic subject may disappear, but only to make way for the life of the mind, heroically cogitating against the massive unreason. The subtleties and blasphemies of this relationship are explored at length by Rachel Killick in her essay on Valéry, but certain essentials may be expressed thus: 'I was there, therefore I know. I saw the Man intimately, so I heard the Work truly. Witness to his life and death, I can execute the Meaning and speak in his Name.'[24] Such propositions should sound familiar to students of almost any literary reputation, but in Mallarmé's case—given his delicate cultivation of figures of anonymity, absence, and suicide—the violence of their misrecognition is all the more shocking. The same goes for the proto-fascistic fantasies of Mallarmé as some sort of artistic SuperMan rising above the *vulgus mobile* of democratic culture and exchange. I shall spare you the more grotesque aspects of such delusions. Less offensive but equally deleterious is the projection of Mallarmé as decadent or deficient, despite the poet's appeals to the contrary:

> J'ai mal à la dent
> D'être décadent![25]

(My teeth will give way / To moral decay!)

Very neatly, Leo Bersani has demonstrated the close links that bind these narrative and exegetical impulses:

> The Mallarmean text is treated as if it were sick, as if it were *deficient in narrativity*. The assumption has been that Mallarmé's work could be appreciated only if it were first straightened out . . . The history of Mallarmé criticism—at least until quite recently—has been that of an amazingly successful deradicalization of the Mallarmean text.[26]

Morally or psychologically something is missing from Mallarmé's personal make-up. In his poetic life, therefore, this will inevitably lead to problems of nonsense, contrariness, and socio-political irresponsibility. Melancholic, impotent, marginalized, psychotic, the

maladies of Mallarmé are as multifarious as the pseudo-medical gazes
trained upon him.

It is important to grasp here that the relative degree of sympathy
or antipathy to Mallarmé's cause is not a determining factor in this
debate. The antipathetic readers might even have the merit of
expressing their incomprehension more strikingly. One thinks, for
example, of the incomparably vitriolic Léon Bloy:

> Stéphane Mallarmé—Dessiner en marge tout ce qui peut paraître
> symbolique de ce qui est impénétrable. Des portes verrouillées
> et garnies de triples barres, des murs de clôture surmontés de
> culs de bouteilles; des 'cartons' soigneusement cadenassés; une
> serrure monstrueuse fermant un tout petit endroit; une vieille
> fille hermétiquement boutonnée et gardée par deux dragons, etc.
> etc.[27]

> (Stéphane Mallarmé—Draw in the margin anything that might
> seem symbolic of impenetrability. Bolted doors furnished with
> triple bars; enclosing walls covered in broken glass; carefully
> padlocked boxes; a monstrous lock sealing off a tiny little place;
> an old woman hermetically buttoned up and guarded by two
> dragons, etc. etc.)

Hard to imagine a better formulation of 'Mallarmé l'obscur'! This is
why it is valuable to trace the evolving sentiments of Mallarmé's
contemporary sympathizers such as Valéry, Claudel, Dujardin, et al.
In their various memoirs and recollections, we see the full range of
deceit and conceit, fidelity, treachery, awe. There is a study to be
written, for instance, about Valéry's apparent freezing of Mallarmé
in the 1870s, the decade of *Hérodiade* and the *Faune*. It would allow
us to evaluate just how crucial Valéry's impact has been to our
twentieth-century formulation of Mallarmé, although in the matter
of corpus-formation Blanchot's focus on *Igitur*, *Un coup de dés*, and
the so-called 'Livre', has been equally influential. In recent times, the
canon has been successfully reformed—thanks to such critics as
Vincent Kaufmann and Roger Dragonetti—and is now more open
to the 1880s and 1890s, as well as to the neglected works such as
La dernière mode or the *Vers de circonstance*. As Burhan Tufail shows

in his piece on the Oulipo group, not only can we dissect the Mallarmé corpus in an infinite number of ways, we can also make quite radical decisions as to what constitutes the cadaver. Amongst the early contemporaries, it is Claudel who stands out, largely for his violent renunciation of the poet he had once reverentially described as the 'Gardien pur d'un or fixe où l'aboi vague insulte!' (Pure guardian of a fixed gold where vague barking insults!).[28] It was his Catholic faith that saved him, of course, enabling Claudel to transcend the spiritual void and literary impasse that Mallarmé had come to exemplify in his eyes. The unfortunately entitled article 'Catastrophe d'Igitur' may be seen as an important relay-point in the development of what we might call the 'disastrous' Mallarmé, the poet as flawed genius, glorious failure, sublime holocaust (although Blanchot is once again the key figure in focusing this particular vision of our poet):

> Mais l'aventure d'Igitur est terminée et avec la sienne celle de tout le XIXe. Nous sommes sortis de ce fatal engourdisse-ment, de cette attitude écrasée de l'esprit devant la matière, de cette fascination de la quantité. Nous savons que nous sommes faits pour dominer le monde et non pas le monde pour nous dominer. Le soleil est revenu au ciel, nous avons arraché les rideaux et nous avons envoyé par la fenêtre l'ameublement capitonné, les bibelots de bazar et le 'pallide buste de Pallas'.[29]

> (But the adventure of Igitur is finished, and with it the adventure of the whole nineteenth century. We have emerged from that fatal numbness, from that attitude of the spirit prostrate before matter, from that fascination with mere quantity. We know we were created in order to dominate the world, rather than the world dominate us. The sun has returned to the sky, we have torn down the curtains and thrown out of the window the plush furniture, the curiosities of the bazaar, and the 'pallid bust of Pallas'.)

Within the autobiographical literature of Mallarmé's young con-temporaries, one could read Claudel's apostasy as the most eloquent and explicit version of a theme common to Dujardin's *De Stéphane Mallarmé au prophète Ezéchiel*, Mockel's *Stéphane Mallarmé, un héros*, Fontainas's *Mes souvenirs du symbolisme*, or indeed a host of analogous memoirs, portraits, and panoramas.[30] In all these histories, Mallarmé may be seen to represent at some level a folly, an extreme, a limit, an absolute, all of which look suspiciously like points which one either cannot represent or no longer wishes to revisit. From our perspective in 1998, this extremist Mallarmé begins to look very much like the radical agent he briefly and improbably became during the exhortations and eructations of May '68. Could we really imagine Mallarmé —other than in a novel perhaps—caught up in the flying *pavés* and teargas-canisters? Strangely enough, the dramatic potential of just such an image had already suggested itself to Camille Mauclair at an earlier moment of social dislocation and revolutionary transcendance. In his 1898 novel *Le soleil des morts*, Mauclair portrays his contemporary as 'Calixte Armel', the brilliantly decadent intellectual overtaken by bloody revolution and historical apocalypse.[31] Such unintentional comedy does help us to dramatize, however, the complex issue of our own contemporaneity, which has discredited so many myths or 'grands récits' but lacks the sense or the courage to live unregretfully without them.

As Mallarmé himself knew perfectly well, the fact of being so far ahead of his time placed him in a paradoxically fresh or young position relative to the avant-garde which he had reputedly fathered. Thus as readers of Mallarmé we are always after or behind him in a banal historical sense, and yet at the same time we see him in advance of us, and beyond us, as if he were patiently waiting for his rather sluggish followers one day to catch him up. Such a position of future anteriority perhaps occupied Mallarmé's commemorative mind when in January 1887 he composed a 'tombeau' for the first anniversary of Paul Verlaine's death:

> Ici presque toujours si le ramier roucoule
> Cet immatériel deuil opprime de maints
> Nubiles plis l'astre mûri des lendemains
> Dont un scintillement argentera la foule.[32]

(Here almost always if the bough should coo / This immaterial grief oppresses with many / A comely fold, the star ripe with tomorrows / Whose scintillation will sparkle on the crowd.)

The poet's future glory will be such a scintillation, a sparkling constellation for an admiring and attentive crowd, composed at present of Killick, Minahen, Holland, Bowie, Terada, Bennington, Tufail, van Orden, ffrench, and Scott. The famous Mallarmean constellations (of the 'sonnet en -yx', for example, or 'Un coup de dés') should be regarded as distinct instants of Mallarmé's intervallic presence, as if each time we looked towards him in the sky it was a different set of light-bulbs we saw in sequence spelling out the dead poet's name:

> Qui cherche, parcourant le solitaire bond
> Tantôt extérieur de notre vagabond—
> Verlaine? Il est caché parmi l'herbe, Verlaine
>
> A ne surprendre que naïvement d'accord
> La lèvre sans y boire ou tarir son haleine
> Un peu profond ruisseau calomnié la mort.

(Who's looking—following the solitary leap / Momentarily abroad of our vagabond—/ For Verlaine? He is hidden in the grass, Verlaine // There to surprise if naively complicit / (The lip does not sip there, nor his breathing run out) / A shallow rivulet that is slandered as death.)

It's no big deal, after all, one hundred years of reading a dead Mallarmé. Little more than a flutter in the heavens ('Rien qu'un battement aux cieux'). At the close of the poem to Verlaine—which is not, of course, a closure but a surprise—we can gain a sense of that flash, flashing in the intervals of the valedictory 'calomnié la mort', as we watch the final hemistich reconfigure itself into the barely audible whisper of a name: m—al—la—r—m—é.

On such a quiet note, let me leave you now, with three prosaic axioms to encourage your enjoyment of these texts, and three slightly fanciful notions of the light in which they might be read. So please don't worry about obscurity. (It's *dur* not *difficile*.) Please don't worry about meaning. (It's *savoir-faire* not *vouloir-dire*.) And please don't worry about life. (It's *vide* not *vie de* . . .) The multiple *battement* of these meetings with Stéphane Mallarmé will thus appear, in that photographed mirror behind you, first as a spectacular interval, second as a flash of eloquence, and third as a blank suspense, between two times.

2

Dis/Re/Membering the Master
Valéry's Écrits divers sur Stéphane Mallarmé[1]

Rachel Killick

An 1891 letter to André Gide provides striking early evidence of Valéry's literary 'will to power'[2] and of his view of literature as a ruthlessly manipulative, territorial activity:

> Je ne dis jamais mon âme en vers ni en toute autre littérature . . . car écrire! ce n'est pas se faire rougir, ni affronter l'indifférence—mais bien l'ambition d'abord de saisir un lecteur idéal et de le traîner sans s'émouvoir—ou encore de l'éblouir, l'étourdir, le réduire par la Vérité supérieure ou la force magique, oui, merveilleuse! de créer tout ce qu'on veut avec de petits signes comme ceux-ci! Ah! mystère magistral! orgueil des Hermès artistes, que de mettre sur du papier avec des ruses fabuleuses les mots âme, larmes, émotion etc., et de faire croire à un homme *très intelligent* que sa vie est moins stupide, et son être moins relatif! et d'obtenir ainsi la vénération de ce Sujet qu'on n'a voulu cependant que traîner en servitude sur le bord des fleuves funèbres, parmi les MORTS![3]

> (I never bare my soul in poetry nor in any other type of literature, for writing is not a matter of one's blushes, nor of confronting the indifference of others—but first and foremost the ambition to seize the ideal reader and subdue him mercilessly or else to dazzle him, stun him, crush him with a superior Truth by the magical, the marvellous power of creating what one will with little signs like these. Ah! mystery of the Master, pride of every artist alchemist, the fabulous cunning of setting down on paper

the words soul, tears, emotion, etc., and of convincing the *most intelligent* of men that his life is less stupid and his being less relative! and thus obtaining the veneration of this Subject whom one only desired to enslave on the banks of the Styx, among the DEAD.)

This perception of the author/reader relationship as a power struggle aimed at the annihilation or enslavement of the receiver has important implications for Valéry not only in his writing but also in his reading.[4] His self-affirmation emphatically requires the submission of the Other. As a necessary counterpart it also emphatically rejects the encroachment of the Other on Valéry's own terrain. Yet this letter is contemporaneous with Valéry's first face-to-face meeting with Mallarmé (10 October 1891) and a direct confrontation with another imperialist impulse which, for all its occultation within a devotion to the ideal of the universal Book, represents a deadly challenge to Valéry's literary and intellectual independence.[5] Worse still, this challenge will remain tacit and unresolved so that, even after Mallarmé's death, a persistent feature of Valéry's literary and personal experience down the years will be the constant linking of their two names and a perceived subordination of his own work to that of his predecessor.

The situation is made more complicated and more emotionally taxing by the close personal attachment between 'débutant' and Master. For Mallarmé, the encounter with Valéry constitutes a return to lost youth, a recovery of the self of the 1860s.[6] His letters reveal his empathy with the young provincial unknown, brought to his attention by Louÿs and Gide, just as thirty years earlier he had himself been encouraged towards the poetic avant-garde by his mentors, Emmanuel des Essarts and Catulle Mendès. But Valéry not only reincarnates the past, he also resuscitates a lost future, his poetic gifts and his closeness in age to Anatole, Mallarmé's son dead in childhood,[7] reawakening for Mallarmé the promise of self-renewal and favouring the rapid development of a father/son relationship, both personal and literary in nature.[8] In an annexatory move, Mallarmé draws his young disciple not only into the broad literary group of the *mardis* but into the inner circle of the faithful, and into the intimacy of the Mallarmé family itself,[9] bestowing on him a unique position as potential successor, heir apparent for the continuation of the Great Work of the poetic transmutation of the world.[10]

Valéry, for his part, gains a 'an ideal father',[11] a role model offering emotional support, artistic encouragement and an entrée into key artistic circles. But the perfection of what he is offered is, by virtue of that very perfection, constraining and disabling.[12] Fathers are inevitably oppressive presences and perfect ones particularly so, especially if their sons are of Valéry's assertive temperament, since they offer no purchase for a justifiable display of filial initiative or difference, forcing their offspring into sentiments of disloyalty and guilt for their desire to affirm their independence. For thirty years Valéry is 'speechless' on the subject of Mallarmé, robbed of his own personal voice by an affectionate reluctance to damage the vision that has been Mallarmé's life,[13] incapable, at Mallarmé's graveside, of formulating the emotional depth of a personal loss, all the more agonizing in that it simultaneously represents an intellectual liberation,[14] unable in his dual sense of personal obligation and frustrated intellectual difference to complete the study of Mallarmé, first projected in 1897, re-envisaged shortly after Mallarmé's death, and still an unrealized preoccupation at the end of Valéry's own life.[15] Valéry's rise to fame with the publication of *La Jeune Parque* (1917) and *Charmes* (1922) seemingly redresses the balance of power. But the respite is only momentary, and in any case more apparent than real. The genesis of these poems is closely entwined with Valéry's revisiting of his early pieces and the Mallarmean ambience in which they were produced. The correspondence shows a well-founded concern with the competition offered by Mallarmé's writing.[16] Though the new poems, with their emphasis on the joys and anguish of human consciousness as it experiences the self as an organic combination of body and mind, are a radical response to Mallarmé's attempt to escape the material world through a sublimation of its contingencies in the transcendency of poetic expression, ill-intentioned critics such as Paul Léautaud, fastening on the personal link and the superficial appearance of an analogous obscurity, readily assimilate Valéry to the orbit of Mallarmé, performing anew the disempowerment earlier experienced in Mallarmé's presence.[17] The opportunity for Valéry to state his case only comes about, when this perceived link, in conjunction with an increasing recognition of Valéry's own eminence, produces requests for authoritative statements on his predecessor's behalf. Though these repeated reminders of a real and a supposed obligation must have been both painful and irritating,[18] they do provide Valéry with a stimulus and a forum for his own version of the Mallarmé connexion. Impelled by the desire to assert his intellectual independence, liberated from the living presence of Mallarmé and his family,[19] supported by the authority of his own poetic and intellectual achievement,[20] Valéry can now publicly present his links with Mallarmé in terms that preserve the emotional warmth of the personal relationship while neutralizing at last the universalizing ambition of Mallarmé's aesthetic vision.

The texts of the *Écrits divers sur Stéphane Mallarmé* which together provide the theatre for Valéry's most public and most influential staging of his relationship with Mallarmé, fall into three main groups depending partly on the time they were written and partly on the occasion and audience for which they were conceived.[21] The first group take a biographical/autobiographical approach, focusing on two crucial encounters: discussion with Mallarmé around *Un coup de dés* in 1897 and Valéry's final visit to Mallarmé at Valvins on 14 July 1898. The second group present specific items of Mallarmé's work. The third group are larger critical studies that either consider the entirety of Mallarmé's work or are incorporated into critical works by other hands. This essay will examine a sample of texts from each group to show the various modes, defensive and offensive, of Valéry's response to Mallarmé's admired but threatening presence.

The concentration of the first group on *Un coup de dés* is seemingly pure circumstance. Valéry's first published article on Mallarmé, 'Le [sic] *coup de dés', lettre au directeur des 'Marges'*, written in 1921 at the urging of Edmond Bonniot, Mallarmé's son-in-law and family guardian of his literary interests, supports Bonniot's refusal to allow a staged performance of the poem. The second, *Dernière visite à Mallarmé*, commemorates the twenty-fifth anniversary of Mallarmé's death. A third text, *Souvenirs littéraires*, the published version of a 1927 lecture of literary reminiscences, naturally includes the 'farewell' scene, reproducing biographical and autobiographical material already developed in the two previous articles. But, more fundamentally, the insistence on the final moments of the lived relationship with Mallarmé pinpoints the symbolic significance of the episode as a crucial event of leave-taking that is as much intellectual as personal. The persistence of the memory over the years testifies eloquently to the trauma of the emotional loss but also to the difficulty of resolving once and for all the crucial issues of aesthetic and intellectual authority. Mallarmé in a sense is never 'dead and buried' for Valéry, but survives as a challenging presence who continues to elicit admiration and respect but against whom the battle for self-assertion must continually be refought.

The first article (*Œuvres* I, 622–30) provides particularly complex illustration of the competing claims of Other and Self. Its primary concern is apparently the protection of Mallarmé's artistic integrity and it is carefully designed to lend weight to Bonniot's uncompromising stance.[22] Valéry is required therefore to demonstrate his closeness to Mallarmé and his authority as an intimate to speak in Mallarmé's place concerning the Master's thoughts and intentions for the poem. Simultaneously though, his own *amour propre* is intimately engaged, for this assumption of responsibility for another's project can all too easily be construed as self-denying surrender to it. It is essential therefore, for Valéry's sense of personal autonomy, that even as he defends Mallarmé's position, he clearly mark his separation from Mallarmé and assert his independent position as poet and intellectual.

These contradictory requirements and impulses inform a variety of textual strategies. Valéry's initial remarks safeguard his own position (he is not, as per the critic of *Marges*, 'un artiste éprouvé' ('an experienced artist'), nor a libellous Jean-Baptiste Rousseau, above all he is not Mallarmé's 'exécuteur testamentaire' ('legal or literary executor')). He does, however, have a privileged insight into Mallarmé's aims and desires. Having marked his superior knowledge vis-à-vis Mallarmé's would-be vulgarizers with a scholarly put-down on a point of information: 'J'ai, peut-être, moi aussi quelques mots à dire sur ce *Coup de dés* que les nouveaux défenseurs de Mallarmé s'obstinent à intituler: *Coup de dé*' ('I too may have a few things to say about this *Coup de dés* which Mallarme's new champions persist in calling: *Coup de dé*') (*Œuvres* I, 623), he further establishes his credentials by a detailed account of his presence at two important moments of the poem's history: the initial revelation of the manuscript and scrutiny, with Mallarmé, of the subsequent proofs. Valéry emphasizes not just his first-hand knowledge of text but also the primacy of his involvement: 'Je crois bien que je suis le premier homme qui ait vu cet ouvrage extraordinaire' ('I believe I was the first person to see this extraordinary work') and stresses the particular importance attached by Mallarmé to showing it to *him* as soon as possible: '*A peine l'eut-il achevé*, Mallarmé me pria de venir chez lui' ('*No sooner had he finished it* than Mallarmé asked me to come and see him' (*Œuvres* I, 623, my emphasis). The particulars of the setting and the unfolding of the actual event are carefully delineated, along with additional information that reinforces the position of Valéry as an initiate:

> Il m'introduisit dans sa chambre de la rue de Rome où derrière une antique tapisserie reposèrent jusqu'à sa mort, signal par lui donné de leur destruction, les paquets de ses notes, le secret matériel de son grand œuvre inaccompli.[23]

> (He took me into his bedroom in the rue de Rome where an antique tapestry concealed the packets of notes, the secret material of his unfinished Work, destroyed after his death on his instructions.)

The reading takes place not in the salon, which was the theatre for the open house of Mallarmé's *mardis*, but 'dans sa chambre', in the bedroom that was also his study. Valéry describes a quasi-religious event, the room a sacred repository of unrevealed mysteries, the table, 'de bois très sombre, carrée, aux jambes torses' ('of very dark wood, square, on sculpted legs'), on which Mallarmé lays his manuscript, endowed with the massiveness of an altar. In this inner sanctum, Mallarmé, in his turn, is portrayed as stage-managing the revelation of his text. In contrast to the polyphonic adaptation now proposed, which would project the poem outwards to a wider audience, Mallarmé's reading is hushed, unaccented, neutral, a reading for himself and for the privileged listener: 'il se mit à lire d'une voix basse, égale, sans le moindre "effet" presque à soi-même' ('he began to read in a low, even voice, with no attempt at emphasis, as if to himself') (*Œuvres* I, 623). The notation emphasizes to the readers of *Marges* the inappropriateness of the ambitious large-scale public rendering for which permission has been sought and refused. It also implies the specular relationship of the participants in the scene.

Mallarmé treats Valéry as an extension of himself; Valéry acquiesces in this assimilation. But the reading is only the preliminary to the full revelation. In the unveiling of the ideograph the illusion of parity is dispelled; Mallarmé, audacious pioneer and prophet of the Word, reduces his compliant audience of one to astounded silence and, benignly dominant, surveys as it were from on high the demolition of Valéry's established frames of references.

Valéry's portrayal of his reaction to this assault on his intellectual security, whilst still stressing the links of intimate personal connexion ('cet homme si simple, si doux, si naturellement noble et charmant' ('such a gentle, unassuming man, someone so naturally noble and charming')), on which his defense of Mallarmé's intentions for *Un coup de dés* is based, rapidly covers the ground from disabling paralysis ('Cette fixation sans exemple me pétrifiait' ('This unparalleled fixing of a thought on the page petrified me') (*Œuvres* I, 624)) to dynamic, self-affirmation:

> Je me sentais livré à la diversité de mes impressions, saisi par la nouveauté de l'aspect, tout divisé de doutes, tout remué de développements prochains. Je cherchais une réponse à mille questions que je m'empêchais de poser. J'étais un complexe d'admiration, de résistance, d'intérêt passionné, d'analogies à l'état naissant devant cette invention intellectuelle (*Œuvres* I, 624–5).

> (I felt myself given over to the diversity of my impressions, gripped by the novelty and strangeness of the poem's appearance, beset with doubts, excited by possible developments. I sought answers to a thousand questions which I stopped myself from asking. I was a complex amalgam of admiration, resistance, passionate interest, dawning analogies as I gazed at this invention of the intellect.)

The fruits of this resistance and of those silent questions, potentially wounding to Mallarmé's self-esteem, condition Valéry's retrospective recounting of the poem. In a counter-move to Mallarme's offensive, he recasts it in the dual perspective of his own physical and intellectual preoccupations, on the one hand privileging the resonances of Mallarmé's reading voice over the Master's desire to promote the autonomy of Language in the text,[24] on the other, limiting Mallarmé's metaphysical quest to a model of mental functioning made visible in its irradiance in language: 'Il me sembla de voir la figure d'une pensée pour la première fois placée dans notre espace . . . L'attente, le doute, la concentration étaient choses visibles'[25] ('I seemed to see the shape of a thought isolated in material space for the very first time. Attentive waiting, doubt, concentration had acquired visible form').

These annexatory tactics are even more evident in Valéry's account of his 30 March 1897 conversation with Mallarmé over the corrected proofs and of his last visit to Valvins. The passage opens ambivalently with a portrayal of Mallarmé's 'admirable smile', which, however, 'ornement du plus pur orgueil inspiré à l'homme par son sentiment de l'univers' ('outward sign of his proud conviction of his universal value'), presents an unspoken challenge to Valéry's own self-sufficient pride. Meanwhile, Valéry's recording of Mallarmé's accompanying remark, ' Ne trouvez-vous pas que c'est un acte de démence?' ('It is an act of madness, is it not?') (Œuvres I, 625), underlines Mallarmé's confidence in a vision beyond the grasp of the multitude whilst discreetly foregrounding a possible reservation on Valéry's part. The ostensible aim of the passage is again to demonstrate to the would-be adapters the essentially typographic nature of Mallarmé's venture and the care in conception and execution invested by him in it which admits of no inappropriate latter-day interference. But Valéry, while indicating a Mallarmé-directed exchange around points of typographic detail, again uses the occasion to display his own alternative vision.

The move is briefly initiated in the description of the 'magnifiques feuilles d'épreuves' ('magnificent proofs') spread upon the sill of a window 'ouverte au calme paysage' ('open onto the calm of the countryside'), a tangible confronting, in other words, of two worlds, the Mallarmean universe of the Book, which seeks to release the imagination from material contingency, and the Valéryan world of the physical universe (body and cosmos) on which all thought depends.[26] Valéry's magnificent account of the splendour of the July night, where he and Mallarmé walk in the darkness among the stars, participants in the living text of the natural world which simultaneously elevates and annihilates the aspirations of mortal man, is his appropriative response to Mallarmé's 'tentative merveilleuse . . . d'élever enfin une page à la puissance du ciel étoilé' ('marvellous

attempt . . . at last to elevate a page to the power of the star-lit sky')
(*Œuvres* I, 626).[27]

For what is it that stands out in the mind at the end of Valéry's
article—the elliptical configurations of *Un coup de dés* (unseen by the
reader of the article) or the expansive rhythms of Valéry's dynamic
prose? Valéry, deftly switching back to *Un coup de dés* ('Laissons mes
souvenirs' ('Enough of my memories')) avoids an answer, but the
closing discussion arguing again the typographical specificity of the
poem through a substantial quotation from Mallarmé on the spatial
dynamics of his poem and paragraphs from Valéry on the con-
substantiality of its *forme* and its *fond*, has the undeniable effect of
leaving the last word to the lyrical power of Valéry's evocation of the
cosmos. If the article defends Mallarmé's unique experiment in *Un
coup de dés*, it also offers a potent statement of Valéry's twin
preoccupations: the workings of the intellect and the interaction of
corps, esprit, monde. The final work and the final visits are thus
transmuted and reconstituted as primal scenes, sites simultaneously
of Valéry's emotional attachment to Mallarmé, his admiration for his
creative audacity, and of his intellectual and imaginative separation
from him.

Two years later in 1923, the twenty-fifth anniversary of Mallarmé's
death involves Valéry in a further public statement on the man and
his poetry. The short piece *Dernière Visite à Mallarmé* (*Œuvres* I,
630–3) provides a compressed version of the final moments of the
personal relationship, telescoping the description of the rue de Rome
visit, the discussion of the proofs and the last meeting at Valvins into
a single event, which this time is explicitly recognized as not only a
literal, but also a symbolic parting of the ways. The starting point
remains the admittance to the inner sanctum, this time the 'cabinet
de travail' at Valvins, the ostensible focus the proofs of *Un coup de
dés*. But the master/disciple relationship is immediately overturned
first by a more developed repeat of the opposition of Mallarmean
space, the enclosed, coffin-like study, 'deux pas de large sur six pas
de long' ('two paces wide, six paces long') (*Œuvres* I, 780) in the
Souvenirs littéraires version, and of Valéryan space, trees, dappled
sunlight, the murmur of the river, entering through the open window,
and secondly by the eliding of the typographical particularity of the
poem into a characteristic Valéryan reflection on the value of the
work of art as a training for the muscles of the mind.[28] The focus

here shifts decisively from Mallarmé's presentation of his poem to Valéry's observation and evaluation of the event. On the one hand, the old order apparently prevails: personal intimacy is intact, Mallarmé's work holds centre-stage. But, at the same time, Valéry already locates the moment in a completed past. Mallarmé, with his finger on the page, in an echo and reversal of the stained glass image of *Sainte*, figures the death, not, as in the poem, of the old religion or of music versus poetry, but of the literary vision itself, centred on the mirage of the universal book:

> Tout était calme et sûr . . . Mais cependant que Mallarmé me parlait, le doigt sur la page, il me souvient que ma pensée se mit à rêver *de ce moment même*. Elle y donnait distraitement une valeur comme absolue. Je songeais, près de lui vivant, à son destin comme achevé (*Œuvres* I, 632).[29]

> (All was peaceful and unchanged . . . But even as Mallarmé was speaking to me, his finger on the page, I remember that in my mind I began to mythologize *the moment itself*, involuntarily ascribing to it a kind of absolute value, seeing his destiny as complete, though the living man was still by my side.)

This superseding of the Mallarmean order is, moreover, clearly announced at the beginning of the article. Valéry stresses from the outset the disaffection from literature which, he is at pains to point out, arose in him independently, before any personal acquaintance with Mallarmé. The nevertheless inhibiting effect of his affection for Mallarmé and his admiration for Mallarmé's artistic achievement conditions a presentation which alternat(iv)ely portrays Mallarmé as scientist or mathematician (assimilating Mallarmean technique to Valéry's own preoccupation with Structure and Method) or (in an elevating and distancing move) as saint or Christ, 'victime supérieure', martyr to a lost literary cause, the pathos of the latter portrayal no doubt increased by Valéry's sense of his complicity in the general rejection.

The end of the article, returning to the final walk in the countryside, repeats the privileging of the Valéryan universe already noted in the article of 1921. Mallarmé, so-called 'poète artificiel', is portrayed as assimilated, with Valéry, to the 'naïve', unreflective splendour of the physical world and at the same time to its ambiguous parameters of infinitude and mortality. In magnificent language, strongly reminiscent of the all-consuming solar imagery of *Le Cimetière marin* (1920), Valéry evokes the surrender of self to being and the deceptive sensation of liberation effected by the loss of restrictive but defining frameworks of individual consciousness. Such a vision ruthlessly exposes the fragility of the constructs of the mind. *Le Cimetière marin* turns inexorably and ironically around the immovable stumbling-block of human mortality, constraining the pretentions of the 'grande âme' and the claim to supremacy of the literary ideal.[30] Similarly, the poetic creativity encapsulated in Mallarmé's final words: 'Voyez, c'est le premier coup de cymbale de l'automne sur la terre' ('Behold, the first golden stroke of autumn's cymbals across the earth') is starkly juxtaposed, at the end of the article, to the bald, typographically detached, announcement of his extinction: 'Quand vint l'automne, il n'était plus' ('When autumn came, he was gone') (*Œuvres* I, 633).[31] Body and mind are extinct, and, along with them, the dream of the Absolute enshrined in the ideal Book. Only the cosmos subsists. Valéry's emotional distress is total, but his valorization of the evolving Self can come into its own, emancipated at last from the pressure of Mallarmean mysticism.

The first group of texts obsessively return to *Un coup de dés* to reconstruct a moment of farewell that is also a moment of liberation. After the anecdotic replay of the final scene in *Souvenirs littéraires* (1927) it seems, however, that Valéry has at last exorcized the trauma of his inner 'execution' of the living Mallarmé. The second group of texts moves away from the 'death scene', concentrating instead as its avowed objective on the presentation of specific items of Mallarmé's work.[32] In *Stéphane Mallarmé* (*Œuvres* I, 660–80), a 1933 lecture with poetry readings to the Université des Annales, Valéry expressly rules out too abstract and theoretical an approach. His starting point, he claims, is an entirely factual one, the modern fame of a poet, castigated in his own time for the difficulty and obscurity of his writing, which still continues to defy the sense-making desire of the reading public. But factual though Valéry's evidence (numbers of editions, number of critical works) clearly is, his choice of starting point is less than innocent. For this evidence serves the needs of an 'observateur de l'univers spirituel' ('observer of the mind') whose interest, defined in the opening words of the lecture, is focused on 'la vie et le destin de Stéphane Mallarmé et le développement de sa gloire' ('the life and destiny of Stéphane Mallarmé and the growth of his reputation') as 'un épisode rigoureusement singulier du drame de la vie intellectuelle' ('a rigorously singular episode of the drama of intellectual life') (*Œuvres* I, 680). In other words, attention, from the first, is displaced from the work itself to Mallarmé, the case-study, from the specificities of Mallarmé's writing to its status as an intriguing phenomenon in the development of the history of ideas. The work becomes subservient to an emphasis on its reception, on its reception, in particular, in the mind of Valéry, consummate investigator of the thinking self.

This implicit re-balancing of Mallarmean and Valéryan power acquires clearer definition as Valéry outlines the method of his investigation. Summarized as 'un simple recours au souvenir' ('essentially memory based'), it incorporates a forceful emphasis on Self as the key element in a discussion of 'un poète qu'on a *soi-même* connu, dont on a pu *soi-même* sur *soi-même* observer l'influence' ('a poet whom one has *oneself* known and whose influence on *oneself* one has been able to study *at first hand*') (*Œuvres* I, 662, my emphasis). Preceding any look at Mallarmé's actual work, a clear statement is provided of the rising and declining curve of his influence on Valéry. Mallarmé's work is thus immediately designated as consumable and expendable. The ambivalence of a method billed as 'la plus vraie (la plus sincère et, d'ailleurs, la plus séduisante)' ('the truest (the most sincere and, moreover, the most seductive)') (*Œuvres* I, 662) is soon apparent in the choice of poems, read aloud to the audience, and the comments provided by Valéry. The first two poems *Brise marine* and *Les Fenêtres* firmly return Mallarmé to the ambience of Baudelaire, an ambience from which the mature Mallarmé sought to distance himself.[33] *Brise marine* recalls 'un Baudelaire plus condensé et d'une sonorité plus délicate' ('a more condensed and phonetically more delicate version of Baudelaire') (*Œuvres* I, 665). *Les Fenêtres* for its part, seen as combining qualities of realism and lyricism, again derived from Baudelaire, is linked with the similarly influenced early poems of Rimbaud[34] and replaced in the distant decade 1862–1872. In the anthology in which Valéry admiringly discovered these poems, 'pièces de clarté immédiate et de valeur incontestable . . . dont je demeurais *entièrement* émerveillé' ('immediately intelligible pieces of unquestionable value . . . which filled me with the *greatest* of admiration', Valéry's emphasis) he also was confronted by 'certains sonnets qui me réduisaient à la stupeur' ('certains sonnets which reduced me to stupefied silence') (*Œuvres* I, 666). None of these, however, is read to the audience or even named, the focus immediately shifting instead to Valéry's manner of overcoming their difficulties. Similarly *L'Après-midi d'un faune* is mentioned but not read to the audience 'car il est de ces poèmes qui demandent à être bien connus avant d'être entendus' ('for it is one of those poems which one needs to know well before one can appreciate hearing it read aloud') (*Œuvres* I, 669). Instead, Valéry offers anecdotal information on the discovery, among the papers of the composer Ernest Chausson, of the initial version, conceived for a stage presentation by Constant Coquelin, and, as an example of a work containing 'les plus beaux vers du monde' ('the most beautiful poetry in the world'), provides a brief, two-line quotation ('Tu sais ma passion, que pourpre et déjà mûre / Chaque grenade éclate et d'abeilles murmure' ('You know my passion, that crimson and richly ripe / Each bursting pomegranate murmurs with bees')) calculated to bring to mind two of his own poems, *L'Abeille* and *Les Grenades* (*Œuvres* I, 118 and 146). His succinct and suggestive characterization of this most Valéryan of Mallarmé poems as combining 'une extrême sensualité, une extrême intellectualité, une extrême musicalité' ('an extreme sensuality, an extreme intellectuality, an extreme musicality') (*Œuvres* I, 670), qualities that are the hallmark of Valéry's own poetry, perhaps suggests that the decision not to read the poem aloud has as much a self-protective as a listener-friendly motivation. His concluding remark on Mallarmé's dissatisfaction with Debussy's musical rewriting of *L'Après-midi d'un faune* is perhaps also to be seen as part of an occulted reflection on the power structures of dependence and ownership and influence and originality.

In contrast to the complex fugue-like construction of *L'Après-midi d'un faune*, the dialogue of Nurse and Hérodiade in 'Scène' lends itself to spoken performance. Part of the once and future text of Mallarmé's writing, it also appears, unlike the texts previously quoted, to offer a long-awaited insight into Mallarmé's poetic vision. But even as Mallarmé's work is put centre-stage, the brief accompanying comments maintain the subtext of Valéry's self-assertion. Minimal observations look not to the specifics of an original text, demonstrating the independence of the author, but to the influence upon Mallarmé of the Parnassians and of Poe. They also emphasize the thematics of purity, virginity, sterility which make Mallarmé's quest for the Beautiful so difficult of access, so inhuman in its coloration. In unstated contrast, Valéry's rewrite of *La Jeune Parque* dynamically displaces the insoluble problem of existence and essence in favour of the continuously self-renewing modulations of the human consciousness.[35]

Meanwhile within the text of the lecture, liberated from the dominance of Mallarmé's actual poems, Valéry again assimilates their author to intellectual and ethical models of mental production. The earlier part of the lecture, echoing Valéry's correspondence of 1889–1891, recalls an initial attraction promoted by the tangible difficulties of distance and unavailability and Mallarmé's reputation for obscurity. In the next phase of the encounter, the pattern is that already outlined in respect of *Un coup de dés*. The difficulties are no longer external; the crystalline sonnets carry their offensive to the centre of Valéry's being, creating as a first reaction stupefied disorientation but as a second, a determined and measured attempt to regain intellectual control which here takes the form of a quasi-scientific analysis of the effect on the reader of their singular combination of musicality and intellectual impenetrability. Valéry records his observation of the seriousness of the writing, the compelling impact of this poetry as a coherent, self-sufficient formal construct and the mnemonic quality which imposes itself on the reader, impelling the mind towards some ultimate limit, towards an idea inherent in the structure of the form itself. This domination of the reader is portrayed by Valéry as an experience of enchantment in both the positive and the negative sense, wonder and admiration strongly imprinted with obverse connotations of conquest and disempowerment. The only way for Valéry to reassert himself is to excise the work, to study its effects rather than its essence, and therefore he chooses to read aloud either poems consonant with the canon or, in the case of 'Scène', a piece which raises ethical as much as aesthetic questions.

The Hérodiade figure combining inviolate Beauty and uncompromising aspiration to its attainment, permits a crucial transition in the closing stages of the lecture from the uncompromising 'aérolithe' of Mallarmé's work and the compliance it ruthlessly demands to its ideal of perfect Beauty, to a defensive symbolization of Mallarmé as the ultimate example of the Valéryan counter-ideal of the creator of the perfect Self. Quotations from letters from Mallarmé to the *félibrige* poet Aubanel[36] are used to strengthen Valéry's position, for the letters reveal both Mallarme's commitment to his idea, a single-mindedness which Valéry commends ('Il se confine en soi-même, en tête à tête avec l'analyse de ses lumières intérieures' ('He shuts himself off within himself, to concentrate on the analysis of his mental activity') (*Œuvres* I, 679)), and the metaphysical bias of his thinking, which Valéry contrives to reject not by an outright refutation, inappropriate in a lecture ostensibly concerned to promote Mallarmé's work, but by the understated no-comment techniques that introduce and complete his summary of Mallarmé's position: a claimed lack of competence to judge: 'Nous ne pouvons que faire des conjectures sur le fond de sa pensée' ('We can only conjecture what his thinking really was') (*Œuvres* I, 679) and an inability to conclude, discreetly embodied in open-ended punctuation . . . The two final paragraphs of the lecture, returning the argument to its start and summarizing Valéry's findings in the curious case of Mallarmé's fame, paradoxically conclude this presentation of Mallarmé's *work* by demoting it in favour of the *man* and the *thinker*:

> Ce n'est point la seule beauté des vers, ni la profondeur des idées, ni les inventions de formes d'une élégance surprenante qui ont fait ce nom grandir, cette Œuvre agir, cette figure s'imposer . . . Mais cet homme qui était à la fois si profond et si gracieux, si simple et si composé, de condition si médiocre mais si digne, mais si noble (car rien n'était si noble que son attitude, son regard, son accueil, son sourire) fut l'exemple le plus pur, le plus authentique des vertus intellectuelles (*Œuvres* I, 680).

> (It is not the beauty of the poetry alone, nor the profundity of the ideas, nor the invention of forms of amazing elegance that have given such prestige to his name, such authority to his work, such stature to his person . . . but this man who combined such depth with such social grace, who was so simple yet so perfect in his manner, so ordinary in his social status, yet so worthy, so noble (for there was nothing so noble as his demeanour, his look, his way of welcoming you, his smile) was the purest and most authentic example of all the intellectual virtues.)

Valéry thus accomplishes a double objective: a personal tribute to a cherished mentor and friend, but also a decisive appropriation of a dangerous literary and intellectual competitor to his own divergent vision.

The third group of texts constitutes the most advanced state of Valéry's self-liberation from the shadow of Mallarmé, for here Valéry, confronting the block challenge posed by the Mallarmean corpus, abandons a policy of tacit or limited reservation vis-à vis Mallarmé's ideas and, turning away from specific Mallarmé texts, moves decisively to incorporate Mallarmé's poetics within his own. *Je disais quelquefois à Stéphane Mallarmé* (*Œuvres* I, 644–60) originally written as a preface to *Poésies de Stéphane Mallarmé* (Société des Cent-Une, 1931) focuses mainly on the linguistic aspects of poetic composition but from a general point of view,[37] Valéry's prime concern throughout being to establish a personal position of strength. Mallarmé's readers, he argues, are all, himself included, natural loners, who empathize with Mallarmé in the single-minded pursuit of the poetic aim which is his *raison d'être*, but each of whom jealously guards a powerful sense of personal uniqueness.[38] Valéry's own position vis-à-vis Mallarmé in 1889/1890 is depicted in contrast as one of vulnerability and dramatic colonization:

> Je suis parti vers la mer assez éloignée, tenant les copies précieuses que je venais de recevoir *Hérodiade, Les Fleurs, Le Cygne* ; et le soleil dans toute sa force, la route éblouissante, et ni l'azur, ni l'encens des plantes ne m'étaient rien, tant ces vers inouïs m'exerçaient et me possédaient au plus vivant de moi (*Œuvres* I, 649).

> (I started off towards the distant sea, holding the precious copies I had just received *Hérodiade, Les Fleurs, Le Cygne* ; and the sun in all its power, the dazzling road, and neither the azure of the sky nor the heady scents of plants made any impact on me, so profoundly did that incredible poetry exercise and possess my innermost being.)

Where the scenarios developed in the first group of articles around *Un coup de dés* offer the expansive sensuousness of Valéry's dynamic triad *corps–esprit–monde* in place of the rarefied spatial tracings of Mallarmé's poem, what is striking in the retelling of this formative episode is the suppression of Valéry's physical Mediterranean universe by Mallarmé's 'immaterial' world of the Book. This invasiveness reaches out into the very syntax of Valéry's account, imprisoning sun, sky, heat, scent, in a web of negation marked as Mallarmé's by the attention-catching, mid-sentence juxtaposition 'et ni' ('and nor'), memorably used by the latter in *Brise marine*, one of the poems to be read aloud to Valéry's 1933 lecture audience. Simultaneously though, Valéry's retrospective staging of his departure, Mallarmé's poems in his hand, towards the distant sea, recalls and points towards the future Valéryan triumph of *Le Cimetière marin* where, in the final stanza, the pages of the book, 'tout éblouies' ('dazzled and over-whelmed') in the tumult of sun, wind and sea, are scattered far and wide from the reader's hand.[39]

This latent scenario of control regained is given an immediate tangible presence in the essay by the dialogue format of the opening section. The title, reproducing the introductory formula, is doubly disarming: a deceptively simple expression of the long-standing familiarity and intimacy which authorizes Valéry's discourse on Mallarmé but which also provides a means for Valéry of taking the initiative and presenting his voice, not Mallarmé's, as the dominant one. There is indeed, only one voice in the exchange, since Mallarmé, looking inwards to his own sense of purpose, refuses dialogue, unwilling to accept judgement or comfort from any but himself.[40] But Valéry swiftly regains the intellectual upper hand by com-prehensively subsuming the hermetic resistance of Mallarmé's work, and the intense effort of reading it imperiously requires, within his own aesthetic of obstacle, effort, and patient construction. Mallarmé's refusal of the facile attraction of narrative or sentiment, his lack of concession to popular taste and the banalities of everyday use of language, his acceptance of the testing demands of musical and metrical constraints, are thus assimilated and reconstituted within Valéry's theorization of poetry as key models of an arduous struggle of reflective calculation against the capricious tyranny of Romantic inspiration.

A yet more drastic disempowerment is performed by Valéry's analysis of literature as a flawed mental activity. For if Valéry, as *poet*, seems momentarily to associate himself with Mallarmé's dream of a total fusion of thought and expression ('que voulons-*nous*—si ce n'est de produire l'impression puissante . . . qu'il existe entre la forme sensible d'un discours et sa valeur d'échange en idées, je ne sais quelle union mystique' ('what do *we* [my emphasis] desire if not to produce the powerful impression that there exists between the tangible form of an utterance and its *intellectual exchange value* [Valéry's emphasis] some indefinable mystical union') (*Œuvres* I, 647)), as an *intellectual* he wastes no time in pointing out its illusory nature, pointing, on the side of the author, to the arbitrariness of the links between sound and idea and, on that of the reader, to the unpredictability of audience understanding and reaction. Thus, though recognizing the force of ancient belief in the magical power of the word, he flatly rejects its mystical orientation, replacing Mallarmé's desire to recover the lost virtualities of language by his own psycho-physiological view of language as the tool by which the Self effects change both within itself and within the mind of the Other. For Valéry, poetry, like prayer, does not so much invoke the divine without as modify the Self within. Poems are manipulative 'charmes' ('magical incantations') 'qui nous intiment de *devenir* bien plus qu'ils ne nous excitent à *comprendre*' ('which do not so much stimulate our ability to *understand*, as impose *change in our way of being*') (*Œuvres* I, 650, Valéry's emphasis). More rigorously for the author, virtuoso exploitation of the medium permits that constantly evolving debate between desire and ability (*vouloir* and *pouvoir*) which reveals the Self to itself and encourages the full exploration of its potential. Valéry thus responds to the challenge of Mallarmé's total poetic corpus by developing a critique of language which, in radical contradistinction to his predecessor, excises Poetry's claim to ultimate supremacy and reduces the chimerical *Grand Œuvre* (the *Masterwork*) to simple *manœuvre*, developmental or manipulative tool.

The end of the article decisively confirms Valéry's elimination of the literary work in favour of the mental process by which it is produced and which its own production helps to further. Like the title and the opening section, though on one level a loving tribute to a cherished Master, it effectively sacrifices Mallarmé to the birth of Valéry, all debate on the intrinsic value of Mallarmé's work engulfed in the development of Valéry's vision of the creation of the Self through language:

Je veux bien que Mallarmé soit obscur, stérile et précieux, mais s'il m'a fait, au prix de ces *défauts*,—et même,—au moyen de

41

tous ces défauts, au moyen des efforts qu'ils impliquent dans l'auteur et exigent du lecteur,—concevoir et placer au-dessus de toutes les œuvres, la possession consciente de la fonction du langage et le sentiment d'une liberté supérieure de l'expression au regard de laquelle toute pensée n'est qu'un incident particulier, —cette conséquence que j'ai tirée de ma lecture et méditation de ses écrits demeure pour moi un bien incomparable et tel qu'aucun ouvrage transparent et facile ne m'en a offert de si grand (*Œuvres* I, 660, Valéry's emphasis).

(Mallarmé may well be obscure, sterile and precious, but if, at the cost of these *faults* —or even—by means of all these faults, by means of the effort they imply in the author and demand of the reader, he has implanted in me as supreme concept, surpassing any individual work, the conscious possession of the functioning of language and the sense of a higher freedom of expression, beside which any single thought is merely a discrete incident, this consequence which I have drawn from my reading and meditation of his work, remains for me an incomparable gift which no transparent, easily accessible work has been able to equal.)

Lettre sur Mallarmé (*Œuvres* I, 633–43), fronting and confronting not Mallarmé's actual work but a work of critical support, Jean Royère's book, *Mallarmé* (1927), develops Valéry's linguistic and ethical arguments in yet more combative mode. Again Valéry's first move, after an initial acknowledgement of his closeness to Mallarmé ('Je ne sais enfin démêler ce qu'il fut de ce qu'il me fut' ('I find it impossible to disentangle what he was from what he was to me' (*Œuvres* I, 634)), is to assert his independence, this time by an extended and cunningly argued general discussion of what constitutes influence, 'cette modification progressive d'un esprit par l'œuvre d'un autre' ('that progressive modification of one person's mind by the work of another') (*Œuvres* I, 634). A forceful demonstration of his own originality is subsequently provided by forthright disagreement with Mallarmé's metaphysical project. The keystone of Mallarmé's vision is briskly demolished: 'le développement de ses vues personnelles, généralement si precises, a été retardé, troublé, embarrassé par les idées incertaines qui régnaient dans l'atmosphère littéraire et ne cessaient pas de le visiter' ('the development of his personal views which were generally só precise, was hampered, troubled, inhibited by the vague ideas holding sway in the literary atmosphere of the time which he could never entirely escape') (*Œuvres* I, 636). Moulding Mallarmé to his own ideal of logical mental function, Valéry argues that the idea of a metaphysical transcendence in art was an aberration from Mallarmé's true being, an accidental *fin de siècle* accretion, deriving largely from the 'prestigieuses et fantastiques improvisations' ('fantastic improvisation and prestigious conjuring tricks') of Villiers de l'Isle-Adam.[41] Valéry's own view unequivocally stated later on in the essay 'Je vais faire à présent un aveu' ('I shall now make a confession') (*Œuvres* I, 638), is that literature has *no* essential function, it is merely 'une province du vaste empire des divertissements' ('but one province in the vast empire of diversion and entertainment') (*Œuvres* I, 638). Authors can only speculate on the uncertain competencies and varying viewpoints of an un-predictable audience; the results of such speculation, good as well as bad, are in Valéry's view an insult to the author's fundamental sense of self-esteem and a threat to his identity as they are produced outside his volition and control. Intellectual autonomy can only be protected by a recognition of the provisional nature of writing and by a redefining of its value not as an end but as a means, as a training, a 'pur *exercice*' (*Œuvres* I, 643, Valéry's emphasis) in the clear articulation of rigorously conceived ideas.

Valéry shows his assertive hand still more clearly with the most developed of all his comments on Mallarmé's ethical significance as a 'héros et . . . martyr de la *résistance au facile*' ('hero and . . . martyr of the *resistance to the facile*') (*Œuvres* I, 641, Valéry's emphasis). He presents Mallarmé's work in the 1890s as producing an effect akin to the Christian message 'par le seul fait de son existence agissant comme charme et comme glaive' ('by the very fact of its existence acting as an enchantment and as a sword'), setting at odds disciples and unbelievers, creating in the former the defensive mentality of a religious cult, sustained by the secret circulation of sacred texts, 'trésor de délices incorruptibles' ('treasury of incorruptible delights') (*Œuvres* I, 638) and in the latter a reaction of incomprehension and injured intellectual pride, angrily manifesting itself in persecution and mockery. Valéry portrays as his own immediate self-protective response the adoption of a detached stance as quiet observer of a singular paradox of mental life, the extremes of unreflective support and unreflective hostility provoked by a work which is itself a model of self-consciousness and care. But Mallarmé's example, insofar as it supports a *literary* ideal, still remains, albeit at one remove, a threat to Valéry's attempt to supersede that ideal by annexing it to a broader intellectual conception. The political metaphor of the well-known 1912 letter to Thibaudet shows Valéry taking a more aggressive line:

> J'ai connu Mallarmé, après avoir subi son extrême influence, et au moment même où je guillotinais intérieurement la littérature. J'ai adoré cet homme extraordinaire dans le temps même que j'y voyais la seule tête—hors de prix!—à couper, pour décapiter tout Rome.[42]

> (I came to know Mallarmé after I had undergone the extreme effects of his influence, and just at the time when I was inwardly guillotining literature.
> I worshipped that extraordinary man at the very moment that I saw in him the one head—beyond all price—to sever, to decapitate all Rome.)

Twenty-five years on, the Revolutionary metaphor opposing rational Republic to obscurantist Church is reformulated as an image of Caesarist self-affirmation and Christian martrydom.[43] Mallarmé is movingly presented as 'sacred head' ('tête mystérieuse'), who has experienced in its entirety the joys and suffering of creative life, who through a long ascesis has purged himself of all mundane preoccupations and attained a peak of aesthetic development from which he can survey the patterns of the universe of the poetic imagination. But such a Christ is dangerous. His indomitable sense of mission and relentless pursuit of perfection in the *univers des mots* elicits admiration and tenderness; but as the embodiment of the literary ideal, representing 'une idée en quelque sorte suprême, une *idée limite* ou une *idée-somme* de la valeur et des pouvoirs des Lettres' ('a more or less supreme idea, an extreme idea or a total idea of the value and power of Letters') (*Œuvres* I, 642, Valéry's emphasis), he must be sacrificed to the emergence of Valéry's wider vision, the dominance of the great intellectual in the *univers des idées*. Valéry's reponse to a message that both fascinates and threatens is the murderous one of the Roman emperors:

Me rendant plus heureux que Caligula, il m'offrait à considérer
une tête en laquelle se résumait tout ce qui m'inquiétait dans
l'ordre de la littérature, tout ce qui m'attirait, tout ce qui la
sauvait à mes yeux. (*Œuvres* I, 642).

(Making me happier than Caligula, he offered to my gaze a head
in which I found all that troubled me in the realm of literature,
all that attracted me, all that saved it in my eyes.)

In the immediate aftermath of Mallarmé's death, Valéry expressed
his determination to ensure that 'ce labeur énorme d'une intelligence
admirable ne soit pas perdu tout à fait' ('this enormous labour of an
admirable mind should not be completely lost'), a promise that Lloyd
Austin sees as magnificently kept in the articles of the *Écrits divers
sur Stéphane Mallarmé*.[44] Valéry's affection for Mallarmé and his
admiration for Mallarmé's work do indeed emerge clearly from these
texts, but the picture presented by the various articles, couched in
the persuasive clarity of a fluent prose far removed from the syntactic
and lexical idiosyncrasy of Mallarmé's writing, very often looks
uncannily like that of Valéry himself. The irreducibly dissonant
feature of Mallarmé's core commitment to Poetry as supreme and
only value, where Chance may perhaps be abolished through a
recovery of the lost fullness of virtuality, is quite simply excised in
favour of Valéry's own locating of virtuality within the chance
determinations of the evolving Self. The topos of decapitation, which
in Mallarmé's *Cantique de Saint-Jean* describes accession to aesthetic
beatitude, is reworked by Valéry as a metaphor for ruthless intellectual
self-preservation and self-development.[45] 'On n'atteint au sommet de
soi-même que par le détour et les secours des autres' ('One only
reaches the summit of oneself by a detour through others and with
their help') (*Cahiers* II, 648) reads a 1926 note; 'CI-GIT MOI /TUÉ
PAR LES AUTRES' ('HERE LIE I / KILLED BY OTHER
PEOPLE') reads an 'Épitaphe' of 1938 (*Cahiers* I, 156). The Other
fulfils a developmental need but is always a lethal threat. The Self to
survive must affirm its separation. The executor must turn executioner
if he is not himself to perish.

3

Poetry's Polite Terrorist
Reading Sartre Reading Mallarmé

Charles D. Minahen

How can it be that Mallarmé, 'this small, kindly, unflamboyant man',[1] could be accused of murder by one well-known critic and of suicide and genocide by another? Interestingly, the first charge, made by Barthes (echoing Blanchot) in *Le Degré zéro de l'écriture*,[2] is more or less contemporaneous with that of the second accuser, Sartre, and is perhaps not surprisingly consonant with the latter's view, since, according to one analyst, *Le Degré zéro de l'écriture* is 'a book that is still situated squarely within the Sartrean problematic'.[3] Even though Sartre tended to associate murder specifically with Genet, the act is clearly understood in the term genocide, which, in Sartre's reading of Mallarmé, envisaged nothing less than the extermination of the entire human race. By focusing on Sartre's position, then, as I intend to do, we will indirectly be examining Barthes's, since the one is, in effect, subsumed within the other.

That Sartre was ever seriously interested in Mallarmé is a fact that relatively few readers are aware of even today. It nevertheless makes sense that 'a philosopher of negation [like Sartre] should be drawn to a poet of negation and absence'[4] like Mallarmé. We know for a fact that the author of *L'Etre et le Néant* discovered the author of *Un Coup de dés jamais n'abolira le hasard* while still a student, sometime during the years of his preparation for and subsequent residence at the École Normale Supérieure (rue d'Ulm), where he spent long hours voraciously reading while cutting classes. The true extent of Mallarmé's impact on Sartre, however, only became apparent in the waning years of his career, when, in certain late published works and interviews, the subject of Mallarmé, which Sartre had addressed and

46

abandoned just after the war, resurfaced. Readers familiar with both of their works might already have discerned an 'existential' affinity between them without knowing that a meeting of the minds had actually occurred in an intertext, more precisely an investigation of Mallarmé undertaken by Sartre, which was never completed. I say investigation because the work is, in effect, an inquest—Sartre frequently uses the word 'enquête'[5] in the elaboration of his existential psychoanalysis—into the facts of a particular case meant to illuminate the essence of that individual. The text in question is Sartre's 'biography' of Mallarmé, which might more accurately be termed a critical, often speculative, existential-psychoanalytical reconstruction, diagnosis, and interpretation,[6] published posthumously in 1986 by Sartre's heir, Arlette Elkaïm-Sartre, under the title *Mallarmé: la lucidité et sa face d'ombre.*[7]

The facts surrounding this text have been thoroughly elaborated elsewhere[8] but can be briefly summarized as follows: it includes the remaining pages of a very lengthy study entitled (apparently by Sartre himself) 'L'Engagement de Mallarmé', most of which was destroyed in the bombing of Sartre's apartment by the OAS in the early sixties;[9] it also includes, with some additions, Sartre's article 'Mallarmé', first published in 1953 and later republished as the preface to the Gallimard edition of Mallarmé's *Poésies.*[10]

But was the Mallarmé project an abandoned *fausse piste* like the *Ethics Notebooks*, with which it was, at its inception, roughly contemporary? Are the *inédits* reliable? Unlike the *Ethics Notebooks* (published posthumously as *Cahiers pour une morale*), part of the *Mallarmé* was, as we have seen, published by Sartre in 1953, and the rest appeared in the journal *Obliques* in 1979 while he was still living, so it was not left untouched, nor was it explicitly renounced, as seems to have been the case with the *Cahiers*. One must not lose sight of the fact, however, that the vast bulk of the manuscript was either lost or destroyed, so there are many important aspects and implications of the *Mallarmé* that are not fully elaborated or explained, such as the *engagement* (commitment) so invitingly announced in the title (about which more will be said later).

'Such as into Himself finally eternity changes him'[11]

Sartre's writings on Mallarmé are part of the existential-psychoanalytical biographical enterprise launched in the mid-forties with his study of Baudelaire, which increased thereafter in importance until it eventually consumed the lion's share of his attention as an author. 'Since the war', Douglas Collins remarks in a book published the year of Sartre's death, 'he has devoted far more pages to biography than to anything else',[12] and Scriven notes the astonishing fact that 'Between 1946 and 1981 approximately four thousand pages [almost two million words] of Sartre's biographical discourse were published' (1). For his work as a whole, then, the significance of these texts, which include biographies of Baudelaire, Genet, Mallarmé, Tintoretto, Flaubert, and an autobiography,[13] cannot be denied, although they have never received the acclaim accorded his literary and philosopical writings. For many readers, there is something resistant, disconcerting, even intimidating about them. Whether it be the unrelenting meanness of the Baudelaire, the subversive perversity of the Genet, the forbidding length and complexity of the Flaubert, or the fragmented disjointedness of the Mallarmé, Sartre's biographies are often provocative to the point of being frustrating, irritating, outrageous. It seems to me, however, that the hybrid nature of his conception of biography, which has passed unchallenged by many of the specialists who approach the works from the Sartrean point of view, might strike the critic, who views the project from the perspective of Sartre's 'victim', as flawed, disputable, unacceptable. How could a Mallarmé scholar, for example, be anything but shocked by Sartre's unrestrained assault upon the 'cher maître'? Such a person, one might conjecture, would rise to the poet's defence and assail the Sartrean position. This indignant Mallarmiste's challenge might run something like this:

When Sartre's critical biographies of writers are compared to his literary works, it is immediately (and perhaps astonishingly) apparent that he treats his literary personages quite differently from the human subjects he analyses. He does not explicitly judge the former, even though there may be an implied judgement, which is nonetheless ambiguously conveyed. By contrast, he ruthlessly cuts up and evaluates his human subjects. Why this disparity? Perhaps because the latter represent the realization *in praxis* of the situations presented hypothetically in his literary works. What the human subjects did counts. Their lives were concrete experiences of being-in-the-world. But there is a puzzling inconsistency in Sartre's approach. As author he creates situations with all their concomitant ambiguity and withholds explicitly judging them, respecting thereby the existentialist maxim that the subject can never really judge with certainty or reliability the other, but as biographer he does not hesitate to dissect, expose, accuse, demystify, even speculate wildly and at times almost irresponsibly. There is, then, a double standard with regard to the imaginary and the real, in which the latter is spared no mercy in contrast to a certain deference afforded the former.

Another peculiarity of Sartre's biographical methodology is the way evidence to document his analysis is selected and used. Speaking of the *Baudelaire*, in particular, Jean-Yves Debreuille notes that Sartre 'uses conjointly and without distinction fragments of poems and fragments of letters to back up his demonstration, without caring about their different manner of signifying'.[14] Sartre indiscriminately gives such evidence the weight of facts. If a fact is indeed a fact, that is, historically anchored in the real, its truth is evident. But a fact, such as the death of Mallarmé's mother, his marriage to Maria-Christina Gerhard, or the birth of his daughter Geneviève, cannot be compared to the recounting of experiences, feelings, or opinions of a letter, where a gap already exists between the letterwriter as subject and object of the writing (letters entail constructs of the self, the projection of an image that could constitute an instance of impure reflection, which, in Sartrean thought, is 'in bad faith'); and works of art are likely to be further removed from the subject, since they may involve constructs that have nothing to do with the self. In the end, Sartre, the phenomenological analyst of intentionality, fails to consider that factor in the way he sifts through and evaluates documentary evidence.

But he did otherwise recognize, although not always consistently, different types of writing, as in the famous distinction between poetry and prose set forth with such conviction after the war in *Qu'est-ce que la littérature*, only to be attenuated and contradicted soon after in such works as 'L'Engagement de Mallarmé', where the title itself reverses the earlier view of poetry as non-committed writing.[15] Late in life, long after the vacillating that followed his position in *Qu'est-ce que la littérature*, Sartre, when queried, made a revealing distinction

49

between philosophical and literary writing, recognizing, in effect, the multivocal nature of literature, as opposed to philosophy which, if not univocal, strives to fashion phrases that have singular, self-contained meanings.[16]

In the case of his existential biographies, however, he rejects not only the difference between types of evidence but also the separation between life and text—'Je m'oppose complètement à l'idée de texte' ('I am completely opposed to the idea of text'), he states in 1971[17]—and it is this lack of separation of the author from the work (the very hallmark of his biographical method) that pits Sartre against the modernist and postmodernist axioms of the death of the author and the primacy of the text. Accepting Sartre's concept of biography requires accepting his complete and indiscriminate identification of the author with the *œuvre*, when in even the most common modes of historical reconstruction, such as occur, for example, in courts of law, degrees of evidentiary reliability are considered crucial to ascertaining the truth of the matter.

Sartre's appropriation of the literary text as a biographical document is particularly critical in the case of a poet. The 'I' of the poet-speaker in lyric verse is easily confused with the poet, and Sartre sees no reason not to do so. But this 'I' is no more the poet than a first-person narrator is the author in a prose text. Certainly there are themes that writers favour, points of view that they tend to take, but these cannot be relied upon as objectifications of the historical self anchored in the world. Gide's compelling and convincing narrators, who ultimately prove dishonest and unreliable, expose the risk of accepting as true the narrating subject's account of things. Even Sartre demonstrates this time and again in his plays, when, as in *Huis clos*, characters insist upon the truth of their bogus recounting of past events. One could not justifiably equate Gide directly with Michel in *L'Immoraliste* on the basis of homosexual tendencies, nor Sartre with Pablo Ibietta in 'Le Mur' on the basis of anti-fascist commitment.[18] Just as Sartre cannot then be reliably identified with his characters, neither can Mallarmé be confused literally with Igitur on the basis of a reflection upon self-extinction or with Hérodiade or the Faun, even if these fictionalized constructs of the artist's imagination display certain characteristics or embody certain privileged themes of the artist. The biographer–analyst who bases his reconstruction on such fictions, merely creates a fiction of a fiction. Put another way, Mallarmé creates a fiction of the self from which Sartre derives another fiction.

This brings us to perhaps the most controversial aspect of Sartre's existential-psychoanalytical biographical method. Wilfully or not—and it often does seem wilful—he, as biographer–analyst concerned presumably with a truthful rendering, does not hesitate to fictionalize and fabricate his subject. Halpern notes that 'Sartre's criticism has always contained an element of fiction or myth that separates it—at least in its intention—from forms of criticism less evidently imaginative and idiosyncratic' (13). The fictionalizing may include not only educated guesses about undocumented elements, but also distortions, misquotations, and misrepresentations of documented evidence, as if the intention were to validate a preconceived opinion of the subject, to which evidence, sometimes taken out of context, is made selectively to conform. It would be too time-consuming to scrutinize every dubious claim Sartre makes in his analysis of Mallarmé, but, in all fairness to the poet, some of the more egregious examples clearly deserve and would even seem to demand a response.

'To black flights of Blasphemy scattered in the future'[19]

Let us begin with the project Mallarmé chooses as a result of a traumatic childhood event. It will be remembered that in the section of *L'Etre et le Néant* entitled 'La Psychanalyse existentielle', Sartre makes his well-known comparison between Freudian (termed 'empirical') and his own existential psychoanalysis. While he embraces the concept of psychoanalysis, he rejects Freud's deterministic version. Rather than a determining complex, there is a freely taken *'choix originel'* (EN, 615), predicated upon an original, presuppositionless liberty: 'La psychanalyse existentielle ne connaît rien *avant* le surgissement originel de la liberté humaine' ('Existential psycho-analysis recognizes nothing *before* the original upsurge of human freedom') (615). In the existential-psychoanalytical biographies, the choice is inevitably preceded by an early childhood crisis that overwhelmingly influences the choice. For Mallarmé, the choice to be a 'poet of nothingness'[20] comes as a direct result of his mother's death when he was five years old. Sartre very vividly (and indeed imaginatively) portrays young Stéphane's struggle to cope with so sudden, devastating, and incomprehensible a loss. One reads the reconstruction like a novel whose narrator is omniscient and ubiquitous, and it is rendered all the more credible by extensive quotations from Mallarmé's letters and literary and critical works. The account is so eloquent that, according to the book's editor, Sartre 'gives to his own discourse a quasi-poetic wholeness', and she extols in particular 'the pages where he highlights the link between the maternal Gaze and the quality of presence in the world' (9). While these pages are indeed beautifully written, the reader, especially one familiar with Mallarmé, cannot help wondering whether or not they have anything to do with what Stéphane Mallarmé actually experienced as a child. Often, when the evidence is checked, the accuracy of a claim becomes immediately suspect.

One telling example is the description of the abandoned child's search for his missing mother, 'La Disparue' ('the Departed One'), against the backdrop of the world's 'massivité sombre' ('dark massiveness'). Sartre imagines the boy mistaking an apparition for 'la présence palpable de la morte' ('the palpable presence of the deceased') (100). He then quotes the following lines from *L'Après-midi d'un faune*:

> Si clair,
> Leur incarnat léger, qu'il voltige dans l'air
> Assoupi de sommeils touffus. (*Œuvres complètes*, 50)

> (So clear,
> The light blush of their flesh, that it floats in the air
> Drowsed in dense slumbers.)

But these lines express a mature male's lusty desire to seduce nymphs. Can they be credibly interpreted to represent a child's ephemeral vision of his lost mother? The overt incestuousness of such a reading might not be surprising in a Freudian analysis, but Sartre's emphasis is upon the mother as an image of absolute presence/absence, upon her all-encompassing gaze, not upon her eroticized body as the locus of an incestuous cathexis. The example thus seems altogether unsuitable and inappropriate.

Another instance related to the trauma of his mother's premature death is the child's perception that he 'ne sera jamais *lui-même en personne*' ('will never be *himself as a distinct person*') (85), since he comes from two lines of faceless functionaries. Noting that the child 'peut incarner tous les ancêtres à la fois puisqu'ils sont tous pareils' ('can incarnate all his ancestors at once since they are all alike'), Sartre quotes the following verses: 'De frigides roses pour vivre/Toutes la même' ('Frigid roses to live/All the same') and then adds, 'ont produit cette rose en bouton' ('have produced this rosebud'). These verses, from the 'Éventail' ('Fan') for Mallarmé's mistress, Méry Laurent, teasingly evoke her aloof 'frigidity', which the poet, speaking through the fan, will melt into laughter. To offer this playfully flirtatious image as evidence of Mallarmé's stark realization that he is just another clone in a long line of insignificant bureaucrats requires an extraordinary leap of imagination that borders on the ludicrous.

Eventually, Sartre claims, the young Mallarmé comes to see himself condemned by his ancestry to a sombre destiny of civil service and intractable *ennui*:

> Puisqu'il sera un fonctionnaire et que le fonctionnaire est déjà tout fait, l'orphelin, de noir vêtu, entre ces messieurs en noir qui lui ressemblent comme des frères, a conscience d'être achevé. Sa vie est là, totalité finie, bouclée, circulaire. (106)

> (Since he will be a functionary and since the functionary is already a finished product, the orphan, clad in black, between these gentlemen in black who resemble him like brothers, is conscious of being fully formed. His life is there, a closed, circular, finished totality.)

It seems that there are two rather surprising and perplexing conclusions to draw from Sartre's psychoanalysis: first, that it is, in effect, a very Freudian scenario—Sartre's anti-Freudian stance notwithstanding—complete with obsessive fixation on the mother, rendered all the more acute by her early death and, as Sartre goes on to argue, hatred and *ressentiment* of the father and of the entire paternal line; and second, that the impact on Mallarmé is as deterministic as the Freudian Oedipus complex, since it will effectively dictate his 'original choice' of a life project. Mallarmé is thus portrayed by Sartre as, to quote Scriven, a 'victim . . . of circumstances beyond [his] control', who undertakes 'a vengeful writing project' (78).

But how can this scenario of irresistible determination be reconciled with Sartre's theory of unrestricted freedom, set forth in

L'Etre et le Néant (along with the tenets of existential psychoanalysis), whereby an individual's liberty and responsibility are total? Moreover, how can Mallarmé ever hope to be authentic, if, from the tender age of five, he is hopelessly steeped in *ressentiment* and, by consequence, bad faith? And finally, is it really reasonable to maintain that a single childhood trauma can so overwhelm a person that it remains the paramount event of his or her entire life, never to be superseded by any other?

In the matter of the effect of the mother's death upon the five-year-old, Sartre himself mentions the 'seule information' ('single piece of information') available, to him at least, that describes the child faking a tantrum, upon hearing someone speak of the recent misfortune, because he was 'embarrassé de son manque de douleur qui ne lui donnait pas la contenance due' ('embarrassed by his lack of grief which did not give him the appropriate demeanor') (SM, 86). Sartre considers the source of the story 'doubtful', although the source is Mallarmé himself, recorded by Henri de Régnier in his diary and reproduced by Henri Mondor in his biography,[21] a book that is otherwise, for Sartre, a font of numerous reliable facts about the poet's life. More recently, Millan has addressed the issue:

> We need to distrust the temptation (which too many critics have found irresistible) of exaggerating the personal impact of his mother's death upon the young Mallarmé . . . First, Mallarmé was only five years old when his mother died: the whole event may have seemed somewhat remote to him. Second . . . in western Europe of the middle to late nineteenth century death at an early age was very much more commonplace than it is today. We must avoid the temptation of viewing such events with twentieth-century eyes and preconceptions . . . In fact, for Stéphane, the immediate consequences of his mother's death were of a practical rather than an emotional nature. (12–13)

In Sartre's analysis, nonetheless, an irremediable sense of loss, exile, and failure, aggravated by a deep feeling of *ressentiment*, engenders in Mallarmé a negating, annihilating vengefulness that he turns upon himself and the world. That Mallarmé was driven repeatedly to commit suicide and genocide, even figuratively in the poetic act, as Sartre claims, seems completely at odds with the image of the harried, distracted schoolteacher or the frail elderly gentleman with a shawl draped over his shoulders pictured in a late photograph. There is no doubt, as his letters attest, that he suffered many bouts of depression, especially during the years of 'exile' in the provinces where he was assigned to teach by a bureaucratically indifferent and, at times, hostile Ministry of Education. But suicide is only an occasional, not a constantly recurring, theme in his works.

It figures significantly in *Igitur*, a relatively early work written between 1867 and 1870[22] during the period of exile, which Sartre quotes repeatedly. Mallarmé, who at the time may indeed have entertained ideas of suicide, faces his fears by representing a possible scenario, which involves a Poesque descent into the family crypt, the ingestion of, presumably, poison—'la goutte de néant' ('the drop of nothingness') (*Œuvres complètes*, 443)—from a 'phial', for which the word in French ('fiole') is an anagram of the word for madness ('folie'). By juxtaposing these words in the final scene—'La fiole vide, folie' ('the empty phial, madness')—the act of suicide is directly associated with insanity. We know from secondary accounts that Mallarmé, whose health, both mentally and physically, was deteriorating, feared he might be 'going insane' (ML, 93). Assuming that the drama of *Igitur* reflects figuratively his own personal plight, suicide, as an insane act, might be portrayed as the inevitable consequence of Igitur's imagined descent into the abyss, but it is an outcome Mallarmé personally feared and, in his vicarious constructing of the drama, attempted to avoid through the healing catharsis of artistic creation. By so directly confronting his demons, as others have pointed out, he hoped to exorcise them. To cite Fowlie: '*Igitur* seems to be an exercise undertaken by Mallarmé to explain to himself a state of mind from which he is determined to escape. Self-knowledge is a liberation. The act of writing is a remedy' (109). Bertrand Marchal deems the work 'a homeopathy'[23] and adds: 'Henceforth can begin the game of Literature' (267).

In a later work, 'Victorieusement fui le suicide beau' ('Victoriously fled the beautiful suicide') (*Œuvres complètes*, 68), the theme of suicide is announced in the sonnet's first verse, but far from expressing a death wish resulting from a personal crisis, it denotes symbolically the sun's ritual suicide at dusk. Although the darkening purple of the crepuscule, presaging an imminent plunge into night, evokes a fleeting image of the poet's 'tomb', its actual 'absence' inspires mirth—'O rire' ('Oh laughter')—not grief, because death, at that moment, is virtual, remote, whereas the woman, whose head is posed alluringly on cushions, is an immanent, immediate enticement. Here, suicide symbolizes the principle of inevitable self-extinction that governs being-in-the-world, but like the sunset that leaves no trace—'de tout cet éclat pas même le lambeau/S'attarde' ('of all that brilliance not even a shred/Lingers')—extinction, for the moment at least, is 'victoriously fled' and any thought of it overpowered by a pressing, present urge. Marchal puts it this way: 'the poet observes, with a detached air, the funereal purple of the sunset which, for once, is not for him; for once, he does not recognize in it the grief of his vesperal dreams . . . the shadow that will reign is not the fatal shadow of dreams, but that propitious shadow of the poet-lover' (162).

Ultimately, in Mallarmé's last major work, *Un Coup de dés jamais n'abolira le hasard*, suicide is, in effect, abandoned as an option in the existential crisis the poem portrays. Although 'folie' (which can be associated intertextually with the suicide of *Igitur*) does appear as an isolated word at the lowest point of the wave trough of the fifth double page, it immediately yields to the 'tourbillon' ('whirlpool') that is literally sketched in the ideograph of page six. The madness of suicide is thus symbolically rejected in favour of a surrender to the forces of chance, which the subsumption of the master/captain/poet into the vortex effectively depicts. Rather than provoke death in a wilful act of self-annihilation, the poet will go with the flow, since, willing or not, the relentless pull of the streamlines will convey him incrementally and inevitably to extinction in the vacuum-void of the vortical core.

'from the simple fact that he can cause darkness by blowing on the light'[24]

Mallarmé's obsession with absence is thus not an impulse to annihilate born of vengence for an irremediable childhood loss. Nor is the cancelling technique so often practised in his poetics, as Sartre claims, 'un travail de destruction' ('a labor of destruction') (SM, 157). Rather than a recurring ritual suicide of the poet through the ritual suicide of word-symbols in the poem, it is an enacting through language of the negative, annihilating effect of nothingness on being, that is, a representation of worldly destruction and death via the

immanent-transcendent agency of the word-symbol, with the paradoxical effect of the positive assertion of a double negative. Take, for
example, the oft-cited image of the 'Sonnet en x': 'nul ptyx' ('no ptyx').
The word 'ptyx' is a signifier with no clear signified, echoed by the
'x' which is emblematic of 'the unknown' (ML, 169). Mallarmé's word
choice here is particularly illustrative of the nothing that a word
paradoxically is. If it has a referent—and this term does not, I
believe[25]—it represents the absence of the thing named. Here, the
'ptyx', which stands for nothing, neither thing nor concept, is itself
cancelled by 'nul', which negates the nothing of the word but at the
same time affirms the process of negation.

Consider, further, the famous dictum 'un coup de dés jamais
n'abolira le hasard' ('a dice-throw will never abolish chance'), which,
among numerous possible interpretations, might be read: 'an attempt
to freeze chance in the phenomenal world will never abolish the
concept of chance' or 'the phenomenon of the poem will never abolish
the concept the poem actualizes'. What issues from the paradox is
the existence of the poem itself, which enacts the cancelling operations of contingency but in so doing affirms them. The poem *is*
nothing.

From a reversed perspective, then, it can be said that just as
nothingness cancels being, so too does being cancel nothingness, and
while this is a more vulnerable, unstable condition, it is one that
Mallarmé evokes. Take the example of the opening verse of 'Salut',
the opening poem of *Poésies*, which Sartre himself cites: 'Rien, cette
écume, vierge vers' ('Nothing, this froth, virgin verse') (*Œuvres
complètes*, 27). Noting the privileged placement of 'Rien' on the first
page, Sartre reads it to mean that 'le poème est suicide de l'homme
et de la Poésie' ('the poem is the suicide of man and of Poetry') (SM,
163), when in fact the line demonstrates just the opposite: an original
nothingness from which springs the ephemeral froth of matter and
its subsequent transmutation into the virgin verse of the poem.
Something emerges out of nothing, even if it is immediately
threatened by nothingness, specifically by the negatively limiting 'ne
. . . que' phrase of the following verse: 'A ne désigner que la coupe'
('designating only the cup/cut'). Although being must inevitably
recede back into the nothingness from which it emerges, Mallarmé
portrays both the surging—*surgir* is a favoured word—and the
vanishing of being against the backdrop of the void. Hence, it is

neither the absolute affirmation nor the total negation of the world that the poem exclusively enacts but rather 'its vibratory near-disappearance':

> A quoi bon la merveille de transposer un fait de nature en sa presque disparition vibratoire selon le jeu de la parole, cependant; si ce n'est pour qu'en émane, sans la gêne d'un proche ou concret rappel, la notion pure.[26]

> (What good is the wonder of transposing a fact of nature into its vibratory near-disappearance according to the play of the word, however; if it is not to derive from it, without the bother of a near or concrete recall, the pure notion.)

If the poetic sign is an empty signifier that opens into a *mise-en-abyme* of emerging and receding signifieds, its sound is a perturbation of the air capable of evoking the pure absence of the idea. Mallarmé is not, as Sartre suggests, annihilating nature with the word, he is affirming its possible disclosure as a pure notion. Poetry is not for him a vengeful, destructive act, it is an attempt against all odds to fix the effervescent, evanescent real in its surging and vanishing. Although the first word of Mallarmé's *Poésies*, 'Rien', is significant for its assertion of nothingness as a ground, the last salient word-image, 'Un Coup de Dés', capitalized by the poet, is even more significant for the solution it proposes to that nullity, namely, the dice-throw of the poem, which captures the pure idea and renders it as durable and illuminating as a constellation.

Sartre's charge of suicide, then, is fundamentally without merit, and that being the case, it follows that his accusation of genocide, since it is as he himself admits an extension of the former, is similarly baseless:

> il tenait le destin de la Race entre ses mains. Il a dépendu de lui que l'Homme disparût ou non de la terre. Le suicide, devenu génocide, lui semblait un acte 'parfaitement absurde'. (SM, 141)

> (he held the destiny of the Race in his hands. It depended on him whether or not Man would disappear from the earth. Suicide, become genocide, seemed to him a 'perfectly absurd' act.)

Suicide is one thing, but genocide suggests a misanthropy on Mallarmé's part that even the evidence Sartre selectively cites belies. For the most part, this alleged evidence, such as the words 'parfaitement absurde' quoted from *Igitur* in the above passage, is drawn either from Mallarmé's literary texts (a dubious source of information concerning the man) or from his correspondence. In the case of the latter, if we focus only on 'L'Élu' ('The Chosen One'), the section of Sartre's study that concentrates specifically on Mallarmé, the notes identify seventy-one dated quotations from Mallarmé's correspondence: sixty-eight of them (all but three) date from the 1850s and 60s, and of those, fifty-eight are from a six-year span, 1862–67, when Mallarmé was 20–27 years of age, a recognized period of extreme crisis in his life. And yet Sartre's analysis of Mallarmé as obsessively suicidal and genocidal rests almost entirely on selected evidence from that brief period, as if Mallarmé was from then on frozen in time and never changed—as Sartre doubtless would have it—which is not supported by the facts. What Sartre (re)constructs, then, is much less a true-to-life portrait than a myth.

'he/his puerile shadow/caressed and polished and rendered and washed'[27]

When, as if the accusations of suicide and genocide were not shocking enough, Sartre states that 'l'holocauste des mots s'accompagnera de l'holocauste des choses' ('the holocaust of words will be accompanied by the holocaust of things') (160), making of Mallarmé a ruthless extirpator, it is clear that he is employing hyperbole either with reckless abandon or, one begins to suspect, with shrewd and callous calculation. But why would Sartre intentionally write in such an irresponsible and inflammatory manner? Why has he no qualms about so flagrantly mixing fact and fiction? This is due, Halpern claims, to Sartre's 'determined effort to use the text, to make of criticism something that goes beyond the subject matter of analysis', to present 'fictional messages' and 'injunctions' to his contemporaries (14). Scriven, attempting to explain 'Sartre's systematic manhandling of canonized cultural figures' (24), may well out-Sartre Sartre himself when he terms the latter's anti-bourgeois assault in *Baudelaire* a 'rape':

If, as Sartre maintains, the reader is an oppressive 'other', a disorientated vacillating presence, a passive acquiescing female, there is only one possible solution for the virile, active and committed writer: rape. The post-war middle-class reader must be forcefully demystified not generously seduced. Such a reader must be penetrated and overwhelmed by the virile existential ethic of the authentic writer. (52)

In order to jolt readers out their complacency, particularly the bourgeois intellectual elite, he attacks their icons: savagely and mercilessly in the case of Baudelaire; aggressively, if less maliciously, in the case of Mallarmé. But to accomplish his iconoclastic aims, Sartre had to find or create a new, dynamic means of expression.

Regarding the shifting preferences of one genre or form over another throughout Sartre's career, Scriven argues persuasively that his abandonment of the novel represented 'the rejection of an archetypal bourgeois literary form' in favour of a form more consistent with his evolving revolutionary agenda. While it is clear that theatre provided a more effective means of making contact with people and thereby promoting social change, Sartre was also looking for an appropriate narrative vehicle. What he did, in effect, was invent a new hybrid form, the existential-psychoanalytical biography, which is rooted in the real, can have symbolic and even propagandistic impact, provides a textual space for the application of existential principles on the metaphysical, philosophical, psychological, and ethical planes, and possesses a mythic or mystical dimension (an important element of literary aesthetics for Sartre that is also very telling, as we shall see).

Rather than supplanting the novel, the novel becomes subsumed into the new form.[28] The grafting of the novel's fictive, figurative, and mythic elements onto biography thus allows Sartre to transform the latter into something more effective than a dull accumulation of facts. Like a novelist he can present his subject, not from the dispassionate neutral position of the old realist narrative (or the old biography, for that matter), but from the perspective of the committed revolutionary. And like a biographer, he can document his case with facts gleaned from the life and times, so his account will have social and historical significance.

But the question then arises, what version of Mallarmé is thus produced: the factual man whose becoming through time involved a series of choices that determined an essence for which he is both responsible and morally accountable, or the mythical 'knight of nothingness',[29] whose transformation of 'the Failure of Poetry' into 'The Poetry of Failure' (SM, 144) represents an apotheosis of the vengeful nihilism advocated by the post-1860 generation of French writers? The first version would be that of the author of *L'Etre et le Néant* and would reflect Sartre's concern with ethics in that early work. The second version would be that of the Marxist theorist attempting to identify a historical totalization through the figurative reconstruction of Mallarmé as a 'singular universal'.[30] But Sartre cannot have it both ways, portraying Mallarmé simultaneously as man and myth. He cannot exaggerate and otherwise distort the facts of his life and also hold him ethically responsible for that ersatz essence. In the end—and it seems to me this is the only way one can understand his portrait of Mallarmé—Sartre opts for myth.

A cynical critic might even go so far as to claim that Sartre thus abandons ethics in favour of politics, existential authenticity in favour of propaganda, that, as a committed revolutionary and pragmatist, he does not care about the factual accuracy of his portrait. In the name of the death of the bourgeoisie, he is ready to sacrifice the individual for the cause. Too bad if a few writers get soiled in the process. Like his admitted alter ego Hoederer in *Les Mains sales*, who dirties his hands as necessary, placing praxis over principle, Sartre will continue assailing and undermining bourgeois culture by destroying its icons, even if it means doing violence to the remembered essence of an individual life or two.

But even as myth, the portrayal of Mallarmé must issue from the reality of the man anchored in history. For, as Barthes has shown, myth is a 'meta-language', a secondary sign derived from the primary 'sense' of a sign-turned-signifier ('form') that connects with a new signified ('concept') to produce a new mythic sign or 'signification'.[31] There must therefore be a direct link between the original semiological sign and the derived mythic signification, which is not the case of a Mallarmé allegedly obsessed with suicide and genocide, since, as I have attempted to show, it is a primary sense that has no substantial and thus no credible basis in fact.

What can justifiably be included in the myth of Mallarmé are those attributions that do have such a basis. Often, it seems, Sartre seizes upon an aspect of Mallarmé's poetic practice that, despite his intention to mock the poet, emerges instead as an insight into the genius of his aesthetic project. Consider, for example, his remark that 'sous le regard réflexif, le Non se change en Oui. Impuissant à chanter, il chantera son impuissance' ('beneath his reflective gaze, No is changed into Yes. Impotent to sing, he will sing of his impotence'), (129) to which he later adds:

> impuissant qui chante son impuissance, Mallarmé convertit son échec personnel en impossibilité de la Poésie; puis par un nouveau retournement il transforme l'Echec de la Poésie en Poésie de l'Echec. (144)

> (impotent poet who sings of his impotence, Mallarmé converts his personal failure into the impossibility of Poetry; then in a new reversal, he transforms the Failure of Poetry into the Poetry of Failure.)

Here Sartre—notwithstanding his negative critical intention—seems sensibly, if unwittingly, to suggest that, far from emerging from a vindictive suicidal or genocidal obsession, Mallarmé's original crisis grew out of a feeling of futility in the face of pervasive nothingness. The sterility of the blank page produced sterility in the poet. There being nothing to say, he could say nothing. Then he realized that the inability to produce meaning could itself be a subject for poetry, that language could enact the cancelling operations of nothingness and thus transform the failure to express into the successful expression of failure in the poem.

In another context, regarding Mallarmé's grief and aloneness after the death of his sister, Sartre summarizes the poet's existential crisis as follows:

> En un mot, il n'a d'être que pour se nier, de la même façon que, par exemple, nous prêtons un être au Vide ou au Néant par le simple fait de leur donner un nom. Ce miroitement fixe et terne, c'est le non-Etre de l'Etre passant dans l'être du non-Etre pour redevenir non-Etre du Néant. (SM, 114)

> (In a word, he possesses being only for it to be negated, in the same way that, for example, we lend being to the Void or to Nothingness by the simple fact of giving them a name. This

fixed and drab shimmering is the non-Being of Being passing into the being of non-Being to become again non-Being of Nothingness.)

Although Sartre's tone is, as usual, sarcastic, he very cogently describes the way Mallarmé, as a poet, found himself empowered by the capacity of language to name and thereby signify (i.e., 'lend being to') the dialectic of non-being and being as a process of cancelling and cancelling of cancelling: specifically, the immanence of ubiquitous nothingness as a ground ('as pure virtuality'),[32] the surging of things out of nothing into being, the shimmering of their momentarily positive but ephemeral 'near-disappearance', their vanishing back into nothing, the nullity of their no longer being, their remembered absence as a pure notion of having been, and their ultimate total annihilation in the oblivion of the nothingness they 'become again'.

'he . . . to whom they attribute the introduction, to Society, like an explosive, of a concept that is too new'[33]

Of all the insights into Mallarmé that Sartre seems to have had in spite of himself, however, there is one that more than any has magnified and energized the Mallarmé myth. Noting that Mallarmé 'pourra écrire que "le poème est la seule bombe"' ('will be able to write that "the poem is the only bomb"') (SM, 157), which is a misquotation of the statement 'Je ne sais pas d'autre bombe qu'un livre' ('I know of no other bomb than a book') that a journalist elicited from him the evening an anarchist had exploded a bomb in the Chambre des Députés,[34] Sartre presciently discerns in Mallarmé's poetry a subtle terrorism, its violence not overt but concealed behind a facade of imperturbable politeness:

> Une bombe est une chose au même titre qu'un fauteuil Empire: un peu plus méchant, voilà tout; que d'intrigues et de compromissions pour pouvoir la placer où il faut. Mallarmé n'est pas, ne sera pas anarchiste: il refuse toute action singulière; sa violence—je le dis sans ironie—est si entière et si désespérée qu'elle se change en calme idée de violence. Non, il ne fera pas sauter le monde; il le mettra entre parenthèses. Il choisit le terrorisme de la politesse; avec les choses, avec les hommes, il conserve toujours une imperceptible distance. (151)

(A bomb is a thing just like an Empire armchair: a bit nastier, that's all; how many intrigues and shady deals to find the right place to put it. Mallarmé is not, will not be an anarchist: he refuses any individual action; his violence—I say this without irony—is so total and desperate that it transforms itself into the calm idea of violence. No, he won't blow up the world; he will bracket it. He chooses the terrorism of politeness; with things, with men, he always keeps an imperceptible distance.)

Sartre's dismissal of any possible involvement on Mallarmé's part with anarchism is more sweeping than the facts indicate. In reference to his discussions of the subject with Mallarmé, Henri de Régnier records Mallarmé as stating: 'Il n'y a qu'un homme qui ait le droit d'être anarchiste, Moi, le Poète, puisque seul je fabrique un produit dont la société ne veut pas, en échange duquel elle ne me donne pas de quoi vivre' ('There is only one man who has the right to be an anarchist, Me, the Poet, since I alone make a product that society does not want, in exchange for which it does not give me anything to live on') (IM, 82). If not a politically active anarchist, Mallarmé clearly was a poetic sympathizer. Moreover, rather than remaining aloof from others and disdaining any individual action, as Sartre avers, Mallarmé proved his willingness to get involved when he intervened on behalf of Félix Fénéon, who was arrested for alleged anarchist activities. Risking possible implication himself, Mallarmé not only spoke out and wrote in defence of his friend and fellow artist, he actually gave testimony before the Cour d'Assises on 8 August 1894 (IM, 80).

Although Sartre did later consider Mallarmé more fully committed,[35] in this earlier text he denies him any political *engagement* while recognizing him nonetheless as *engagé*: 'Il fut tout entier poète, tout entier engagé dans la destruction critique de la Poésie par elle-même' ('He was entirely a poet, entirely committed to the critical destruction of Poetry by itself') (167–8). That a poet can be considered a committed writer represents an evolution in Sartre's thought from the contrary view expressed in *Qu'est-ce que la littérature*; hence, the encounter with Mallarmé proved to be a turning point in his formulation of the concept of *engagement*.[36] But even though Sartre rightly discerns Mallarmé's commitment to a terrorism of politeness, he misunderstands, in the previously cited passage and repeatedly elsewhere in his study, Mallarmé's motivations and intentions. Mallarmé's commitment is not aimed, as I have tried to show, at the destruction of self, humanity, and poetry, in revenge for the childhood loss of a cherished mother. A commitment to so total an annihilation would mean the annihilation of commitment itself. His strategy, rather, is to wage a kind of guerilla warfare from within the bourgeois system of authoritarian values and received ideas, which is the true object of his attack and which he will attempt to undermine by discreet acts of linguistic sabotage.

But how could this most seemingly bourgeois of men, who entertained friends on Tuesday evenings and spent vacations sailing his boat on the Seine, also be an anti-bourgeois terrorist? On the other hand, how could the anti-bourgeois terrorist Sartre, privileged alumnus of the exclusive École Normale Supérieure, enjoy long lunches, often with friends and admirers, seated not on the 'common' side but in the 'fancy', 'aristocratic' section of his favorite café-restaurant, La Coupole?[37] There is no doubt that Sartre recognized (at least eventually) the limitations imposed upon him by the historically determining effects of the bourgeois milieu he was born into and brought up in. He could not realistically metamorphose into a proletarian any more than the middle-class family man Mallarmé could become an anarchist activist. But both had reasons to distrust and despise the particular form of bourgeois culture in which, as Frenchmen, they lived. Mallarmé had suffered many indignities as a schoolteacher-functionary at the mercy of an all-powerful, autocratic, and arrogant civil administration, which condemned him specifically for writing poetry; Sartre suffered through the blatant hypocrisy of such government-sanctioned policies as Nazi collaboration and colonial oppression and exploitation only to find himself, as an outspoken critic, marginalized and shunned.

To remedy the situation through armed revolt would be futile, as the lesson of La Commune all too clearly demonstrated. So both Mallarmé and Sartre, it could be said, take their cue from Rimbaud, who, in the wake of the failure of La Commune, realized he could more effectively subvert the system on the level of language. Sartre chooses the overt form of the polemic, a prime example of which would be the existential biography we have been examining. Like Nietzsche, he will philosophize with a hammer and destroy such bourgeois idols as, ironically enough, Mallarmé. He will strafe the

65

establishment with a hail of words like a machine-gun; he will toss inflammatory books like Molotov cocktails.

Mallarmé, always the gentleman, will take a more subtle, polite course. Recognizing that the conventions of bourgeois culture are signified and transmitted through conventional language, he will assail those conventions, not so much by wreaking havoc upon the signifying operations of the sign—for example, creating shocks and ruptures between signifier, signified, and referent—as had Rimbaud, but by exploiting the cancelling operations inherent in language to explode conventional meanings and expose the nothingness upon which they are predicated. What better anarchy than to make words appear and vanish before the reader's stunned gaze and thereby undermine the conventions they convey. In this sense, Mallarmé is a very contemporary kind of anarchist. His poetic bomb is an illuminating burst with a destructive potential more like that of a computer virus, ingeniously devised, cryptically encoded, clandestinely insinuated into the signifying system, and lying there silently undetected until just the right moment, when a sudden flash erases everything, the system crashes, and nothing remains but an empty blank screen.[38]

4

Lacan and Mallarmé
Theory as Word-Play

Malcolm Bowie

Prose pour des Esseintes	*Prose for des Esseintes*
Hyperbole! de ma mémoire	Hyperbole! can you not
Triomphalement ne sais-tu	Triumphant, today a rune
Te lever, aujourd'hui grimoire	From my memory stand out
Dans un livre de fer vêtu:	In a book clad in iron:
Car j'installe, par la science,	For through knowledge I ensconce
L'hymne des cœurs spirituels	The hymn of spirited hearts
En l'œuvre de ma patience,	In the work of my patience,
Atlas, herbiers et rituels.	Books of maps, of herbs, of rites.
Nous promenions notre visage	We took our face on a trip
(Nous fûmes deux, je le maintiens)	(There were two of us, for sure)
Sur maints charmes de paysage,	Round many charms of landscape,
O sœur, y comparant les tiens.	Comparing yours, O sister.
L'ère d'autorité se trouble	Authority grows restless
Lorsque, sans nul motif, on dit	When with no motive we say,
De ce midi que notre double	As our twin unconsciousness
Inconscience approfondit	Is deepened, of this midday,
Que, sol des cent iris, son site,	That—if so, they have noted—
Ils savent s'il a bien été,	Its site, soil of the hundred
Ne porte pas de nom que cite	Irises, was not quoted
L'or de la trompette d'Été.	When Summer's gold horn thundered.

Oui, dans une île que l'air charge	Yes, on an island perfumed
De vue et non de visions	More with first then second sight
Toute fleur s'étalait plus large	Each flower more flagrantly bloomed
Sans que nous en devisions.	Without our discussing it.
Telles, immenses, que chacune	So that they all, enormous,
Ordinairement se para	Were adorned with clear outlines
D'un lucide contour, lacune	Commonly, a hiatus
Qui des jardins la sépara.	Between them and the gardens.
Gloire du long désir, Idées	Ideas, glory of long
Tout en moi s'exaltait de voir	Longing, my all leapt to see
La famille des iridées	The tribe of the iris throng
Surgir à ce nouveau devoir,	To fulfil this fresh duty,
Mais cette sœur sensée et tendre	But that sister, wise and kind,
Ne porta son regard plus loin	Looked and gave a smile—no more—
Que sourire et, comme à l'entendre	And, as though to understand,
J'occupe mon antique soin.	I give all my ancient care.
Oh! sache l'Esprit de litige,	Let the captious spirit know,
A cette heure où nous nous taisons,	At this hour of our silence,
Que de lis multiples la tige	That the stem where lilies grow
Grandissait trop pour nos raisons	Grew too much for our reasons
Et non comme pleure la rive,	And not as the shore will grieve,
Quand son jeu monotone ment	When its dull game murmurs lies
A vouloir que l'ampleur arrive	Wanting fullness to arrive
Parmi mon jeune étonnement	Amid my youthful surprise
D'ouïr tout le ciel et la carte	To hear heaven and the map
Sans fin attestés sur mes pas,	Which my ceaseless steps attest,
Par le flot même qui s'écarte,	By the very waves that lap,
Que ce pays n'exista pas.	That this land did not exist.
L'enfant abdique son extase	The child forswears ecstasy
Et docte déjà par chemins	And prematurely solemn
Elle dit le mot: Anastase!	Says the word: *Anástase!*
Né pour d'éternels parchemins,	Born for eternal vellum,

68

Avant qu'un sépulcre ne rîe	Before a grave can be gay,
Sous aucun climat, son aïeul,	Its grandsire, in any clime,
De porter ce nom: Pulchérie!	With this name: Pulcheria!
Caché par le trop grand glaïeul.[1]	Hidden by too tall a bloom.[2]

Separare, séparer, ici se termine en *se parere*, s'engendrer soi-même. Dispensons-nous des faveurs certaines que nous trouvons dans les étymologistes du latin, à ce glissement du sens d'un verbe à l'autre. Qu'on sache seulement que ce glissement est fondé dans leur commun appariement à la fonction de la *pars*.

La partie n'est pas le tout, comme on dit, mais d'ordinaire inconsidérément. Car il faudrait accentuer qu'elle n'a avec le tout rien à faire. Il faut en prendre son parti, elle joue sa partie toute seule. Ici, c'est de sa partition que le sujet procède à sa parturition. Et ceci n'implique pas la métaphore grotesque qu'il se mette au monde à nouveau. Ce que d'ailleurs le langage serait bien embarrassé d'exprimer d'un terme originel, au moins dans l'aire de l'indo-européen où tous les mots utilisés à cet emploi ont une origine juridique ou sociale. *Parere*, c'est d'abord procurer —(un enfant au mari). C'est pourquoi le sujet peut se procurer ce qui ici le concerne, un état que nous qualifierons de civil. Rien dans la vie d'aucun ne déchaîne plus d'acharnement à y arriver. Pour être *pars*, il sacrifierait bien une grande part de ses intérêts, et ce n'est pas pour s'intégrer à la totalité qu'au reste ne constituent nullement les intérêts des autres, et encore moins l'intérêt général qui s'en distingue tout autrement.

Separare, se parare: pour se parer du signifiant sous lequel il succombe, le sujet attaque la chaîne, que nous avons réduite au plus juste d'une binarité, en son point d'intervalle. L'intervalle qui se répète, structure la plus radicale de la chaîne signifiante, est le lieu que hante la métonymie, véhicule, du moins l'enseignons-nous, du désir.

C'est en tout cas sous l'incidence où le sujet éprouve dans cet intervalle Autre chose à le motiver que les effets de sens dont le sollicite un discours, qu'il rencontre effectivement le désir de l'Autre, avant même qu'il puisse seulement le nommer désir, encore bien moins imaginer son objet.

Ce qu'il va y placer, c'est son propre manque sous la forme du manque qu'il produirait chez l'Autre de sa propre disparition. Disparition qu'il a, si nous pouvons le dire, sous la main, de la part de lui-même qui lui revient de son aliénation première.

Mais ce qu'il comble ainsi n'est pas la faille qu'il rencontre

dans l'Autre, c'est d'abord celle de la perte constituante d'une de
ses parts, et de laquelle il se trouve en deux parts constitué. Là
gît la torsion par laquelle la séparation représente le retour de
l'aliénation. C'est qu'il opère *avec* sa propre perte, qui le ramène
à son départ.[3]

Separare, separating, ends here in *se parere*, engendering oneself.
Let us dispense with the obvious gems we find in the works of
Latin etymologists concerning the slippage in meaning from one
verb to the other. One should simply realize that this slippage
is grounded in the fact that they are both related to the function
of the *pars*.

The part is not the whole, as is said, though usually without
thinking. For it should be emphasized that the part has nothing
to do with the whole. One has to come to terms with it; it plays
its part [*sa partie*] all by itself. Here the subject proceeds from
his partition to his parturition. This does not imply the grotesque
metaphor of giving birth to himself anew. Indeed, language
would be hard pressed to express that with an original term, at
least in Indo-European climes where all the words used for this
purpose are of juridical or social origin. *Parere* was first of all
to procure (a child for one's husband). That is why the subject
can procure for himself what interests him here—a status I will
qualify as "civil". Nothing in anyone's life unleashes more
determination to succeed in obtaining it. In order to be *pars*, he
would easily sacrifice the better part of his interests, though not
in order to become part of the whole [*s'intégrer à la totalité*],
which, moreover, is in no way constituted by others' interests,
still less by the general interest which is distinguished therefrom
in an entirely different manner.

Separare, se parare: in order to take on the signifier to which
he succumbs, the subject attacks the chain—that I have reduced
to a binary, at its most elementary level—at its interval. The
repeating interval, the most radical structure of the signifying
chain, is the locus haunted by metonymy, the latter being the
vehicle of desire (at least that is what I teach).

It is, in any case, through this impact—whereby the subject
experiences in this interval something that motivates him Other
[*Autre chose*] than the effects of meaning by which a discourse
solicits him—that he in fact encounters the Other's desire, before
he can even call it desire, much less imagine its object.

What he will place there is his own lack, in the form of the lack he would like to produce in the Other through his own disappearance—the disappearance (which he has at hand, so to speak) of the part of himself he receives from his primal [*première*] alienation.

But what he thus fills up is not the lack [*faille*] he encounters in the Other, but rather, first of all, that of the constitutive loss of one of his parts by which he turns out to be made of two parts. For the subject operates *with* his own loss, which brings him back to his point of departure.[4]

Lacan was a devotee of word-play in his writings and spoken performances, and at the same time the originator of a theory of subjectivity which conferred upon word-play a special intellectual dignity. He was not of course the first philosophical writer to place a double pressure of this kind on what is now familiarly known as 'the play of the signifier'. Plato, Erasmus and Heidegger, to take just three widely spaced examples, all share a taste for verbal jests and poetic etymologies, and all attempt to supply theoretical justification for their habit. Those who study such thinkers do not feel obliged to place any particular emphasis on the local details of their practice as writers, although most commentators will draw attention to key moments of semantic slippage or ambiguity. What is singular about the response of Lacan's commentators to such elements of his work is that they have often found his stylistic habits contagious. Rather than seek to understand, say, the tactical advantages and dis-advantages of word-play within the strategic framework of Lacan's theory as a whole, they have become second-order punsters, hoping to acquire authority in the handling of that theory by the docile imitation of certain Lacanian *effets d'écriture*. What follows is an attempt to slow discussion of Lacan down by examining closely a specimen of his writing, and to ask what the structure of his puns tells us about his theoretical writing in general. For comparative purposes I shall set Lacan's paragraphs against a work by one of the undisputed 'masters of the signifier' in modern France: Mallarmé.

Mallarmé's 'Prose pour des Esseintes' (1885) and Lacan's 'Position de l'inconscient' (1960) share a single pun (on derivatives of the Latin *separare* and *parare*), exhaustively over-determine that pun, bathe it in a more general atmosphere of erudite etymologizing and at the same time suggest ways in which puns of this type might be thought of as strictly and necessarily without content. Both texts set forth a paradigm in which an air of semantic plenitude and overflow is set against, and punctured by, an insistent intimation of vacuity, of something that might be there but is, for now, actively and invasively not there. In addition both texts are witty, conceited and ingenious, and ask themselves how far they can go in the direction of tautology and repetition without losing momentum or sinking into the mire. Both are intellectual performances of great subtlety that willingly take chances with sense, and allow a pre-articulate, pre-semantic babble to weave its way through the delicately differentiated and phased arguments that they set forth. I have chosen these texts also because the combined seriousness and levity that Mallarmé and Lacan achieve by way of their word-play will help me, towards the end of my discussion, to make a polemical point about the status that word-play is currently accorded in the sprawling world of verbal endeavour that goes under the obligingly imprecise name of 'theory'.

Mallarmé's celebrated poem has a pun at its centre in the form of a *rime équivoquée* on *se parer/séparer*. Two things about this rhyme are plain: (i) that it marks the end of the first half of the work and ushers in the astonishing visionary climax contained in quatrain 8; (ii) that the contrast it enacts, between the conceptual motifs of *separation* on the one hand and *decoration* or *dress* on the other, is elaborated elsewhere in the text. This, after all, is a poem about the *separation* of the transcendent from the terrestrial order, and about the separation of the mental faculties appropriate to the perception and articulation of each order; and it describes, and recreates in its gorgeous apparel of tropes, the inescapable rhetoricity or dressiness of poetic speech. Moreover, there is a grand metaphysical jest in Mallarmé's pun, for the quality of ideality that separates the transcendent flowers from the fibrous, earth-nourished organisms that horticulture knows is here seen as an artfully applied cosmetic preparation. The ideal flowers separate themselves from their terrestrial counterparts by the daily exercise— 'Ordinairement se para'—of decorative artifice: the 'lucide contour' by which they indefinitely outshine and out-exist mere garden flowers is held in place by an active reminiscence of ordinary human ingenuity, the sort of thing that makes earthly gardens look good. These ideal flowers are *dressed up* in the qualities that define them.

All the ultra-rich rhymes in the middle quatrains of the poem catch up within themselves a gap, iron out in the second member of the rhyme-pair a disjunction that the first member had left intact: 'motif on dit' > 'approfondit', 'de visions' > 'devisions', 'se para' > 'sépara', 'désir, Idées' > 'des iridées', 'de voir' > 'devoir'. Two words melt into one, or two discrete phonic units become a phonic continuum. But the singularity of the 'se para'/'sépara' rhyme is that it catches up between the members of the rhyme-pair the very word, the most *juste* of *mots justes*, needed to characterize gaps of this kind: *lacune*. The argument of the poem is such that the lacunary character of rhyme becomes as it were the minimal index of a lacunary cosmological scheme, in which an unbridgeable gulf exists between two orders of being. The word *lacune* marks another kind of hiatus too, and one that the text as a whole again favours: between metre and syntax. 'Lacune' is the first word of an extended appositional phrase that is to be completed at the end of the following line, and by the device of *contre-rejet* the non-adequation between metre and syntax becomes, in the word *lacune*, a self-naming and autotelic verbal event.

Here, then, is a poem that presents reference works—the book of spells, the atlas, the herbal—as emblematic books and praises the arts of classification for bringing order, in the wake of Linnaeus, to the natural world—'lis multiples', 'cent iris', 'iridées'—but that places at its very centre an imp of the perverse, a genie of vacancy, which dismantles and discredits all taxonomic schemes. *Lacune*, as staged here in the interference zone between rhyme, syntax and metre, is not the principle of differentiation that all acts of classification require—class must be sealed off from class—but the non-commensurability between adjacent systems, their askewness each from each. An earnest philology is at work in the poem, sorting and counterposing individual meanings, and a sober manual of scholarly method is present that refers us repeatedly to the slowness, the studiousness, and the unprepossessing apparatus that science and the writerly arts alike require. Yet all this patient toil has at its core a zone of absence and unmeaning. In Mallarmé's pun-laden central quatrains an unstoppable pulse of desire is seen to thrive upon the closeness of all desiring transactions to an unthinkable but in-extirpable emptiness. It is not part of this poem's business to explain or to *theorize* the connections between desirousness and the lacunary state, but it ties these two psychological and philosophical motifs together into a tight semantic knot.

If we turn abruptly to *se parare/separare* as reincarnated in Lacan's 'Position de l'inconscient' we are likely to be struck first of all by the supercharged philological whimsy that Lacan extracts from their phonetic resemblance. Where Mallarmé had placed the pun at a fulcrum-point in the unfolding of his poem, Lacan sends it echoing in all directions at once. He is rather like an organist who wants to display the huge resources of his many stops and manuals in the shortest possible playing time.

As in 'Prose pour des Esseintes' *séparer* and *se parer* are unveiled as a necessary preliminary to the summative unveiling of *desire*. 'Gloire du long désir' in Mallarmé's eighth quatrain and 'la métonymie véhicule du désir' in Lacan's central paragraph are alike in that, once the full force of separation has been registered, desire cannot be conceived of as other than long to the point of interminability. It is a process of displacement that can never, short of death, have a stop. The clinching power that this piece of word-play has in the centre of Lacan's philological cadenza has been prepared for by a different but related play upon *se parare/se parere*. This launches a parade of witticisms that runs through the entire text: separation is here set against self-appearance, and offers us an appearance of the subject for which the subject cannot be held solely or fully accountable, a self-generation that takes place in the eyes of, and at the hands of, the Other and can be construed only in terms of the otherings, occultations, intervals and disappearances that this encounter brings with it. Lacan's seemingly subordinate verbal echoes and filiations are all motivated by a doctrine of subjectivity as intermittence that is by this period firmly in place within his teaching. *Pars* → *part* → *partie* (in its two senses) → *partition* → *parturition* → *appariement* → *disparition* → *perte* → *départ* are a tribute to the intervallic structure of the signifying chain, to the gaps that keep it going: the pun is valued as a sameness that includes difference, as a difference that recapitulates sameness, and as a backwards- and forwards-referring movement caught up inside the unarrestable momentum of signifying process. (Lacan or his editor or his proof-reader have, by the way, got something wrong. In a context where *erreur* and *errance* fade into each other seamlessly, one hesitates to press a charge of error, but Lacan surely means *parare* and not *parere* in the middle of his second paragraph: in Latin it is *parare* and not *parere* that has the sense of *procurer* given here.)

All the care that Lacan takes to make his specimen section of signifying chain into a visibly, audibly and self-declaringly concatenated and fluidly self-transforming thing, to make it become what it describes, should not, however, tempt us into understating the firm underlying structure of argument that the passage has. Putting that argument in its simplest terms, and remembering the metaphor/metonymy antithesis that Lacan had borrowed from Roman Jakobson,[5] we could say that Lacan is here seeking to revalorize metonymy at the expense of metaphor: metaphor occurs only in the highly pejorative phrase 'métaphore grotesque' and the would-be self-replication, the (for Lacan) fatuous cult of self-identity, that this sentence as a whole seeks to indict may be thought of as one of the perils or follies of metaphoricity at large. He or she who merely metaphorizes is trying to create an isolated and timeless island of identity in the time-bound flow of desire. Metonymy, triumphantly displayed at the mid-point of this excerpt, is the desire-trope *par excellence*.

A subsidiary argument sets metonymy against synecdoche, with which it is often confused: the conditions of subjectivity rule out any recourse to a *pars pro toto*, reveal it as an impossibility; the 'parts' which metonymy aligns, and out of which it produces its intervals and its propulsive force, can never be totalized. The *pars* defined in this way has nothing to do with the whole, and all talk of wholes—within the human subject at least—is a pitiful attempt to refuse what cannot be refused: the scansion, the rhythmicity, the uncompletable, unconsummatable processiveness of desire.

If the debate between metaphor and synecdoche on the one hand, and a triumphant and unmasterable metonymy on the other, provides the plot for the first half of the passage, the second half is governed by the invisible, subtextual agent that had produced the primary alienation and the endless metonymic displacement of desire in the first place. Lacan names this agent by not naming it, by allowing its or his effects to ripple through the verbal texture. What is the phonemic pattern that belongs in part to these *parts*, *séparations*, *départs*, *pertes*, and *disparitions*, but is not identical to any of them? It is *père*, of course, but not loudly proclaimed as in the *nom du père*, or in the parting gnomic aphorism of Lacan's *Télévision*: 'De ce qui perdure de perte pure à ce qui ne parie que du père au pire' ('From that which perdures through pure loss to that which wagers only on Dad to worse').[6] Lacan's *père* in this passage appears only in the rustling of the text, dispersed into other words and encroaching upon all the key terms. He is most explicitly present in the *opère* of the last sentence, and the proximity of this to *ô père* brings us close to the language of liturgical address. Lacan's 'father' is here rather like the dissipated first cause of Valéry's *Ébauche d'un serpent*:

> Il se fit Celui qui dissipe
> En conséquences, son Principe,
> En étoiles, son Unité.
>
> (He became He who fritters away
> His Primal Cause in consequences,
> And in stars his Unity.)[7]

Perhaps there is a male pregnancy phantasy here somewhere: metonymy is a process of continual parturition for which fathers not mothers, and fathers to the exclusion of mothers, have sole responsibility. Within the phonic substance of this passage, certainly, the divisive legacies of the father—the first destructive *Autre*—are everywhere re-enacted.

The supremely exciting central thing in this passage is not, however, metonymic displacement itself, nor desire, nor the scattered traces of the paternal interdict but the rhythmic pattern of empty intervals that provides the signifying chain, and the human subject, with their firm backbone: 'L'intervalle qui se répète, structure la plus radicale de la chaîne signifiante . . .' ('The repeating interval, the most radical structure of the signifying chain . . .') This is not *lacune* as in the Mallarmé poem—dangling, ripely overdetermined, and caught up in the complex cross-currents of octosyllabic verse—but *lacune* in and as rhythm. We are so accustomed to the stabilizing and mythologizing of individual signifiers, Lacan proposes in this passage, that we forget the necessary articulating spaces that come between them. Yet those spaces, in their emptiness and in the scansion they afford, are central to our humanity: speech-creatures are creatures of the gap, the divide, the lacuna, and if desire has a structure, a principle in terms of which it can be grasped and theorized, these reside in an organized procession of vacuities. 'Long' desire is not for Lacan a spiritual striving as it perhaps still was for Mallarmé, nor yet an insistent animal appetite as it often was for Freud: it is what keeps the signifying chain going and what gets you across its gaps.

The Mallarmé and Lacan texts both adhere, then, to a rule that Lacan was to announce in his seminar on *Les Psychoses* of 1955–56: 'le signifiant comme tel ne signifie rien' ('The signifier as such signifies nothing').[8] Both of them do this, in part, by artfully positioning a multi-faceted pun, and in such a way as to draw attention to the discontinuity between its facets, the snags within sense out of which the promise of new sense arises. And both writers use the pun not simply to assert an intermittence, and to pay tribute to the organizing power of repetition, but to suggest that on the other side of their elaborations and conceits there is something impossibly ordinary and terrible: a nothingness that threatens every aspect of human endeavour, and is only minimally held at bay by the lacunary rhythms that run through our lives.

The comparison between Mallarmé and Lacan could be taken much further in this direction. We could examine the many other works in which the two writers calculate their intermittences, articulate their vacuities, and run their readers right up to the brink of the abyss. We could set the multi-dimensional and polyrhythmic spatiality of *Un coup de dés*, for example, against the topological obsessions of Lacan in his final seminars, and we could see both authors in their late years producing graphic devices that are informed, and given their last unthinkable twist, by a sense of mortality that will not go away: both writers glimpse a last desperate opportunity for the structure-seeking imagination in the task of picturing how things cease to be. Mallarmé and Lacan are both catastrophists, we might say, predicting and pinpointing the minimal inflections of space by which we all finally lose the game. But when we have said all this, and gone out into the highways and byways of their works armed with a conviction that 'abyssal' structures explain almost everything that their works contain, we have taken no more than a first step in understanding why 'Prose pour des Esseintes' and 'Position de l'inconscient' are such astonishing artefacts. Decorativeness and separateness as punned upon in these texts do indeed explain each other, complexify each other, and form a convenient binary structure in terms of which much useful analytic work can be done.

But what a strange fate *pleasure* has if we look at matters in this way solely: it is either written out of the text altogether, or written in as a mere side-effect of the metaphors, metonymies, and metrical patternings by which a disconsolate vision takes textual shape. 'Prose' and 'Position' are pleasure-driven and festive, however, and do much more with their gaps than eroticize them in a death-haunted fashion.

Mallarmé's poem contains a recurrent emblem of extremity and excess. Irises appear as a multitude spread out upon the earth: a hundred saw I at a glance ('sol des cent iris'). Each of them spreads itself broadly ('Toute fleur s'étalait plus large'), and the genus to which they belong ('les iridées') *rises up*—initially in a dutiful and reasonable-sounding way ('Surgir à ce nouveau devoir') but later at the end of an impossibly long, expansible, upwards thrusting stem ('de lis multiples la tige/Grandissait trop pour nos raisons'). The poem's last flourish ('le trop grand glaïeul') recapitulates these indications of length and strength, and seems to move us definitively from the horizontal to the vertical axis of floral growth. But despite the overt phallicizing of the flower images here, Mallarmé is far from suggesting that male sexuality offers a royal road, or even an obviously efficient road, to pleasure. It is not just that the thrusting flowers appear in a dubitative textual setting, but that there is much in the poem to suggest that ecstasy, when it occurs, comes in the form of sudden, unwilled transport. There it unaccountably is, not as a result of planning or choice, not as a big reward for any bigness that the individual may seek or assume or boast about, but adventitiously, unannounced, as a gratuitous grace. When it comes it calls upon the individual to stop talking, ratiocinating, litigating and staking his claim. Mallarmé in 'Prose' creates a lattice-work between different modes of sexual feeling, and between different styles and intensities of delectation. What I was calling a moment ago the lacunary rhythm of his text is part of the overall lattice: the gaps and vacancies that Mallarmé insistently sets forth are adjacent to, and at moments give access to, *joy*. Death and joyfulness are brought together in an elaborate verbal comedy.

Lacan's wit in the passage I have been looking at is of course less grand than Mallarmé's, less shot through with exalted perspectives and extreme forms of *jouissance*. Indeed, the tone is often, for all the erudition Lacan displays, reminiscent of the low punning that can be heard any day of the week in the schoolyard or in the executives' washroom. Listen, for example, to the complicit nudges that direct our attention from one key term to the next in an etymological labyrinth like the following:

> Qu'on sache seulement que ce glissement est fondé dans leur commun *appariement* à la fonction de la *pars*.
> La *partie* n'est pas le tout, comme on dit, mais d'ordinaire inconsidérément. Car il faudrait accentuer qu'elle n'a avec le tout rien à faire. Il faut en prendre son *parti*, elle joue sa *partie* toute seule. Ici, c'est de sa *partition* que le sujet procède à sa *parturition*.

> (One should simply realize that this slippage is grounded in the fact that they are both related to the function of the *pars*.
> The part is not the whole, as is said, though usually without thinking. For it should be emphasized that the part has nothing to do with the whole. One has to come to terms with it; it plays its part [*sa partie*] all by itself. Here the subject proceeds from his partition to his parturition.)

Punning of this kind has both a local and a general doctrinal point to make. The local one has already been noted: it has to do with the dividedness and untotalizability of the human subject; the subject, for Lacan, is never the sum of his or her parts. There is no sum, no summation, no consummation. Parts, scanned and concatenated in this way or that, are all we have and all we are. But the more general point has to do with what Jean-Pierre Richard in a different context has called 'l'optimisme du signifiant'; and I shall pause here for a moment to remember what a peculiar amphibious creature Lacan's *signifiant* is.[9]

The signifier, in the special, enlarged and not very Saussurean sense that Lacan gives the term, turns all other technical terms in the direction of polysemantic play. The signifier needs the tribute of word-play, we might say, to offset the implacable legalities with which language hedges us about. Word-play of the *pars* → *part* → *parti* → *partition* kind, or of any other kind, is the speaking subject's optimistic riposte to the simple fact of being trapped inside a language that she/he did not create and whose rules she/he has no real power to affect or mitigate. The theorist as punster speaks, plays, on behalf of all speaking creatures, invites all empty, decentred, intervallic subjects to a festival . . . Lacan's theory motivates his word-play, and his word-play takes us back, sometimes directly, sometimes circuit-ously, to the theory from which it takes its cue. When it works with robust inventiveness, as I think it does in 'Position de l'inconscient' and the three long papers of the mid-1950s,[10] it supplies a constant sense of openness, potentiality and copiousness to a doctrine that could otherwise easily become flatly doctrinaire. Lacan like Mallarmé —as I said earlier—takes chances with sense, runs the gauntlet of multiple meaning, willingly runs the risk of babble and hocus-pocus. It is this shared quality that brings me to the polemical point I announced at the beginning of these remarks.

What can criticism do when faced with verbal and intellectual performances like these? One thing it does do, noticing the word-play, and the theoretical work that puns do, and the legitimacy they enjoy from 'theory', is join in the game. And the results are sometimes dismal. It ought to be obvious that word-play easily gets attenuated, complacent, and shallow if it remains unchallenged. We arrive at a most curious paradox when we are dealing with a theory like Lacan's, which issues an insistent invitation to textual playfulness: follow his advice too literally and you are lost. Pun yourself this way and that in the Lacanian manner, and re-using perhaps certain of the Lacanian master puns for guidance, and you are likely to emerge as a literal-minded loyalist of the dullest sort. The Mallarmé and Lacan texts that I have talked about could be thought of as exemplary in this regard. Their own word-play takes place under conditions of great stress: on the one hand it is reduced at a culminating moment in each text to an intimation of empty, contentless structure, and on the other hand it becomes a variety of passion and sensual engage-ment with experience. Word-play itself is subject to the Freudian *fort/da*, to a rhythmic intermittence, to an interleaving of sense and nonsense, sensuality and anaesthesia, gravity and levity. Dare one imagine a theoretically self-aware criticism in this mould? One that resisted as well as endorsed its master texts? One that knew when the punning had to stop?

5

From Crisis to Critique
Mallarmé for Blanchot

Michael Holland

Die Kritik ist also gefährlich und mühsam (Novalis)[1]

In 1941, more or less one hundred years after being born, Stéphane Mallarmé finally came into a life. It was written by Henri Mondor.[2] Mondor was, in Jean-Pierre Richard's words, 'le premier, par de patients et nombreux travaux . . . à donner à Mallarmé une vie réelle, une biographie et un visage' ('the first, by dint of patient and numerous efforts, to give Mallarmé a real life, a biography and a face').[3] In that year, 1941, thirty-three years after being born, Maurice Blanchot first acquired the signature by which we identify him today: on 16 April of that year, there appeared in the *Journal des Débats* the first of what would become over 170 'Chroniques de la vie intellectuelle' (Chronicles of Intellectual Life), written between 1941 and 1944. With one or two exceptions, the chapters that make up the first book by Blanchot the critic, *Faux pas* (1943),[4] are taken from among these 'Chroniques'.[5] In that same year, 1941, the year Mallarmé acquired a life and Maurice Blanchot a signature, Blanchot stepped *out* of a life he had already stopped living. That is to say: in a manner that is unique, and which lies at the origin of Blanchot's originality as a writer, the move by which 'Maurice Blanchot' became the identifying mark on a growing body of writing, severed all links—both present and past—between that name and a person leading a life in the real world and answering to that name. In this extraordinary move, as it were by coincidence, the name 'Mallarmé' plays a key role.

If this appears to be coincidental, it is because nothing would seem to justify Mallarmé's role in the move I have described, except the very tenuous fact that the centenary of his birth (which is when he acquires a 'real life') more or less coincides with the German Occupation of France and what seemed to many to be a slide into the abyss. Yet this coincidence becomes the basis for a relation between Mallarmé and Blanchot which, it is generally acknowledged, is of primary significance. Blanchot's readings of Mallarmé have acquired an authority among authorities on Mallarmé. They are something which, agree with them or not, critics feel necessarily obliged to take account of.[6] I should like, therefore, to begin to explore this transformation of coincidence into necessity—it being, quite literally, a matter of life and death.

The first of Blanchot's 'Chroniques de la vie intellectuelle', dated 16 April 1941, begins as follows:

> Les peuples meurtris qui ne peuvent exprimer les sentiments qui les agitent se rejettent dans la lecture . . . Lire, apprendre, connaître quelque chose, chacun a découvert en soi ce besoin, comme si le seul moyen d'imposer silence à un monde trop bruyant eût été d'entendre quelques voix intérieures prises au plus près de leur source.[7]

> (Wounded peoples, unable to express the feelings which agitate them, fall back on reading. Everyone has discovered within himself the need to read, learn or know something, as if the only way to impose silence on a world grown too noisy were to hear one or two inner voices drawn from as close as possible to their source.)

And it concludes with the following observation:

> Beaucoup d'écrivains . . . se sont condamnés au silence, moins à cause des difficultés extérieures qu'ils pouvaient rencontrer qu'en raison d'une véritable épreuve de stérilité. Ils se sont tus et ils continuent de se taire parce qu'ils croient qu'ils n'ont plus rien à dire. Une nuit aride est tombée sur eux. Après de nombreuses années où ils s'agitaient vainement, ils ont enfin

entendu leur propre silence. Combien de temps durera cette crise?

(Many writers have condemned themselves to silence, less as a result of the external difficulties they may have encountered than owing to a veritable ordeal of sterility. They have fallen silent and continue to be silent because they believe they have nothing more to say. An arid night has descended upon them. After many years of vain agitation, they have at last heard their own silence. How long will this crisis last?)

It is noteworthy that while both readers and writers find themselves reduced to silence in 1941, there would also seem to have been a reversal of roles within 'intellectual life'. Whereas to enjoy the passivity of being a reader and hear 'one or two inner voices' is *actively* to impose silence on the world, to be a writer now means to have ceased all writerly activity and become *passively* receptive to 'one's own silence'. The medium within which intellectual life continues is therefore *silence* in each case. But in each case, the silence is not quite the same: reading entails creating the conditions for a repetition of what has already been said, while writing entails ceasing to speak altogether. At one level, the silence is undeniably of the same nature: a silence occasioned by the inability to speak, a loss of *voice*. Readers are people 'unable to express the feelings which agitate them', while writers believe, 'after many years of vain agitation', that 'they have nothing more to say'. But between the silence of readers and the silence of writers, no continuity exists. Looked at from the reader's point of view as Blanchot presents it, this appears to be a simple matter: for readers, the silence affecting writers at present is part and parcel of the silence which they as readers have imposed upon the outside world, in order to hear again the 'inner voices' which, as the term anachronistically indicates, are voices belonging to the past.[8] The voices of today, 'outer' voices compromised by the 'vain agitation' to which they contributed in previous years, are merely part of the noise upon which readers have imposed silence. Within the silence necessitated by events, in short, writers have been displaced by readers, who now consider themselves to be those best placed to sustain intellectual life.

Seen from the writer's point of view, however, this displacement within silence is less straightforward, and the break in continuity that it effects is less easily located. Whereas silence, for readers, is the result of silencing 'too noisy a world', the silence of writers has, according to Blanchot, nothing directly to do with that. 'External difficulties' created by what is going on in the world do not play the role they seem to play from the reader's point of view. If writers have at last 'heard their own silence', therefore, this is not because they have been silenced by events in the present. Yet nor is it because they have had silence imposed upon them by readers who prefer to listen to 'inner voices' belonging to the past. They have silenced *themselves*, silenced the 'vain agitation' of previous years in response to 'a veritable ordeal of sterility' which seems to bear no direct relation to what is going on in the outside world. Hence, while readers are using silence to withdraw entirely from the present, writers are neither seeking to complement that move by imposing their own silence on 'too noisy a world', nor are they letting themselves be confined within that world by having silence imposed upon them by readers. Though squarely *in* the present, they cannot be located there by means of a topology of 'outer' versus 'inner', or a chronology of 'present' versus 'past'. The space and time they inhabit are those of 'an arid night', resulting from a decision to be silent that has already been taken ('they *have condemned* themselves to silence' 'they *have fallen* silent'). Though each results from an inability to speak, the silence of readers and the silence of writers are thus not coextensive. Rather, they coincide and intersect with each other in such a way that, within the *simplicity* of silence itself, considered as the opposite of voice, a distortion takes place and a displacement occurs. This introduces another borderline between readers and writers, one which does not align itself with that fixed one that separates 'outer' and 'inner', nor that mobile one lying between past and present and noise and voice (both of which define the reader as a central point, centred in silence, as a pure agent of silence considered as a pure means), but runs through the middle of silence itself considered as what has replaced voice, as an absolute act of reflexivity (*hearing one's own silence*), which both divides readerly subjectivity from writerly subjectivity and divides subjectivity from itself. Which is to say, it is a borderline lying not just between readers and writers considered as distinct subjects in language, but between reading and writing on the part of the same subject, within the silence that has currently overtaken intellectual life. While silence allows readers to hear again the voices of those writers they have made their own, writers, in the present which for readers has ceased to count, but at an absolute remove from events and from language as voice, allow their silence to double back and become, within the negative, a mode of reflexive self-awareness which is topographically and chronologically distinct and original. Within the silence that has overtaken intellectual life, and which is at one level the same silence for writers and for readers, events have introduced a complex set of displacements between past and present, voice and silence, inner and outer worlds, and made *readers* the agents of silence and the nexus of those displacements. Displacing those displacements, dislocating the field in which they happen and in so doing encompassing the dualism of their alternation within a permanent doubling back or reflexivity, the silence of writers exists both as an alternative to voice and as a supplement to it, a threat to conscious reflexion in language and the offer at least of an entirely original mode of reflective consciousness (*hearing one's own silence*).

That being so, it is noteworthy that, in his first 'Chronique de la vie intellectuelle', between the reader's silence with which it begins and the writer's silence with which it ends, Blanchot introduces a third perspective. After briefly surveying the fictional output there has been since the Occupation, he goes on to observe that the works which have attracted most attention are 'des œuvres de critique intellectuelle et littéraire'. This extension of the same term, *la critique*, to embrace both the intellectual and the literary (in that order) cannot be overlooked, in this the first article signed by Blanchot the critic. For what he is talking about, using one word: *la critique*, is something which in English really calls for two: *criticism* when he is talking about 'la critique littéraire', but when he is talking about 'la critique intellectuelle', the more appropriate word would be *critique*—which is to say, the analysis of the basis of knowledge. Hence, the works which have recently 'attracted most attention' are works of both criticism and critique. As with the term *le silence* therefore (not to mention the term *agiter*),[9] the simplicity of the term *la critique* immediately suffers a displacement when it is applied to the complex reality of intellectual lfe in 1941. In other words, Blanchot's observation does not imply a simple taxonomy of current output (novels etc.

85

on the one hand, essays etc. on the other), as is made clear by the first example that he chooses to illustrate his point:

> On ne saurait trop penser à l'ouvrage que M. Henri Mondor vient de consacrer à Stéphane Mallarmé. C'est le fruit d'un long travail, et c'est un travail heureux.

> (One cannot be too attentive to the work that M. Henri Mondor has just devoted to Stéphane Mallarmé. It is the fruit of considerable effort, and that effort has been successful.)

The choice of a literary biography as an example introduces a further level of complexity into the already complex significance of 'la critique intellectuelle et littéraire'. And as we shall see, it also throws further light on the silence within which intellectual life goes on in 1941. Biography, as a genre, would appear to lie entirely outside the domain of *la critique* (whether we understand this term as 'criticism' or as 'critique'). Furthermore it would appear to reverse the entire thrust of a writer's relation to the world, be he a writer of fiction or a thinker, insofar as it is a condition of the operation of both the imagination and the mind that the world, the real world, be set at a distance. By bringing back a writer's world for that writer's readers, the biographer would seem unavoidably to be working *against* any form of critical reading, indeed to be violently interfering with the very essence of the writer–reader relationship. More precisely, the 'too noisy world' that readers in 1941 have silenced in favour of 'inner voices' is restored, by Mondor's biography, to a supremacy which seems to threaten the very existence of Mallarmé as a poet.

Indeed, the way Blanchot goes on to describe Mondor's project appears to confirm this:

> Le docteur Henri Mondor a rassemblé des textes admirables qui éclairent d'une extraordinaire lumière le destin de ce prince de l'esprit. Il a réussi, grâce à une recherche patiente parmi un très grand nombre de lettres, à *tirer des paroles* et même des confidences de l'écrivain le plus silencieux, le plus dépouillé, le plus capable de *pudeur intellectuelle*. Il a *restitué une histoire* à un homme dont toute l'existence a été dans son œuvre, elle-même toute proche du néant par son prodige même. Il l'a montré dans la simplicité de son orgueil. (My emphasis)

(Dr Henri Mondor has brought together some admirable documents, which throw extraordinary light on the destiny of this
Prince of the Mind. Through patient research among a vast
number of letters, he has succeeded in *extracting words* and even
confidences from the most silent and concise of writers, a writer
more capable than any of *intellectual modesty*. He has *restored to
history* a man whose entire existence lay in his work, the wonder
of which was that it was itself as close as possible to being
nothing. He has displayed him in all his proud simplicity.)

Torture, rape and general coercion are what come to mind on reading
the terms in which Blanchot describes Mondor's undertaking. Yet it
is, he says, 'a successful effort'. Although the texts on which it is
based—letters for the most part—seem destined, both as writing and
by virtue of the life which they reflect, to obscure what makes
Mallarmé Mallarmé, namely an existence entirely given over to
literature (and thus to nothingness), on the contrary they 'throw
extraordinary light on the destiny of that Prince of the Mind'. But
what sort of light, other than the *ordinary* light of the world, can
biography shed on the writing of a man who sought to withdraw
from the world? What *critical* perspective on Mallarmé can Mondor's
Vie possibly open up? From what perspective is Blanchot writing
when he concludes his brief account of Mondor's work by saying:

> C'est aujourd'hui pour l'esprit une facile, mais agréable revanche
> que de contempler un homme qui dans une complète et obscure
> solitude sût dominer le monde par l'exercice pur d'un pouvoir
> d'expression absolu?

> (Today it is easy but sweet revenge for the mind, to contemplate
> a man who, in complete and obscure solitude, was able to
> dominate the world by the pure exercise of an absolute power
> of expression.)

Can a mind *getting its own back*, in 'easy but sweet revenge',
by contemplating what Mallarmé wished to remain hidden, be
described, by any stretch of the mind or the imagination, as working
in a *critical* frame?

But let us be clear about what this *spirit of revenge* is actually
directed against. On the surface, and following the argument that

Mondor has *forced* Mallarmé to speak, *overridden* his modesty and *restored* him to history, it is tempting to think that revenge is being wreaked against Mallarmé himself, against the pretension summed up at the outset of his career in such statements as 'I *wished* to be forgotten' or 'I am completely dead'.[10] On closer examination, however, things turn out to be less straightforward. This is revenge 'for the mind' in its relation to a man whom Blanchot calls 'that Prince of the Mind'. The critical faculty—here *critique* not *criticism*—is therefore satisfied after all, it would seem, by Mondor's *Vie*. What is more, it is a faculty shared with the subject of the biography, who is presented as one of its supreme exponents. Far from obscuring what made Mallarmé unique, therefore, 'the extraordinary light' shed thanks to Mondor's biography is extraordinary because, taking Mallarmé as a 'Prince of the Mind' and not 'the Prince of Poets' as he was ultimately crowned,[11] it obliges the reader to revise his perspective on Mallarmé, to consider him as a poet, but as such, because of the *way* he was a poet, as also more than a poet: as the equivalent of a thinker, a philosopher (*un homme d'esprit*).

In fact, therefore, the *sweet revenge* afforded the mind by Mondor's *Vie* is not directed against Mallarmé at all. The contemplation in which it consists is not the intrusive, ultimately prurient scrutiny of a private life: it is contemplation of the way a man who sought to cut himself off from the world entirely (rather like a *reader* in 1941 according to Blanchot) succeeded thereby in exercising an absolute domination *over* the world, by means of a language which was paradoxically that of 'the most silent of writers' (making him seem rather like the *writer* as Blanchot describes him in 1941). If there is revenge, therefore, it is not against the man or the mind. It is against the world on the one hand, which for Mallarmé was not merely silenced but dominated through language; and against language on the other, in so far as it is considered identical to *voice*. At a moment when the world has collapsed into such chaos that reading alone seems capable of preserving the mind against it, it is satisfying, says Blanchot, to be reminded of a *writer* who, not content simply to silence the world so as to make silence his own, succeeded in dominating the world by means of language alone, while remaining 'the most silent of writers'.

In short, positioned in Blanchot's first 'Chronique de la vie intellectuelle' between *readers* silencing the world in order to hear again what have become 'inner voices', and *writers* discovering, in place of their own voice and at a remove from 'external difficulties', 'their own silence', Henri Mondor's *Vie de Mallarmé*, presented as belonging to the category of 'œuvres de critique intellectuelle et littéraire', fulfils its critical role while functioning as what it is (biography), by revealing in Mallarmé an author who neither simply silenced the world, nor simply fell silent, but rather, by exploring the limit separating voice and silence, silence and world, turned silence itself into a reflexive quantity: a 'significatif silence' founding a new and original relation between mind and world. It is thus that Mallarmé emerges as not just a prince of poets but a prince of the mind, who with his mind, exercised as 'an absolute power of expression', dominated the world to which he had ceased to belong, by means of what would appear to be a totally original act of intellectual *critique*. Thanks to coincidence, therefore, Mallarmé offers Blanchot, at the point where he emerges as a critic (a figure in whom reading and writing come together), the model for a *critique* in which the intellectual and the literary will no longer be distinguishable as they usually are. It nevertheless remains unclear why it should take a biography to reveal this, in the case of a writer determined to set the world, and life in the world, at a distance; nor why it should be Mondor's work that attracts the title *œuvre de critique* and not Mallarmé's. Prince of the Mind Mallarmé may have been, but if Blanchot is right, the intellectual critique he proposes would appear incapable of standing on its own. To explore this question further, we must look at how Blanchot's attention to Mallarmé develops in subsequent 'Chroniques de la vie intellectuelle'.

The paragraph on Mondor contained in the first 'Chronique' of 16 April 1941 is followed up with a full review of volume 1 of the *Vie* on 23 April, then a review of volume 2 a year later, on 1 April 1942.[12] Together these form chapter 1 of the section in *Faux pas* entitled 'Digressions sur la poésie', under the title 'Le silence de Mallarmé'.[13] In these two articles, Blanchot develops his seemingly paradoxical assertion that by restoring Mallarmé to life and to history, Mondor's *Vie* casts *extraordinary light* on what it is about him that lies outside of life and history, namely 'the destiny of that Prince of the Mind'. This paradox is now augmented by another one. For, curiously, what

Blanchot extols about Mondor's achievment is the *ignorance* in which it leaves the reader. This is a peculiar sort of ignorance, however. By definition, ignorance is incompatible with biography. The only ignorance that would seem to result from knowledge of an author's life is one affecting our ability to know his work:

> Il y a de très grands artistes qu'on devient incapable de connaître, dès qu'on connaît leur vie . . . Les vers que nous lisons ne sont plus que les points de repère d'une histoire. La biographie a tout dévoré. (117–18)

> (There are great artists whom one ceases to know, as soon as one knows about their lives. The lines we read are no longer anything but reference-points in a story. The biography has devoured everything.)

The same cannot be said of Mondor's biography, according to Blanchot. In his case, despite the minute detail which it provides, 'la biographie ne cache pas l'œuvre' ('the biography does not hide the work'). This is because 'elle n'est que le reflet d'une merveilleuse vie intellectuelle' ('it is merely the reflection of a marvellous intellectual life') (118). In other words, any light it sheds on the 'outer' life of Mallarmé the poet is drawn from the 'inner', intellectual life which made him a poet. A clear reversal is in operation here, recalling the action of readers silencing the world so as to hear the voices within. But if this move removes the initial paradox in Blanchot's thinking, by defining Mallarmé's life first and foremost as an inner life of the mind, the paradox remains that if it does not 'hide the work', the knowledge that the biography provides still somehow maintains the reader in a state of ignorance as to the origins of the work. For as biography, it is focused squarely on the outer life of the poet. The marvellous inner life, which *made* him a poet, is given priority only as the *source* of a light of which the outer light is merely a reflection. It is not itself revealed either directly or indirectly by that light. Because, Blanchot continues, when we have read Mondor's *Vie*:

> on s'aperçoit qu'on savait déjà tout ce qu'elle nous a appris et néanmoins on garde le sentiment heureux de ne rien savoir. Notre ignorance est restée pure. (118)

90

(we realize that we already knew everything it has taught us and yet we continue blissfully to feel that we know nothing. Our ignorance remains pure.)

Pure ignorance, made perfect through knowledge of all that is knowable, is thus presented by Blanchot as the only truly critical mode in which to approach Mallarmé's work, or more precisely, the *intellectual life* of which the work is a part. Hence, if the *extraordinary light* shed thanks to Mondor's *Vie*, illuminates or clarifies (*éclairer*) what Blanchot calls 'the destiny of that Prince of the Mind', it does not therefore simply throw light on it. All that is illuminated in that way is the outer life, which appears in all its familiarity in a reflection of the true light which the biography sheds. If that light is *extraordinary*, this is because, within the inner life where it has its source, if it illuminates, it does not make visible, and if it clarifies, it does not make known. If it is light, therefore, it is the light of ignorance.

Yet according to Blanchot, by creating what for some readers will be a disappointment, Mondor turns the gap in knowledge that his work produces into 'une vérité positive' ('a positive truth'):

> C'est maintenant un fait qu'on ne saura jamais que peu de chose sur le travail de Mallarmé et presque rien sur les relations de son esprit avec l'œuvre qu'il méditait. Il y a un silence, d'une qualité particulière, qu'il n'y a plus d'espoir de voir se dissiper jamais et qui est d'autant plus remarquable et mystérieux qu'aucun secret délibéré ne semble en avoir établi le règne. (121)

> (It is now established that we shall always know very little about Mallarmé's poetic labours, and almost nothing about the the relations between his mind and the work he was planning. There is a silence of a singular quality that we can now never hope to see dispelled, and which is all the more remarkable and mysterious in that no deliberate secrecy seems to have established its reign.)

In so doing, what is more, he is merely following Mallarmé's example:

> Mallarmé . . . n'a jamais dissimulé ses projets. Il a fait allusion plusieurs fois à l'œuvre qu'il préparait et dont il a proposé sous

diverses formes la justification théorique . . . Il a donc, autant
qu'il est possible, écarté le voile et rendu public son esprit. (122)

(Mallarmé never concealed his projects. He alluded on several
occasions to the work he was preparing and for which he
provided a theoretical justification in various forms. As far as is
possible, therefore, he drew aside the curtain and made public
what was in his mind.)

All of which leaves us, Blanchot concludes, with an enigma:

D'où vient alors cette énigme, comment, ayant parlé autant et
plus que beaucoup d'autres, peut-il donner l'impression de s'être
tu si profondément? (122.)

(Whence comes this enigma, therefore: how, having spoken as
much as anyone, indeed even moreso, can he give the impression
of having kept so utterly silent?)

However, the interest and significance of Blanchot's paradox for us
does not lie in his attempt to pursue it further in the form of a
question. This simply leads him to speculate about the possibility of
a sort of parallel biography, 'l'histoire du silence de Mallarmé' ('the
history of the silence of Mallarmé'), in a move which results in a sort
of Valéryesque fantasy:

Une telle étude, grâce à M. Henri Mondor, sera peut-être un
jour entreprise, si, du moins, il est permis de rêver l'étude d'un
esprit, à partir de ce qu'il a fait et de ce qu'il n'a pas fait, et
comme ébauche des possibles qu'il a été. (122)[14]

(Such a study will one day, thanks to M. Henri Mondor, perhaps
be undertaken, if, that is, we may dream of the study of a mind
in terms of what it has and has not done, and so to speak as an
outline of all the possibilities of which it has consisted.)

What is of interest, in his paradox, is the way it reflects something
more complex than anything paradox can express. For the Mallarmé
of whom we remain ignorant precisely to the extent that we know
all there is to know about him, and in whom therefore nothing is

simply hidden, is not just a *paradoxical* Mallarmé, but also, and more fundamentally, a dual and therefore dislocated 'Mallarmé'. At the heart of his inner intellectual life there lies not merely a contradiction but rather an enigmatic quantity, whose *effects* may give rise to paradox, but whose reality cannot be reduced in that way because the only way we can know it is through ignorance.

In reversing the usual biographical relation between life and work, therefore, Mondor is doing more than merely follow the lead being given by readers in 1941. For at the heart of the inner intellectual life which he reveals in Mallarmé, where readers for their part expect to hear 'inner voices', there is something unreadable and at the same time inexpressible: the enigma of an *extraordinary light* whose counterpart is a *silence of a singular quality*. Hence, having aligned Mallarmé with the readers of 1941 in an initial reversal, Mondor's *Vie* aligns him, in a second reversal, with the writer of 1941, whose silence too is of a singular quality according to Blanchot. The silence which in 1941 divides reader from writer is thus encompassed by Mallarmé in both its simplicity and its reflexivity. In short, Mallarmé as a writer is both the reader and the writer of 1941, and hence also the complex displacement that forms the borderline between them. In revealing this, Mondor is thus offering both reader and writer a way out of the impasse into which each has been driven. For unlike them, Mallarmé does not use his intellectual life simply to silence and suppress the world and eschew language. While doing those things he also reveals the world fully and gives it full expression. In him, 'arid night' is a source of 'extraordinary light', while silence is the mode in which language becomes 'an absolute power of expression'. This means, however, that his existence as Prince of the Mind cannot be embraced in a single act of comprehension (if that is attempted, the result is paradox), because it both attests to and so calls forth a frame of mind which is absolutely original, one which subsumes the positions of both reader and writer in 1941, supplements them with ignorance considered as 'a positive truth', and so turns what for writers, reflecting upon their own silence within the silence imposed by readers, can be no more than a *crisis*, into an *esprit critique* of a non-unitary nature.

Once again, however, it is difficult ultimately to see why Mondor's *Vie* should deserve the title *œuvre de critique*, save possibly as a reflection of what it reveals about Mallarmé. But in that case, why should the extraordinary originality of Mallarmé's critique require a biography to become accessible? Especially given the fact that what makes Mondor's *Vie* a critique, according to Blanchot, is not its revelation of the enigma at the heart of Mallarmé's intellectual life. The ultimate truth revealed by Mondor is that, as enigma, it is not subject to revelation: we are, and can only remain, *ignorant* as to its reality, and oblivious of the complex, decentred reflexivity linking 'extraordinary light' and 'singular silence' which it generates. In short, biography, in his hands, simultaneously reveals its own irrelevance to an understanding of Mallarmé, and reveals Mallarmé to be beyond understanding. At best, therefore, it remains the prisoner of paradox, whereas what it reveals about its subject is an enigmatic quantity and a source of critique that exceeds paradox.

Extraordinarily, Blanchot overcomes this limitation by pursuing the terms of the biographical paradox (ignorance/knowledge) beyond the limits within which paradox confines them. In other words, he takes Mondor a step further. Towards the end of 'Le silence de Mallarmé', he recalls that in the years leading up to his move to Paris, Mallarmé's letters frequently evoke the suffering he endures as a poet. In Blanchot's words: 'Une sorte de nuit stérile semble l'enveloper' ('a sort of sterile night seems to envelop him') (122). In the years following the composition of *Igitur*, however, these complaints disappear from Mallarmé's correspondence. While it is possible that he was simply hiding them, Blanchot argues, another explanation also presents itself:

> Un voile est jeté sur le drame profond de son esprit aux prises avec lui-même; le désespoir qui était à la fois l'ombre, la voie et le ressort de sa lucidité, s'évanouit, soit que le souci de ne plus le laisser paraître ait tari les confidences, soit qu'une découverte fondamentale lui ait par-dessus ses doutes et ses fatigues donné une confiance souveraine dans la direction de sa pensée. (123)[15]

> (A curtain is drawn over the profound drama of his mind as it grapples with itself; the despair which was simultaneously the shadow, the way and the motivation of his lucidity vanishes,

either because the desire no longer to show it dried up his confidences, or else because a fundamental discovery gave him, over and above his doubts and his weariness, a sovereign confidence in the direction of his thought.)

This confidence—the confidence to eschew confidences—was to remain with him for the rest of his life, says Blanchot. Henceforth, his response to his silence will be silence. The silence which condemns us to ignorance therefore originates in a deliberate act. As silence, furthermore, it is two-fold in nature.

In choosing to see Mallarmé's silence as an act of confidence, however, Blanchot is also taking confidence himself in the perspective he has opened up in 1941, thanks to Mondor's *Vie*, on that silence. The early Mallarmé and his torments, he says, are not merely repressed thanks to what *Igitur* has allowed. The 'sterile night' of his suffering (which recalls the 'arid night' endured by the writer in 1941) is totally dispelled by what Blanchot will later call the *experience* of *Igitur*[16] and the confident certainty with which it fills Mallarmé. But what dispels 'night' must not simply be understood as its opposite, namely *light*:

> Cette certitude . . . [était] . . . peut-être éprouvée au cours d'une nuit douloureuse *non pas* comme l'éclair d'une révélation énigmatique mais comme le point extrême d'une méditation entièrement consciente . . . (123; my italics)

> (This certainty was perhaps experienced during the course of a painful night, *not* as a flash of enigmatic revelation but as the extreme point of a process of entirely conscious meditation.)

In other words, night seems here not so much to have been dispelled as to have been displaced by what Blanchot has already called the *extraordinary* light of Mallarmé's inner intellectual life, a light which neither illuminates nor clarifies that inner life, and hence does not make intellectual activity a mode of visibility or its opposite. Mallarmé's sudden silence regarding the activity of his mind does not hide anything therefore. It marks a discovery on his part which, if it takes the form of an enigma for us, does not conceal any 'enigmatic revelation'. On the contrary, it is a moment of total lucidity, 'a process of entirely conscious meditation', but one whose reality lies solely in the displacement it effects. In the rest of 'Le silence de Mallarmé', it is to the extraordinary nature of this enigmatic lucidity that Blanchot turns his attention.

He concludes the article with an assertion which reflects the increasing critical confidence he himself now feels: Mallarmé's choice of silence is of significance, he says, not because it marks the absence of the 'Book' or 'Work' he spent his life projecting; nor either because it leaves us ignorant about the relations between the 'Grand Œuvre' and the works he actually published; it is significant solely because:

> Si l'on présume que quelque chose de grand s'est perdu, ce sentiment vient moins du Livre qui n'a pu voir le jour que des réflexions par lesquelles il l'avait préparé et qui . . . n'ont pas survécu à sa disparition. C'est là le mystère qui recouvre sa vie de poète. (124)

> (If we assume that something major was lost, this feeling comes less from the Book which never saw the light of day than from the reflections with which he had prepared it, and which did not survive his death. That is the mystery that shrouds his life as a poet.)

What Mallarmé's silence reveals as most significant about Mallarmé thus has nothing *directly* to do with what makes him Mallarmé for his reader today and what gives him a signature, namely authorship of a body of work either real (*une œuvre*) or projected (*un œuvre*)—in short, with what makes him primarily a Prince of Poets. It has to do solely with what Blanchot goes on to call 'la conscience claire . . . des moyens [de] . . . son art', 'son jugement méthodique', 'son travail réfléchi' ('the clear consciousness of his artistic means . . . his methodical judgement . . . his reflective labours') (124). Which is to say, with what would make him exclusively a Prince of the Mind. However, we know already that what truly makes Mallarmé significant for Blanchot, and what Mondor's *Vie* promotes, is our *ignorance* of that 'reflective labour' (of which the biography itself is a mere reflection): 'Nous ne savons rien de ce qu'il nous importerait infiniment de savoir' ('we know nothing about what we have an infinite need to know') (125). In other words, what is absolutely significant about Mallarmé's life as a writer is not only lost to us, as the biography reveals, so that it is significant *precisely to the extent* that we shall never know about it: it has nothing directly to do with anything he ever wrote. Far from constituting the true substance of Mallarmé's intellectual life, therefore, so that its loss limits our capacity to know his work definitively, his 'reflective labour' is totally cut off from his work as we know it, so that the ignorance by which we apprehend it also requires of us that we ignore his work entirely. As an intellectual act—an act of critique—it is thus without significant content for us. And if it appears to us as an absolute enigma, that is because it draws us, under the name of Mallarmé, into the limbo of indeterminacy which lies between two states of ignorance.

By now, however, the question must surely arise as to the status of this 'Mallarmé' upon whom Blanchot ultimately focuses. Following on from that, one can only wonder about the standing of Blanchot as a critic. For the Mallarmé he identifies is essentially without definition. In so far as he is significant neither for what he actually wrote, nor for what he aimed to write, but solely for what he thought in aiming to write; but even then, not for what we *know* he thought, but to the extent that we shall never know what he thought, Blanchot's Mallarmé could be anyone, or more likely: no one. He is a name without an identity. Yet—to return to my initial perspective —in 1941, Maurice Blanchot emerges as a literary critic whose authority is destined to become considerable; and Mallarmé becomes established as an author over whom Blanchot's authority is generally acknowledged. Jean-Pierre Richard, surveying the field of Mallarmé criticism in 1961, observes that in Blanchot and Georges Poulet, Mallarmé had found 'deux grands critiques capables de marcher à son pas et de respirer à sa hauteur' ('two major critics capable of keeping in step with him and breathing at his altitude').[17] More striking still, the first volume of Mallarmé's *Correspondance*, published by Henri Mondor in 1959, has as its epigraph none other than the opening paragraph of Blanchot's 1941 article 'Le silence de Mallarmé', devoted to Mondor's *Vie*.[18] How is this possible, given what has emerged as the true status of 'Mallarmé' in the article which Mondor cites?

The answer lies in the fact that Blanchot is not just reading Mallarmé in 1941, he is also reading Mondor. Thanks to Mondor, we are reminded of what we knew already: at a certain point in his career, what made Mallarmé essentially Mallarmé became totally inaccessible to anyone else:

> Aux autres, même ceux qui lui étaient le plus proches, il a tu ce qui lui était essentiel, dérobant son intimité sous des réticences charmantes et ne se laissant deviner que dans un au-delà insaisissable, aussi éloigné de son moi public que pouvait l'être de ses œuvres partielles le grand œuvre secret dont il n'a montré que l'absence. (125)

> (With others, even those closest to him, he kept silent about what was most essential to him, concealing his intimacy beneath charming reticence, and only allowing himself to be glimpsed in an elusive beyond, as remote from his public self as the great secret work, of which he revealed only the absence, could be from his partial works.)

Thanks to Mondor, too, we now know for certain that that essential Mallarmé will remain forever inaccessible to us. Mallarmé's silence must be matched by our ignorance. If Mondor's *Vie* is a work of critique, therefore, critique would appear to consist in placing an abyss between Mallarmé and the present. That is the *paradox* of Mondor's undertaking. However, what Blanchot sees is that the abyss which Mondor's *Vie* opens up also offers the means wherewith to span it. For the abyss does not simply mark out the limits of knowledge and the inaccessibility of what must remain unknown. Such an abyss could only foster the hope that, one day, something more may be revealed and the enigma solved. Mondor's revelations take things a step further, as we saw, by placing us, in the present, in a limbo of ignorance which is as 'elusive' for the mind as the 'beyond' in which Mallarmé's silence confines him. The mind's relationship to the abyss is thus one of confusion and disorientation. The ignorance by which the reader 'knows' the essential Mallarmé is an abyss within an abyss. This, according to Blanchot, introduces into the field, determined by the opposition between knowledge and ignorance, a supplementary dimension which disrupts it decisively:

> Si le silence de Mallarmé ne pouvait d'aucune manière être rompu, s'il était naturel et raisonnable que l'homme qui avait le

plus clairement organisé et suivi le cheminement de son esprit ne laissât de son effort qu'un témoignage énigmatique, couronné par quelques œuvres inimitables, *il n'est pas moins important* que ce silence, ce fait d'être resté silencieux au milieu de tant de paroles puisse apparaître comme le secret même dont l'existence ne devait pas nous être révélée. (125; my italics)

(If there was no way in which Mallarmé's silence could have been broken, if it was natural and reasonable that the man who had organized and followed the progress of his mind as clearly as possible should have left behind only the most enigmatic evidence of his efforts, crowned by a few incomparable works, *it is no less important* that this silence, the fact of having remained silent in the midst of so many words, should appear as the very secret whose existence should not have been revealed to us.)

What Blanchot encounters *by chance* in Mallarmé, therefore, in 1941, thanks to the coincidence of a centenary and the revelations of a biography, is something quite extraordinary: a silence whose significance lies not in what it hides and should be made to reveal, nor even in the revelation that it hides nothing, but in the fact that, until Mondor's *Vie*, it remained hidden itself and ought never to have been revealed. In short, silence itself is the secret, not what it conceals or does not conceal. So that our knowledge of it, even though it is equivalent to ignorance, is, as ignorance, the penetration of a secret and therefore essentially illicit: the ignorance regarding what makes Mallarmé essentially Mallarmé to which we are condemned by Mallarmé's silence is something of which we ought to have remained oblivious. Hence the knowledge of that ignorance which Mondor's *Vie* provides does more than merely confine us to paradox: the knowledge that our ignorance corresponds to a silence which renders it definitive constitutes an act of *transgression* which exceeds the confines of reason entirely. In other words, if Blanchot can be said to take Mondor a step further, this is to the extent that Mondor allows his reader to overstep the mark. To be 'in step' with Mallarmé as a critic (*marcher à son pas*) is to take what Blanchot will much later call a 'step beyond' (*un pas au-delà*).[19] Critique would thus appear not simply to consist in dividing 'Mallarmé' from what he wrote and turning him into an enigma without content, but to lie in the emergence of the new, non-unitary frame of mind which the enigma

99

of Mallarmé calls forth after Mondor. Critique is therefore not a new *activity* of the mind (a biography, after all, *does* nothing of an intellectual nature), but rather a *condition* brought about by the encounter, both accidental and illicit, with the necessity and the justification of ignorance in the case of what makes Mallarmé Mallarmé. The abyss which biography opens up between Mallarmé and his readers, by turning Mallarmé into an enigma once and for all, is ultimately the product of the transgressive knowledge that penetrates the enigma to reveal that Mallarmé's silence hides nothing from us, and that therefore there is no abyss. In short, the abyss has always already been spanned by the transgressive step (the *faux pas*) by which it is opened up. At the same time, the displacement effected through transgression means that the abyss can never cancel itself out. For the illicit knowledge that there is no enigma, by leaving the mind in a limbo of ignorance, opens up an abyss within the mind that is more radical than any by which it finds itself separated from 'Mallarmé'. The 'knowledge' that has always already closed the abyss is so disorienting and abysmal for the mind that the only way in which it can sustain a relation to what 'Mallarmé' signifies is to reopen the abyss which separates it from what makes Mallarmé Mallarmé. If critique is not an activity of the mind, therefore it is not merely a *state*. It engages the mind in an endless exorbitant loop from which there would appear to be no escape. The enigma of Mallarmé's silence is thus a trap. It either has *no* reality for the mind, in which case something essential about Mallarmé is simply ignored, or else it acquires the reality which makes it an enigma through an act of transgression by the mind, which reveals that there is no enigma and at the same time makes Mallarmé unlocatable. In short, the enigma of Mallarmé's silence exists only in the mind which seeks to penetrate it. To the extent that the mind seeks to penetrate it, enigma becomes the mind's mode, taking it over and emptying it of content, while dislocating it so that it embraces something that is other than rational: the abyss which has now opened up within its own field. If the knowledge that Mondor's *Vie* provides makes it a work of critique, therefore, the condition in which it places the mind is a critical one in more than one sense. Far from marking the accomplishment of rational activity, on a par with 'the extreme point of a conscious meditation' from which Mallarmé's confidence derives, it entails the *subjection* of the mind, which, by dislocating the field of its exercise and making its object unlocatable, would seem to drive it to the edge of breakdown.

Yet it is precisely here, where Blanchot's critical relation to Mallarmé is at its most controversial, that it is at its most confident. The *critical condition* emerging as the sole authentic response to the enigmatic 'Mallarmé' upon which Blanchot focuses via Mondor may well subject the mind to endless displacement: this condition is destined to become the critical mode to which Blanchot's name is attached, as the following lines, written in 1967, confirm:

> L'Œuvre comme livre conduit Mallarmé hors de son nom. L'Œuvre où régit l'absence d'œuvre conduit celui qui ne s'appelle plus Mallarmé jusqu'à la folie: entendons, s'il se peut, ce *jusqu'à* comme la limite qui, franchie, serait la folie décidée.[20]

> (The Work as book leads Mallarmé outside his name. The Work in which the absence of the work holds sway leads he who is no longer called Mallarmé to the point of madness. If we can, let us understand this *to the point of* as the limit that, once crossed, would be decisive madness.)

Before it can be understood how this move acquires its coherence, however, a final issue remains to be addressed: why is the knowledge that Mallarmé fell silent *illicit* knowledge? Why is his silence a secret that ought never to have been revealed to us? What is there about it that the mind must not *know*? Without an answer to these questions, it is difficult not to see Blanchot's critical position as little more than sophistry, well deserving the scepticism displayed by Malcolm Bowie in response to his 1941 reading of Henri Michaux:

> This is an admirable account of the possible power of a possible literary work. But as an account of the works in question it is an extravagant piece of whimsy.[21]

To find an answer, it is necessary to go back and reflect carefully on Blanchot's assertion that Mallarmé's silence both allows him to become totally confident in the direction of his thought, yet at the same time directs his thought entirely away from others. It follows from the latter fact that the knowledge, provided by Mondor, that Mallarmé did fall silent can prompt no more than speculation

regarding the reason why. According to Blanchot, the most that can
be said about what happened following the completion of *Igitur* is
this:

> On peut croire que cet esprit si lucide, si contraire aux hasards
> et aux ombres, s'était en lui-même énoncé tout entier, s'était dit
> et s'était vu complètement. (133)

> (We may assume that this mind, so lucid and so incompatible
> with chance occurrences and with shadow, had, in itself, given
> utterance to itself entirely, had expressed itself and seen itself
> completely.)

Yet what Blanchot is proposing in this uncertain mode is decisive
when it comes to defining the critique in which he engages after
Mondor. For by his account, rather than emanating from a source
that remains contemporaneous with Mallarmé's writing in the post-
Igitur period, so that the supplementary dimension it contributes to
the language that he continues to use is actively sustained as part of
the activity of writing, Mallarmé's silence results from an *event* of the
mind, which happens once, and once and for all: a single act of seeing
and saying which, taking place in time, puts an end to rational
reflection by allowing the subject of reflection both to understand
itself and to express itself completely, and, by so fulfilling its task, in
effect deprive itself of any reason to go on existing. If Mallarmé chose
to respond to the painful silence of his early years by falling silent,
therefore, the ignorance in which this leaves his readers concerning
the source of what he continued to write reflects more than mere
reserve on his part. It is ignorance that no possible knowledge could
ever dispel, because it results from the willing relinquishment of the
processes of knowledge on Mallarmé's part: the abdication of the
rational subject following an act of total, and hence terminal,
reflection.

If the knowledge of this ignorance is illicit, if Mallarmé's silence
is something that ought never to have been revealed to us, this is
quite simply because it is knowledge of what puts an end to
knowledge in Mallarmé's case: the willed extinction of identity and
of voice, following which Mallarmé ceased to exist in contemporaneity
with himself. What the reader goes out to meet, in overstepping the

mark and penetrating Mallarmé's silence, is itself revealed to be a transgressive step beyond the confines of language and subjectivity that has already been taken. The 'knowledge' thus obtained is therefore not illicit because it is a violation of Mallarmé's privacy. Were the aftermath of *Igitur* to have led to absolute silence on his part, the result might have remained a mystery, knowledge of the mystery would not have been transgressive in itself. Between silence and the work, as in Rimbaud's case, the line would have been clearly drawn. Knowledge of the silence would not so much have been illicit as irrelevant: a private matter concerning Mallarmé alone. What displaces that line in Mallarmé's case, so that knowledge of ignorance is an overstepping of the mark by his reader, is the fact that, having chosen to respond to silence with silence, Mallarmé continued to write, indeed discovered a new lease of life, so to speak, as a writer. What is transgressive about our knowledge of his silence is therefore our encounter *in* language with the fact that the assumed subject *of* language has absconded, that the Prince of the Mind is so by virtue of his abdication, that the 'Mallarmé' who lives on through language could indeed be anyone. Mallarmé is thus neither mysteriously located within his own silence, nor identifiable with the voice that continues to speak in his name. Rather, the limbo of disorientation in which the enigma of Mallarmé entraps the mind, leaving us perpetually ignorant both of Mallarmé's work and of the source of his work, is in fact the condition of the mind which produces Mallarmé's writing after *Igitur*. By depriving our reason of its central focus, enigma thus induces in our minds that extinction of subjectivity which occurred once and for all for Mallarmé through an act of total self-appraisal and total self-expression on his part. The enigma of Mallarmé amounts to a transgression of the limits defining our own subjectivity.

Critique would thus appear to amount to making an act of intellectual suicide which took place in the 1870s into the pre-condition for intellectual life in 1941. If the enigma of Mallarmé is all in the mind of his reader (so that 'Mallarmé' could be anyone), the critical condition this induces is a replica of the condition willingly endured by Mallarmé. Yet the two-fold ignorance which the illicit knowledge of that act induces in the mind seems rather to plunge it into terminal crisis and threaten it with breakdown. The endless exorbitancy of enigma seems insurmountable. According to Blanchot, however, writers in 1941 are *already* in the grip of crisis: 'they have at last heard their own silence. How long will this crisis last?' Yet as his question reveals, if things have reached a term ('they have *at last* heard'), the crisis this precipitates does not exclude a beyond. In order to see how it is the critique made possible by Mondor's *Vie* that provides that beyond, it is important to distinguish between the two moments in Mallarmé's experience when silence became the condition of the writer. The first is recorded in a famous letter to Cazalis of 1867, and belongs to the period of *crisis* when silence simply meant the inability to write:

> Je viens de passer une année effrayante: ma Pensée s'est pensée, et est arrivé à une Conception Pure . . . je suis complètement mort, et la région la plus impure où mon Esprit puisse s'aventurer est l'Eternité, mon Esprit, ce solitaire habituel de sa propre Pureté, que n'obscurcit plus même le reflet du Temps . . . C'est t'apprendre que je suis maintenant impersonnel, et non plus Stéphane que tu as connu,—mais une aptitude qu'a l'Univers Spirituel à se voir et à se développer, à travers ce qui fut moi.[22]

> (I have just spent a terrifying year: my Thought has thought itself, and arrived at a Pure Conception. I am completely dead, and the most impure region into which my Mind can venture is Eternity—my Mind, that solitary, used to frequenting its own Purity, and which is no longer darkened by even the reflection of Time. Which amounts to telling you that I am now impersonal, and no longer the Stéphane you knew,—but an aptitude of the Spiritual Universe to see itself and develop through what once was me.)

The second is the moment following the completion of *Igitur* when, according to Blanchot, Mallarmé acquired the confidence not primarily to write, but to remain silent about the silence to which writing condemns him. The letter he wrote to Cazalis at the time is crucial to an understanding of the position which Blanchot is seeking to circumscribe:

> Je redeviens un littérateur pur et simple. Mon œuvre n'est plus un mythe. (Un volume de Contes, rêvé. Un volume de Poésie, entrevu et fredonné. Un volume de Critique, soit ce qu'on

appelait hier l'Univers, considéré du point de vue strictement *littéraire*.)[23]

(I have gone back to being a literary man, pure and simple. My work is no longer a myth. (A volume of Tales, so far only dreamt of. A volume of Poetry, glimpsed and hummed through. A volume of Critique, which is to say: what in the past was called the Universe, considered from a strictly *literary* point of view.)

What these two quotations reveal is that, by responding to silence *with* silence, Mallarmé turned a sterile crisis, during which he found it almost impossible to write, into a new departure for *literature*, one of whose dimensions would be *critique*. Unlike for the writer of 1941, caught as he was in a night as arid as Mallarmé's was sterile, the reflexivity he introduced into silence did not result in paralysis: in him, the self-defeating passivity resulting from *hearing one's own silence* was transformed into a reflexive *activation* of silence. Whereas the former could only put an end to writing, by placing the writer outside language, in the latter that outside—silence—has itself become articulate, so that language in its turn is subject to a displacement which inscribes within it a reflexivity of a non-rational and non-unitary nature.

   The price to be paid for this was considerable, entailing a cosmic alteration of the very conditions of subjectivity. For as the second letter to Cazalis reveals, the 'I am completely dead' of 1867 was mere histrionics: Mallarmé may have considered himself impersonal and effectively dead to the present, but 'l'Univers spirituel', in other words the mind (*l'esprit*) in the absolute, offered apotheosis in exchange. At most, to use Blanchot's terms, this left Mallarmé out of a name (*hors de son nom*). In his own name, therefore, he could write nothing, and crisis was the result. Nevertheless, *sub specie æternitatis* and albeit silently, Mallarmé continued to exist through language and in the present. With the experience of *Igitur*, however, and the decision to respond to silence with silence, this refuge in the absolute suffered absolute disruption. Henceforth, time and identity could no longer survive loss of name thanks to the ascendancy of the Universal: after *Igitur*, the Universe too was a thing of the past ('what in the past was called the Universe'). The entire frame within which the mind exists and pursues its goals through language had fallen away in time and come apart. Two-fold alienation—from self, from Universe—was all that was left to the mind in the disjointed 'present' in which Mallarmé's *je littéraire* made its transgressive 'step beyond'.

Yet it is this move which takes Mallarmé beyond crisis, and towards what he himself calls critique. In 1941, on what seemed the edge of an abyss of collective rather than individual proportions, Henri Mondor's *Vie*, by revealing the true secret behind Mallarmé's 'death', offered the writer (which is to say: Maurice Blanchot) that same step beyond. Much remains to be explored concerning the conversion of crisis into critique whereby Blanchot acquires the signature by which he is known today. For reasons alluded to at the outset, and which relate to the loss of the political signature by which Blanchot was known throughout the 1930s, it is, in Novalis's words, 'gefährlich und mühsam': a dangerous and difficult undertaking.[24] Yet as the following lines from another article on Mallarmé of 1942 reveal, it is one that Blanchot himself identifies from the outset as being central, in its eccentricity, to the task that will be his:

> Est-il tourment plus pur que cette critique de la raison par soi et cette division pendant laquelle elle s'éprouve au voisinage de ce qu'elle ne peut toucher? Elle en reçoit l'impression, non d'être déchue, mais d'approcher infiniment ce qu'elle accepte de ne point saisir selon son mode.[25]

> (Was there ever a purer torment than this critique of reason by itself, and this division during which it experiences itself in the vicinity of what it cannot touch? It thereby receives the impression, not of having been deposed, but of coming infinitely closer to what it willingly refrains from grasping according to its own mode.)

De Man and Mallarmé
'Between the Two Deaths'

Rei Terada

Paul de Man's interest in Mallarmé lasted a lifetime, but absorbed him with particular intensity during two periods of at least seven years on either side of his 1960 dissertation on Mallarmé and Yeats. De Man mentions Mallarmé's *Igitur* in his first published English text,[1] then cites Mallarmé's poetry again and again—especially *Hérodiade*, *Igitur*, and *Un coup de dés*—in at least twelve essays he publishes between 1953 and 1970.[2] In the beginning, Mallarmé was for de Man the poet *par excellence* of 'becoming', sometimes paired off (with qualifications) against Baudelaire, a poet of 'being' (the pairing itself borrows from Mallarmé's opposition between 'essential' and 'immediate' poetry in *Crise de Vers*).[3] In de Man's dissertation, Mallarmé 'begin[s] his career as a naive pantheist' (PRP, 5), then 'turns away . . . in horror' from the feminized organic world (PRP, 8), only to find that this horrified turning is involved in what it turns from, and will be perpetual. While Mallarmé's poems thematize a struggle against the organic, de Man traces the implicit parallel path of the poet experimenting with representational and non-representational language. At stake in the discussion is the possibility of dialectical development. But the question is even larger as well, literally a matter of life and death: is continuance of *any* sort possible and desirable? De Man's attitude toward Mallarmean dialectic registers the effects of his well-known and much-pondered shift from phenomenological to rhetorical analysis. Much of the dissertation argues for Mallarmé's development by negation, yet already characterizes 'development' in peculiar, ironic terms; 'Lyric and Modernity' (1970) is more decisive, asserting, for example, that 'the Mallarmé–Baudelaire relationship is exemplary . . . in that it illustrates the *im*possibility of a representational and an allegorical poetics to engage in a mutually clarifying dialectic' (italics mine).[4] Although de Man's earlier Mallarmé readings are comparatively ambivalent on the subject, I'll argue here that they suggest, sometimes in spite of themselves, that development is *not* possible, and that for that very reason, continuance is.

The result of de Man's rejection of dialectic by 1970 is that Mallarmé seems heavily associated with an early phase of de Man's career whose principles come to seem rough and unsatisfying to de Man himself. Mallarmé's appearances in de Man's work rise and fall with his pursuit of 'development'; de Man never published his dissertation analyses of *Hérodiade* and *Igitur*, and references to Mallarmé, unlike references to Wordsworth and Hölderlin, fall off after 1970. What kind of precursor, then, is Mallarmé for de Man? Through no fault of his own, Mallarmé seems to lead de Man down a blind alley. Blindness turns out to be the point, however, when the collapse of dialectic into the recurrence of error turns out to be *the* form of continuance de Man can endorse. Like Rousseau, Mallarmé then seems to de Man to have always already recognized this pattern, while de Man has to reread his own readings of Mallarmé in order to discover it. This rereading process is predicated on de Man's systematic identification with Mallarmé. By 'systematic', I mean structural; de Man does not want the reader to think he empathizes with Mallarmé psychologically (although in fact he does that too), just as he refuses to claim that Mallarmé identifies psychologically with the obsessions of his poetic personae (autoeroticism and suicide, for example). Rather, the identification between them lies in the persistence of this 'just as', adjusting the positions of protagonist to poet and poet to critic.

We can watch this correlation forming when de Man simply asserts—more or less without evidence—that the 'Ouverture' to *Hérodiade*

> must express the consciousness of the protagonist as well as that of the poet who describes her, while also describing the dramatic relationship that develops between both; hence the persistent multiple structure, from the echoing 'aboli' in the first lines till

the final identification between the two participants, Hérodiade and the poet (ll. 91 ff).[5]

Once this 'persistent multiple structure', the continuous parallel between protagonist and poet, has been set up, there is no way to limit the mirror-game to two participants. As the poet reads himself in the protagonist, the critic reads himself in the poet and so on. De Man's model of the text–reader relationship is, throughout his career, specular and dramatic. Discussing Baudelaire, for example, de Man notes 'the construction and the undoing of the specular structure that is always involved in a reading';[6] elsewhere, he suggests that 'the observation and interpretation of others is always also a means that leads to the observation of the self'.[7] The specularity between text and critic can be antagonistic, as in de Man's essay on Kleist, in which critic and text play fencer and bear. De Man's work on Mallarmé is an early instance of such specularity, in which Mallarmé's negations of his former poems correspond to negations by de Man of his own previous readings of Mallarmé. De Man's rereading of his Mallarmé interpretations produces not a synthesis, but a self-reflexive recognition of critical error—and, eventually, the reading model of *Blindness and Insight*—at which, he believes, Mallarmé arrived before him. The repetition of error, in turn, reveals itself to be the pulse of consciousness, so that even if error were not intrinsically repetitious, we would have to try to repeat it. While de Man's impulse to link Mallarmé to Hegel is not unusual, then, his interpretation of Mallarmé's Hegelianism is. De Man's Mallarmé embraces a *stalling* dialectic, redefining continuance as what happens after dialectic has broken down.

De Man's engagement with Mallarmé, then, helps us to understand why both de Man and Mallarmé find failed dialectic absorbing. Both Mallarmé and de Man can seem to be going around in circles, and it is critically unsatisfying to conclude that they must be describing futility. Therefore, it's important to see that for both Mallarmé and de Man, broken dialectic comes to mind during dramas of suicide. Sartre argues that having 'very seriously contemplated suicide', Mallarmé conceives his poems to be 'both the suicide of man and of Poetry';[8] a similar view recurs (less crudely) in Blanchot, who believes that *Igitur* and *Un coup de dés* promote the existential force of suicide. For this reason, de Man directs his readings of both poems against

Blanchot. It is interesting to note that de Man's analysis of Mallarmé's long poems coincides with his exploration of other authors and works associated with suicide, Hölderlin's *Empedokles* especially.[9] To some extent, de Man's readers have recognized the relevance of suicide to his work. Neil Hertz has shown in vivid detail that the circumstances of de Man's mother's suicide enter de Man's conceptual vocabulary as images of suspension (literally, of hanging).[10] A few critics have also noticed that de Man's family dynamic, in which the uncle Hendrik de Man figures prominently, seems to influence his thought about genealogy; Robert Caserio half-seriously speculates, along these lines, that de Man's uncle metaphorically or literally takes the place of his father.[11] The conjunction of suicide and avuncular family romance circles back again to the Mallarmean image-repertoire of *Hamlet* and *Igitur*. Although it isn't my point simply to say so, the suicide de Man considers between 1955 and 1966 seems potentially to be his own as well as his mother's. But his reading of Mallarmé resists the temptation of suicide as it resists the potential self-monumentalization of dialectic. Universalizing the self, either by recuperating self-negation or—in what amounts to the same thing—by transfusing identity from an organic to a literary body, ends by killing it, de Man implies. The only way to survive 'le Jeu suprême' is to manage never to get to the end of *The Phenomenology of Spirit*. De Man would be such a survivor. And it is to this end that he builds suicide-linked motifs based in Mallarmé—maternal and paternal varieties of succession, an electric zone of indetermination between them—into an affirmation of temporal suspension and material continuance. The suicide subplot suggests that de Man's and Mallarmé's attraction to failing dialectic should be understood as the desire to conceive a time in which to think and, therefore, live.

Necessary Degradation and 'la balsamique Mort'

In his dissertation work on *Hérodiade, Igitur*, and *Un coup de dés*, de Man sketches a Hegelian evolution in which the poet comes to realize that his work is necessarily self-destructive, and, moreover, that self-destruction, thematized and made continuous, is the stuff of which the suspensive time of poesis is made in the first place.[12] Although de Man goes out of his way to disqualify psychological interpretations of Mallarmé's development, Mallarmé's story can nevertheless be understood as a contest between the maternal and the paternal and symbolic order, accompanied by fears of apocalyptic death—fears that the entire symbolic system might fail. Mallarmé's poesis is 'a hazardous act putting into play the disappearances of the symbolic', as Julia Kristeva observes.[13] The contest between gendered orders is represented in the poetry not by things on the one hand and language on the other, but by two kinds of language, representational and nonrepresentational; de Man sees Mallarmé's emphasis on nonrepresentational language as an effort to sublate the eroticism of feminine being. When eroticism proves resistant to dialectic, de Man eventually reconsiders dialectic itself.

'Poetic Nothingness: On a Hermetic Sonnet by Mallarmé' (1955) previews parts of de Man's dissertation, using Mallarmé's 'Une dentelle s'abolit' as its example. Within de Man's narrative, as in so many other critics', 'Une dentelle . . .' depicts a moment when the poet, having repelled the organic world, tries to distinguish the aftereffects of its disappearance:

> Une dentelle s'abolit
> Dans le doute du Jeu suprême
> A n'entr'ouvrir comme un blasphème
> Qu'absence éternelle de lit.
>
> Cet unanime blanc conflit
> D'une guirlande avec la même,
> Enfui contre la vitre blême
> Flotte plus qu'il n'ensevelit.
>
> Mais, chez qui du rêve se dore
> Tristement dort une mandore
> Au creux néant musicien
>
> Telle que vers quelque fenêtre
> Selon nul ventre que le sien
> Filial on aurait pu naître.[14]

(A lace to the light may give way / In doubt of the ultimate Game / As it opens onto the shame / Of absence where a bed once lay // Such a blank unanimous pain / Of a garland with another / Seems less to hold than to hover / If against the pale

window pane // Or the golden dream room wherein / There
sleeps a maudlin mandolin / With its hollow musical nought //
May have carried to the window / From a womb induced by
mere thought / The still born son one cannot know)

De Man scripts for Mallarmé a struggle between the negative power
of poetic consciousness—its capacity to show how the recognition of
objects depends on the possibility of their absence—and a 'feminine',
'direct, maternal' 'world of a spontaneous contact with things' (CW,
23). Mallarmé's shift from bed to music, in this 1955 reading, attacks
a series of conventionally feminine values—'the sensual world', 'the
eternal feminine', and 'natural, elementary rhythms'—'summed up in
the one symbol-word *lit*' (CW, 23), replacing these with the values
of hypothesis and development beyond the empirical. De Man's
contrast here is not explicitly between the maternal and the paternal,
but between the maternal and something—unnamed and ungendered
—linguistic and abstract. It is as though, since to name 'would be to
destroy the hope that remains' (CW, 27), the conventionally paternal
capacity of negation appeared as a literal negative space, elided and
therefore undiminished by representation. As a consequence, the kind
of language opposed to maternal language appears naturalized simply
as 'language'. The maternal 'bed' stands for barrenness in the sense
that it maintains existence at the expense of development; although
de Man does not remark on it, the verbal level of the poem supports
the idea that 'bed' is ominous by embedding 'lit' in 's'abolit' and
'ensevelit'.[15] In the terms of de Man's early vocabulary, bed per-
petuates 'being' at the expense of 'becoming'; as de Man puts it,
'Mallarmé would say with Hegel that mere "life" has no history' (CW,
25).[16]

Over the years, many Mallarmé critics have constructed similar
anti-erotic readings of this poem. But it would be more precise to
say, with others who have investigated Mallarmean pleasure,[17] that
'Une dentelle . . .' is really about the eroticism of chastity and vice
versa. A 'dentelle' is a text made of material loops, as a poem is made
of inky ones (the 'l's in 'dentelle', for example). The poem's first line
suggests the way a loop slips into a straight line, undoing itself, when
the right part of the thread is pulled. The poem literally *opens*, then,
with a kind of undressing that also opens onto something, though
only an 'absence éternelle de lit' is revealed. De Man's anti-erotic

DE MAN AND MALLARMÉ

interpretation is unable to explain why this innocent revelation is still 'comme un blasphème'. As de Man observes, 'Une dentelle' is a poem of palpable negations; I would suggest, first, that absence is like a blasphemy because a blasphemy, too, is a negation. A blasphemy, negating the sacred, makes the sacred seem to exist. Thus Rebecca Saunders has argued recently that 'Mallarmé constructs his "purity" out of the materials of ritual and philosophical defilement'.[18] At the same time, in the poem's context of seduction, the anticlimax of absence—of 'nothing but' absence—is itself a comical 'blasphème', in the way that an unconsummated marriage would be obscenely chaste. By presenting this anti-primal scene, Mallarmé implies that layers of doubt precede and produce effects of sanctity, arousal, and significance. Possibly he makes fun along the way of Plato's bed, another originary non-bed: Mallarmé's bed, like Plato's, is not really *a* bed, but bedness, a missing ideal that grounds the apprehension of objects. Poetically, absences are at least as generative as presences, as de Man suggests. But it does not follow that the matrix of the poem could be, as de Man puts it in 1955, 'a sleepless night, *impregnated* with nervous fatigue and *an entirely mental excitement*' (CW, 21; italics mine). No realm, exciting or not, can be 'entirely mental'—not to mention fatigue and excitement that one would want to call impregnating. Rather, Mallarmé's nonexistence of bed constitutes the illicit quality of the striptease: the form of secrecy creates titillation, even when the secret happens to be empty. Mallarmé's exposure of nothing-to-expose recalls Lacan's notion of the symptom as a product of more and less than subjective discourse.[19] In Slavoj Žižek's extrapolation, 'there is nothing "behind" the fantasy; the fantasy is a construction whose function is to hide this void, this "nothing" '.[20] The French word-play in which a woman's genitals are 'nothing' makes it all the easier to consider a striptease to be the erotic exposure of nothing-actually-illicit. Most importantly, *contra* de Man, the Lacanian symptom is formed with pleasure. The symptom knots itself not to defend against pleasure but because 'that to which [it] gives[s] satisfaction by the ways of displeasure is . . . the law of pleasure'.[21] Mallarmé's teasing sonnet seems to work in the same way, with what Roger Pearson calls 'alluring sterility'.[22]

De Man's later readings of Mallarmé pass to a more pliant understanding of poetic language, in which the recurrence of pleasure makes sexuality immune to dialectical negation. In 1955, the problem with Mallarmé's poetic asceticism is that it 'ends by annihilating form', so that 'henceforth, form can no longer be taken seriously' (CW, 25). In the 1960 dissertation analysis of *Hérodiade*, however, the problem is that 'poetic asceticism' is a contradiction in terms: 'the poet has in fact merely substituted the sensuous enjoyment of a linguistic form for the sensuous enjoyment of nature which he was trying to transcend' (PRP, 32). Therefore, while 'Poetic Nothingness' pits a mental realm against a passionate one, the dissertation opposes 'auto-erotic love' to 'a different, natural passion' or 'natural, maternal, affection' (PRP, 22–3). Hérodiade chooses a '*kind* of erotic experience . . . linked, from the start, with poetic creation, death, and self-reflection' (PRP, 21; italics mine).

This time around, de Man does not celebrate the 'poetic' negation: its new-found eroticism makes it impossible for him to do so. Hérodiade's death, 'instead of being the heroic renunciation out of which a new work was to be born', seems to him an auto-erotic physical extinction (PRP, 27). To an extent, the difference in de Man's attitude is explained by Hérodiade's gender; in dismissing the 'lit', the female protagonist dismisses *herself*. Therefore, de Man figures her refusal as a suicide. In support of this idea he recalls 'Hérodiade, the erotic rose' in 'Les fleurs' (PRP, 20), where artificial flowers suggest suicide:

> The deadly power of the flowers, suggested in the stanza on 'la blancheur sanglotante des lys', becomes quite explicit in the line
> Calices balançant la future fiole
> 'La future fiole', here also called 'la balsamique Mort', is a recurrent Mallarmean symbol for suicide by poison. (PRP, 21; *Œuvres complètes* 33–4)

But the equation between femininity and poetic suicide also works the other way around: Hérodiade stands for all poets—all Parnassian poets, at least—who are consequently feminized *through* her contempt for 'natural passion'. Because de Man's discussion of Mallarmé does not follow the chronology of Mallarmé's poems—the reading of 'Une dentelle . . .' precedes the reading of *Hérodiade*—the figure of the poet implied by de Man's reading seems to *become* feminine between 1955 and 1960. This makes sense in that between 1955 and 1960, de Man gives up the idea of a truly *un*feminine language. Now, in rejecting Hérodiade's preference for 'death [and] self-reflection', and particularly in calling that choice 'auto-erotic', de Man also rejects the interpretation of Mallarmé he offered in 'Poetic Nothingness'. De Man refers to the 'lit' image in the same way in 1960 (see below), implying that the reading of Hérodiade is also a *re*reading of 'Une dentelle . . .'. In the sonnet Mallarmé does treat the lace's dissolution in auto-erotic terms, calling attention to its self-undoing and describing this act as a 'blanc conflit / D'une guirlande avec la même'. Because de Man now perceives the auto-erotic charge of the poem he once called 'purely mental' (CW, 20), he interprets Hérodiade as dramatizing a false renunciation, a rejection of eroticism that merely re-eroticizes language in a no less sexualized way; and at the same time, interpreting Hérodiade in this way entails rereading 'Une dentelle . . .'. When he concludes, then, that with Hérodiade, Mallarmé's poet has 'discovered that he has sung and praised language, not as a depository of absolute truth, but as if it were a part of the warm, natural, sexual realm symbolized by "lit" ' (PRP, 32), de Man sounds as though he were describing his discovery of his own mistake in 'Poetic Nothingness'. It is as strange to believe one could overcome poetic pleasure by writing Parnassian verse, it seems, as to believe one could overcome eroticism by pursuing auto-eroticism. According to de Man, the recognition that pleasure is interminable marks a strong break in Mallarmé's poetic project, which 'will now have to realize that it always and necessarily brings about its own destruction' (PRP, 34).

With the word *necessary*, poetic self-destruction distinguishes itself from suicide, since suicide is above all voluntary. Mallarmé's poet *must* 'chanter le lit', must mistake bed for the bedless ideal, cancelling out his aims: that's what poetry does, and what de Man himself does in 'Poetic Nothingness'. The moment of necessity proves to be crucial in de Man's thinking: eventually, necessary self-destructiveness carries de Man to the claim that 'necessary degradation' is the core of interpretation—'the necessary degradation of melody into harmony . . . of metaphor into literal meaning'—since 'the rhetorical character of literary language opens up the possibility of the archetypal error: the recurrent confusion of sign and substance' (BI, 136). Although de Man, like Mallarmé, is thought of as a lapidary writer, the sensuality of 'substance' is never really repressed in his prose—as his own argument here implies. When we understand that the 'lit' persists in 'literal' as much as in 'abolit', 'degradation' no longer seems like an inexplicably strong word for literal interpretation.

The context of Mallarmé interpretation suggests that de Man also deploys the idea of 'necessary degradation' as a shield against suicide. *Igitur*, with its echoes of *Hamlet*, is sometimes seen as Mallarmé's suicide text—his 'to be or not to be' soliloquy. Blanchot's view of *Igitur* matches de Man's 1955 reading of Mallarmé, in which, if poetry is suicidal, it is because its negative power is self-consuming: 'words, having the power to make things "arise" . . . also have the power to disappear . . . This act of self-destruction is in every respect similar to the ever so strange event of suicide which, precisely, gives to the supreme instant of *Igitur* all its truth.'[23] De Man, however, insists on interpreting *Igitur* as *anti*-suicidal (and in this, opposed to *Hérodiade*), twice bringing up Blanchot simply in order to disagree with him on this point:

> 'L'acte qui s'accomplit' (IV, 3) is not Igitur committing suicide in order to defy his finite nature by asserting his freedom (an interpretation suggested by Maurice Blanchot but not confirmed by the text);[24] it is rather the decision of a consciousness to keep asserting itself after the absurdity of all thought has been revealed. Igitur experiences the supreme negation: '. . . il a enlevé à l'Absolu sa pureté, pour l'être . . .' (IV, 5) and his thought, confronted with the impossibility of defeating chance, remains in existence by meditating on this impossibility. It is condemned to live on the verge of its own destruction and to reflect on its inevitable downfall. (PRP, 90)

Yet, de Man strangely mixes resistance to suicide with sympathy for its goals. Hérodiade's error is not her will to die, or more generally, her desire to quit the senses; her error is believing one *can* escape desire. And in de Man's concurrent narrative of Mallarmé's poetic development, the poet's mistake lies not in his having been attracted to an antiseptic language, but in his assumption that there is no sensual thrill in linguistic austerity. The existential consequence of this conclusion is that suicide is peculiarly futile and ironic, but not for the reasons that people usually think. According to the Mallarmé readings, it is not incoherent for a living consciousness to want to die; that is the part that seems intuitive. What is incoherent is that the act of suicide *only makes sense as an expression of a desire to live,* that is, of desire in its most general form.

De Man stumbles, as it were, upon the deconstruction of suicide: suicide 'always and necessarily' cancels itself out because it is a *constructive* attempt to create or correct a symbolic identity. Therefore, every suicide is a double negative—a suicide *of* suicide—and as such, a singularly meaningless hollow. De Man's figure for this black hole is the corpse: while suicides plan to become symbolic beings, they become instead the material waste products of their own acts, on a level with the rags and cans at the bottom of Yeats's ladder—objects de Man calls 'the utterly worthless content of reality' (RR, 238). The corpse image appears with striking violence in the non-Mallarmé half of de Man's dissertation, in his treatment of Yeats's 'Her Vision in the Wood'. This is Yeats's most violent poem, and de Man's analysis is equally hideous. In the poem, mortal lovers (echoing Venus and Adonis) sacrifice themselves to Dionysus in a 'violent but voluntary death'. The woman is a Hérodiade-like figure, for whom 'death is the passion for prenatal light as opposed to *Hysterica Passio*, the passion for the natural womb' (RR, 133). The poem suggests that the lovers' blood ought to turn into wine, but the transfiguration doesn't take. De Man lingers mercilessly over the fact that 'the turning point that marks the dramatic climax of the poem', narrated by the woman, 'reintroduces the natural substance of "blood"':

> That thing all blood and mire, that beast-torn wreck,
> Half turned and fixed a glazing eye on mine, . . . (RR, 237)

De Man is drawn to this poem, to *Hérodiade*, and to Hölderlin's *Empedokles* because they all stage the vulgar ambition of suicide. Hérodiade anticipates her death as a glamorous withdrawal (as in her direction to the Nourrice, 'si tu veux, clos les volets . . . / . . . je déteste, moi, le bel azur!' (*Œuvres complètes* 48)) ('if you wish, close the shutters . . . I detest the beautiful azure!'). Like Garbo, she wants to be alone. A brief look at de Man's reading of *Empedokles* confirms his interest in suicide as delusory gesture. De Man refers to Hölderlin's verse drama in 'Heidegger's Exegesis of Hölderlin' (1955) and in 'Process and Poetry' (1956). In the former, de Man quarrels with the critic Beda Allemann's interpretation of the poem; according to de Man, Allemann sees in Empedocles' leap into Mount Etna's volcano 'an absolute reconciliation'. De Man, however, sees 'death' in quotation marks—' "death" in the Hegelian sense' that leads 'to a higher level of consciousness, which in Empedocles' case is historical consciousness' (BI, 264–5). Allemann's version, in other words, is the reading of 'being' as opposed to 'becoming'. Empedocles makes a good representative of being, since he plunges himself into the *earth*, a symbol of origin and permanence. As Kenneth Burke notes in a discussion of Matthew Arnold's 'Empedocles on Etna', 'the destruction terminates in imagery of a homecoming, a return to sources probably maternal'.[25] De Man's version of the story thwarts the plot of being, so that there is 'nothing more than the notion of becoming . . . there is never any effective reconciliation' (BI, 265). De Man offers a key piece of evidence for this interpretation in 'Process and Poetry', pointing to the fact that 'the chorus emphasizes [Empedocles'] death with just one word: Future (*Zukunft*)' (CW, 67). If Empedocles covets a definitive end, this word is the last he would want to hear. In de Man's reading—since his Hegel is, even in the fifties, an uncomfortably open-ended, at-least-half-poststructuralist Hegel[26]—the word 'future' does not signal Empedocles' symbolic universalization, because that stabilization would correspond to the very permanence Empedocles covets. 'Future', de Man concludes, 'would be better rendered by such negative terms as "indetermination" or, thinking of Mallarmé, by "chance" ["hasard"]' (CW, 67) . De Man's future lasts a long time, to maintain the *in*stability that alone ensures continuance. It is true that the word 'future' allows de Man to interpret Empedocles' death as 'death' for something, toward historical consciousness. But at the same time, the fact that that future, and that consciousness, is figured by a death shows that the very idea of a future should be 'rendered by . . . negative terms'. Indeed, the future *has* to be rendered in negative terms if there is to be a future at all.

Indestructible Temporality

Empedocles' brand of suicide recalls a poet's hope to transfer particular energies to a symbolic existence in poems. Such a suicide makes the final act of life itself a reading of the life—a commentary to dominate all succeeding commentaries. As such, it is an oddly pedantic moral performance. This would-be instructiveness may help to account for the contagiousness of suicide (as in the *Werther* syndrome): overbearingly exemplary, suicide solicits confirmation. But in this, suicide highlights a disturbing feature of all literature, conventionally construed as the rendering of the self's truth in a preternaturally legible form. Mallarmé's elegy for Poe is written in this traditional key, especially de Man's favourite line, 'tel qu'en Lui-même enfin l'eternité le change' (*Œuvres complètes*, 70).[27] Mallarmé's Poe seems to resemble Hegel's 'individual who, after a long succession of separate disconnected experiences, concentrates himself into a single completed shape' (Hegel, 270). Lecturing on Rousseau in 1967—a lecture in which he quotes the beloved line— de Man reflects on the duality created by substitutions like Mallarmé's exchange of 'le' for 'Lui-même':

> here we are faced, at once, with a fatal confusion between two selves: the one specific, particular, historical, and chaotic, the other capable of the lofty lucidity of total self-understanding. The gap between the two is so wide as to have become comically proverbial. (RCC, 27)

The problematic with which de Man concerns himself here has its locus classicus in Boethius, reappears in Hegel, and has been studied by Lacan under the rubric of 'the difference between the two deaths'—the death of an individual and the death of the name, which often occur in syncopation. Speaking of the relationship between individuals and their families, Hegel mentions the example of Antigone, the survivor who disputes her brother's second death.[28] Lacan's interpretation of *Antigone* takes up Hegel's hint, investigating stresses within the universalization of the name.[29] Žižek—whose reading of this seminar of Lacan's is one of his most significant—renders the motif of the two deaths in a memorable simile:

> take the example of video games, in which we deal, literally, with the differences between the two deaths: the usual rule of such games is that the player (or, more precisely, the figure representing him in the game) possesses several lives . . .The whole logic of such games is therefore based on the difference between the two deaths: between the death in which I lose one

of my lives and the ultimate death in which I lose the game itself. (Žižek, 135)

If we return now to the first line of 'Le Tombeau d'Edgar Poe', we can see in it the tensions of the 'two deaths' paradigm. As an epigraph, the line is highly ambiguous, because two incompatible interpretations of it appear in the dissertation. In the first, orthodox view, the poet's identity is decanted into his work; in the second, the attempt to perform this transfer is just more corpse-production, the text now doubling in the role of the dead body.[30] Visible in Mallarmé's phrase is the reification which befalls Hegelian consciousness on its way to universalization. When consciousness universalizes itself, it also becomes a thing (Hegel, 457), growing opaque as it becomes a *figure*.[31] Consciousness evolves in two directions, becoming more concrete as well as more spiritual. Thus, Hérodiade, in trying to become, like Socrates, a hero who undergoes the first death in order to avert the second, likens herself to statuary—a symbol of monumentalization for de Man through 'Shelley Disfigured' (1979)—and, as de Man points out, 'the "tears" of her sacrifice undergo a metamorphosis into "jewels"' (PRP, 25). De Man would come to be known for resisting the idea of critical personification—of taking texts for people—but here he resists the complementary idea that one can take people for symbols. A writer like Poe or Mallarmé (or a figure like Empedocles or Hérodiade) tries to make the self a purely symbolic entity, performing the reverse of personification. In arguing that this is impossible, de Man does not divide 'life' from 'art'. Rather, the mistake is not to remember that *no art, no text* can be transparently symbolic, just as no experience, and no poetry either, can be pleasure free.[32]

The failure of dialectical progression from self to poem recurs in the relations between successive poetic works (and later, in *Blindness and Insight*, between poetry and criticism). Thus, de Man notes that the petrifaction of Hérodiade's tears represents 'a perfect symbolization of the change that separates Mallarmé's Parnassian poetry from his earlier verse' (PRP, 25); and when Mallarmé literalizes the duality between consciousness and its thought of itself in the decapitation of St Jean Baptiste, de Man promptly casts the decapitation in terms of Mallarmé's stylistic modulations:

the poetic work, the 'fraise arachnéenne' . . . separates the head from the body like the scythe which decapitates Saint John in the final section of *Hérodiade*. Similarly, the early poetry is now forever separated from the mature work that will follow *Igitur*. (PRP, 66).

De Man would have us believe that *Igitur* is to Mallarmé's poetry what poetry in general is to existence: the dotted line separating the symbolic from the particular, as St Jean's head is separated from his body. This very position, however, shows that poetry is not itself the symbolic: explicitly, it is the borderland between the two. *Igitur*'s narrator ponders 'le hasard infini des conjonctions' (*Œuvres complètes*, 437), and 'igitur' *is* a conjunction—literally a grammatical connector, metaphorically a coincidence of possibilities. Not only is 'igitur' the name of a borderland, but its territory goes on forever. 'Une chambre du temps', Mallarmé calls it (*Œuvres complètes*, 435). Situated 'between the two deaths'—'a place of sublime beauty as well as terrifying monsters' (Žižek, 135)—the poem is described by de Man as at once open and claustrophobic:

> Igitur is torn between, on the one hand, a stable but unbearable form of memory and, on the other hand, a desire for an impossible future which keeps him suspended outside of his present reality . . . master of a past and of a future that are both equally unbearable . . . in a state of total stability, he is now like a thing. (PRP, 41–2).[33]

The combination of vastness and constraint as de Man renders it here is characteristic of language in general. The domain of language is the 'Angoisse' of Mallarmé's 'sonnet en yx', which, as Paul Allen Miller points out, 'may initially be identified as a personification of the sensation produced by being squarely placed between converging opposites', and etymologically 'derives from Latin *angustus*, meaning narrow or constricted'.[34] Thus, for Derrida, *angustia* names 'the necessarily restricted passageway of speech against which all possible meanings push each other'.[35] (It would be like Mallarmé to have noticed the *ang* common to *ang*oisse and l*ang*age, the additional *u* sound shared in English by *angu*ish and l*angu*age.) De Man's *œuvre* is full of such 'necessarily restricted' places—the channel of

Hölderlin's Rhine, the 'whirligig (*tourniquet*) . . . capable of infinite acceleration' (RR, 71), Baudelaire's description of Constantin Guys's frenetic sketches.[36] This passage from de Man's 1966 essay on Ludwig Binswanger is particularly relevant:

> The artist is suspended as in the 'rhythmique suspens du sinistre' that Mallarmé evokes by a succession of 'suspended' sentences in *Un coup de dés*, carried aloft in the ambiguous time-structure of the monadic work . . . A 1943 article [by Binswanger] has for its theme a quotation from Hugo von Hofmannsthal: 'Was Geist ist, erfaszt nur der Bedrängte.' The term 'der Bedrängte' is difficult to translate. It combines an idea of being locked up in too narrow a space, with the temporal ordeal of being steadily urged on, of being unable to remain at rest. One thinks of Pascal, of course, but also of man in Baudelaire, driven and harassed, 'imitant la toupie et la boule'. (BI, 45)

To construct a set of poles, however (a 'past' and 'future', for example), is also to use suspension as a shock absorber. Through such a structure, experience can appear as recognizable. In the lexicon of *Blindness and Insight* this frame is the 'axis' on which unassimilable experience '[spreads] out' for the benefit of consciousness; in that of 'Une dentelle . . .', it is the lacy frame of doubt through which absence looks like the absence *of* something. Alternatively, de Man's dissertation represents the support of consciousness as a medium, a 'substance' like water; arguing with Blanchot again over *Un coup de dés*, de Man claims that the poet's 'supreme effort of the mind' in 'know[ing] he is about to be annihilated' (PRP, 114)

> is not prompted . . . by the desire to demonstrate the mind's freedom in making its own decision to die at the moment of its choice . . . The poet, or thinker, is a creature in a suspended state, whose downfall is no longer immediate—in the temporal as well as in the philosophical sense of the term—since the language of his thought stands between him and the fulfilment of his destiny. The act of thought does not simply *postpone* his death to a future point in time; in the realm of the mind, a determined future is already a present and, consequently, a delay of this kind would be of no avail. Rather, thought as Mallarmé conceives of it, *engenders* time as the mediating entity between

consciousness and the chaos of immediate reality. The language
of thought contains time as a substance in which consciousness
can remain suspended. (PRP, 115–16)

If the thought of destruction 'contains time' and therefore consciousness, thought staves off suicide to the very extent that it remains
a possibility. Held in the mind, the edge of destruction elongates to
form the ground of consciousness. Like Hamlet, Mallarmé's *'seigneur
latent qui ne peut devenir'* (*Œuvres complètes*, 300), Igitur becomes a
figure of continuance because he fails to decide whether to live or to
die. As Hans-Jost Frey remarks of 'Une dentelle s'abolit . . .': 'We
are left stranded between being and nonbeing. We can therefore
neither say that Mallarmé's poem is nor that it is not . . . It expresses
itself as the missed opportunity to be and not to be.'[37] *Igitur* and *Un
coup de dés*, too, demonstrate the 'possibility of *repeating* the moment
of truth' (PRP, 53), the 'mere succession of such "deaths"' (PRP,
46), and the task of 'admitting forever, by never forgetting, the
given duality' (PRP, 52); in this way they reveal an 'indestructible
temporality' (PRP, 46). This is the sort of time experienced by
a cartoon character—or poetic object—who suffers daily 'deaths'
(by steamroller, dynamite, or falling safe) to live and die again. In
such a landscape, it would be missing the point to commit suicide.
Derrida observes that Pierrot and Columbine, in a chain of texts
metonymically related to Mallarmé, do precisely that. In Gautier's
Pierrot Posthume, for instance, Pierrot 'pretends to die' by mouse-
swallowing and autotickling, 'in the supreme spasm of infinite
masturbation', *then* (metaphysically) considers 'suicide once and for
all'. But Pierrot 'will never have finished killing himself, the "once
and for all" expressing precisely . . . that before which we shall always
burst out laughing'.[38] For Derrida, suicide and virginity alike occupy
the liminal amplitude of de Man's 'indestructible temporality'. De
Man's virtual world, however, is more like Ovid's or Dante's, in which
the population is meant to be able to feel its endless annihilation and
recovery-only-to-be-annihilated: it is, in other words, the *natural*
world. Thus he remarks in 'Shelley Disfigured' that the 'play of veiling
and unveiling', remembering and forgetting, 'is like desire because,
like the wolf pursuing the deer, it does violence to what sustains it'
(RR, 106). In the sixties especially, de Man's interpretation is a long
way from the feathery playfulness of Derrida's Mallarmé; the

phenomenon of de Manian *humour* doesn't really emerge until *Allegories of Reading*. But despite the difference in tone, de Man, too, generalizing on the model of *Igitur*, redefines consciousness as an area 'between the two deaths'.

The indestructibility de Man finds in Mallarmé is ironic, however, and its irony challenges both Hegel and Nietzsche. Hegel is made the victim of a cosmic joke (a 'Jeu suprême'?): by the end of de Man's dissertation, he is still the guiding figure of the project, but only in the sense that we are returned, nightmarishly, to the *beginning* of the *Phenomenology of Spirit*. Igitur does not exactly break down in Hegel's 'sense-certainty', in which 'I, *this* particular I, am certain of *this* particular thing' (Hegel, 58), but he only gets one step further. In the course of connecting particularity to what it is an instance of, a stutter falls upon the 'therefore', and we never get to know what particularity is an instance of. This is to say that the connection, 'igitur', logically precedes the consciousness that utters it; because there is a 'therefore', there is an 'I'. As Andrzej Warminksi observes, 'we begin with certainty and not with the senses'.[39] Perhaps this is clearer in the Cartesian idiom, where 'igitur' may be translated as 'ergo'. In de Man's Mallarmean reasoning, the Cogito would have to read 'Cogito, ergo, ergo, ergo. . . .': to reach 'sum' would be to disappear; it would be to fall through the floor of consciousness. De Man associates this repeated sound, the repeated 'admission of the given duality' (PRP, 52), with the clock in *Igitur*: 'the moment is repeated; it is a rhythmical beat, similar to the ticking of the clock, marking a succession of deaths, an eternal reaffirmation that no future can exist' (PRP, 57). *Igitur*'s ticking clock blurs into 'les pulsations de [son] propre cœur', ('the beats of his own heart') and this same sound, 'le bruit du progrès de [son] personnage' ('the sound of the progress of his character') (*Œuvres complètes*, 438), is also 'le scandement de [sa] mesure' ('the scansion of his measure') (*Œuvres complètes*, 439). Here, in the superimposition of cardiac 'pulsations' and metrical 'scandement', Igitur 'SE PERD DANS LES ESCALIERS' (*Œuvres complètes*, 436). This sound, the sound of thought not in motion but in neutral, is neither natural nor artificial. In de Man's later work it marks the time of Gedächtnis, rote memory that exteriorizes the innermost mental workings, and of 'measure', by which de Man means 'any linguistic [device] of articulation' which can run 'independently of [its] signifying constraints' (RR, 114). A consciousness supported by rhythmic pulsation, we should notice, is as much as ever an auto-erotic one of self-sustaining repetition: it, too, undergoes a continual 'necessary degradation'. It is even amniotic; truly, whatever holds your mind up is your mother.

When I mentioned, at the start of the last paragraph, that the joke might be on Nietzsche as well as on Hegel, I was thinking of the way in which this repetition of a thought—that may also be just the sound of a mental wheel turning—combines the eternal return with Hegel's idea of empty connection from the beginning of *The Phenomenology of Spirit* (a book that taxes the stamina of the eternal return). The kind of 'living on' that de Man envisions in *Igitur* has to be done over in order to be done at all. But would we want to say 'yes' to consciousness, and choose to live it over again, when it gets no further than 'igitur'? De Man's reading of Mallarmé's implicit encounter with suicide assumes that the answer is yes; but it is the *sort* of yes that seems to ironize Nietzsche's. It is a yes by default, and a yes by description rather than by assertion. De Man's interpretations of Mallarmé—like so much of his work—convey a mixture of resignation and passion too curious to call pessimistic. De Man shares this complex of qualities with Mallarmé, for whom 'conceptual and emotional indecision', as Malcolm Bowie notes, 'is neither a morbidity of temperament nor an awkwardness of style: it is the sign of a tenacious and often painful fidelity to the facts of experience'.[40] Gramsci writes of hoping to avoid 'those vulgar, banal states of mind that are called pessimism and optimism';[41] de Man's suspension of dialectic can be understood in a similar way, as transforming 'pessimism' and 'optimism' from the inside. In reading Mallarmé's poems as responses to suicide at a time when he was, apparently, looking for arguments against it, de Man found or invented unsentimental images of continuance that defend themselves against self-destruction *in* their acknowledgment of its power.

7

Derrida's Mallarmé

Geoffrey Bennington

Although 'La double séance' has often appeared to be a daunting and rather mysterious text, its structure and principal arguments seem relatively clear. Analytically speaking, Derrida wants to interrogate the relation between literature and truth, and to show how literature escapes (or can escape) the hold of the ontological question ('What is . . .') in a way which can nonetheless provide something like a 'formalization' of the question of truth. To do this, Derrida is concerned (1) to explicate a traditional, Platonic, schema of *mimesis*; (2) to establish the *theoretical* possibility of this schema's being disrupted by a feature or process he calls the re-mark; (3) to posit Mallarmé as an *exemplary* instantiation of that theoretical possibility; (4) to show firstly, that this cannot be accounted for by a thematic reading, and, secondly, that it entails a practice of reading which takes more seriously than a thematic one ever could the play of syntax, and sub-lexical items in the text. Each of these points is presented in recognizably argued form, and could in principle be the object of critical debate and evaluation.

If 'La double séance' has been a daunting text, however, this is not without good reason. Among the many doublings and duplicities the text's title[1] indicates is a basic doubling of the analytical structure I have just outlined, by a structure we might be tempted (ill-advisedly) to call more 'properly' deconstructive. According to this second, overlaid structure, Derrida wants to show that those disruptions of the Platonic model, which it is heuristically simpler to ascribe to Mallarmé, must in fact already be at work in that Platonic model, so that that model is, already and intrinsically, double and duplicitous. According to this structure of argument, the failure or disruption of the Platonic schema is part of that schema from the start, and so Mallarmé's status as exemplary disruptor is rendered more complicated. According to a duplicity which inhabits the very concept of example, Mallarmé will, on the one hand, be presented as exemplary in the sense that he would be the *best* example, or at least a shining example, to that extent more than *just* an example but a sort of paragon; and on the other as really no more than a *sample*, exemplifying the disruption of *mimesis* just as any text (including Plato's) might be taken to exemplify it, an example more or less randomly picked from a whole range of possiblities.

I want to argue not only that the interest of 'La double séance' lies primarily in the way in which Mallarmé is thus presented as duplicitously *exemplary*, but also that the logic of exemplarity at work in Derrida's text follows, in its structure, that of the 're-mark' Derrida finds exemplarily at work *in* Mallarmé's text (that re-mark being the essential feature of the theoretical possibility of disrupting the Platonic schema of *mimesis* posited in (2) above). This structure places Mallarmé in a curious position which I shall try to explicate, and dictates a certain convergence, both between Mallarmé's more theoretical remarks about language and Derrida's own, and between Mallarmé's textual *practice* and Derrida's own.[2] This will mean that Derrida's text cannot in principle be read exhaustively as theoretical or argumentative (although that is how I shall almost exclusively be reading it, for reasons which go beyond issues of personal competence), and that in some sense it too is, still in this double sense, *exemplary* of the theoretical positions for which it argues.

To make these points, let me first quote Derrida's formalization of the Platonic view of *mimesis:*

> 1° La *mimesis* produit le double de la chose. Si le double est fidèle et parfaitement ressemblant, aucune différence qualitative ne le sépare du modèle. Trois conséquences: *a)* Le double —l'imitant—n'est rien, ne vaut rien par lui-même. *b)* L'imitant ne valant que par son modèle, il est bon quand le modèle est bon, mauvais quand le modèle est mauvais. Il est neutre et transparent en lui-même. *c)* Si la *mimesis* ne vaut rien et n'est rien par elle-même, elle est néant de valeur et d'être, elle est en soi négative: elle est donc un mal, imiter est un mal en soi et non seulement quand cela revient à imiter le mal. 2° Ressemblant

ou non, l'imitant est quelque chose puisqu'il y a de la *mimesis* et des mimèmes. Ce non-être 'existe' en quelque sorte (*Sophiste*). Donc *a)* s'ajoutant au modèle, l'imitant vient en supplément et cesse d'être un rien et une non-valeur. *b)* S'ajoutant au modèle 'étant', l'imitant n'est pas le même et fût-il absolument ressemblant, il n'est jamais absolument ressemblant (*Cratyle*). Donc jamais absolument vrai. *c)* Supplément du modèle, mais ne pouvant l'égaler, il lui est inférieur dans son essence au moment même où il peut le remplacer et être ainsi 'primé'. Ce schéma (2 propositions et 6 conséquences possibles) forme une sorte de machine logique; elle programme les prototypes de toutes les propositions inscrites dans le discours de Platon et dans ceux de la tradition. Selon une loi complexe mais implacable, cette machine distribue tous les clichés de la critique à venir. (212–3, n. 8)

((1) *Mimesis* produces the double of the thing. If the double is faithful and perfectly similar, no qualitative difference separates it from the model. Three consequences: (a) The double—the imitator—is nothing, is worth nothing in itself. (b) Because the imitator only has the value of its model, it is good when the model is good, bad when the model is bad. It is neutral and transparent in itself. c) If *mimesis* is worth nothing and is nothing in itself, it is void of value and being, and is in itself negative: it is therefore an evil, imitating is intrinsically evil and not only when it comes down to imitating evil. (2) Whether similar or not, the imitator is something since there is *mimesis* and mimemes. This non-being 'exists' in some sense (*Sophist*). So (a) adding itself to the model, the imitator comes as a supplement and stops being a nothing and a non-value. (b) Adding to the 'existent' model, the imitator is not the same and even if it were absolutely similar, it is never absolutely similar (*Cratylus*). So never absolutely true. (c) As supplement of the model, but unable to equal it, it is inferior to it in its essence at the very moment it can replace it and thus be 'outdone'. This schema (2 propositions and 6 possible consequences) forms a sort of logical machine; it programmes the prototypes of all the propositions inscribed in Plato's discourse and in those of the tradition. According to a complex but implacable law, this machine distributes all the clichés of criticism to come.)

Let us accept for now that this is an accurate description and that it does indeed provide the means for accounting for all subsequent doctrines of mimesis.[3] We shall see in due course that part of Derrida's point is that this doctrine *cannot* in fact account for mimetic practices in general, so it is in fact predictable that all subsequent doctrines of mimesis (and indeed Plato's own) will in some sense always be escaping its terms, and Derrida's schematic footnote will to that extent come to have a slightly parodic ring, as he shows how Plato's discourse is *also* necessarily escaping the hold of this 'logical machine'. For now, however, this doctrine (insofar as it can be made coherent) is essentially determined by the fact of its referring itself to the *truth*, and, according to our point (2):

> cette référence est discrètement mais absolument déplacée dans l'opération d'une certaine syntaxe, quand une écriture marque et redouble la marque d'un trait indécidable.[4] Cette double marque se soustrait à la pertinence ou à l'autorité de la vérité: sans la renverser mais en l'inscrivant dans son jeu comme une pièce ou une fonction. Ce déplacement n'a pas lieu, n'a pas lieu une fois, comme un *événement*. Il n'a pas de lieu simple. Il n'a pas lieu *dans* une écriture. Cette dis-location (est ce qui s') écrit. De ce redoublement de la marque, qui est en même temps une rupture et une généralisation formelles, *le texte de Mallarmé, et singulière-ment la feuille* ['Mimique'] *que vous avez sous les yeux, seraient exemplaires* (mais il va de soi que chaque mot de cette dernière proposition doit être du même coup déplacé ou frappé de suspicion). (220)

> (this reference is discretely but absolutely displaced in the operation of a certain syntax, when a writing marks and redoubles the mark with an undecidable trait. This double mark withdraws from the pertinence or authority of truth: without overturning it, but inscribing it in its game as a piece or a function. This displacement does not take place, does not take place once, as an *event*. It has no simple place. It does not take place *in* a writing. This dis-location writes; this dis-location is what is written. I am suggesting that *Mallarmé's text, and more especially the sheet you have in front of you* ['Mimique'] *are exemplary* (though it goes without saying that every word in this pro-position must by the same token be displaced or struck with

suspicion) of this redoubling of the mark, which is also a formal break and generalization.)

We need to understand a number of things in this passage. Let's try first to explicate the theoretical possibility of this double mark, and its undecidability, before attending to the status of Mallarmé as an exemplary instance of the practice of it, and, finally, to the problem of knowing what to make of the final parenthetical *mise en garde*.

(1) Mallarmé's text 'Mimique' describes the scene of a sort of radical imitation which in fact imitates nothing, no thing. The 'mime' described acts out, represents, a drama which has no fixable prior referent, no anterior 'reality' of which it is the representation. Mallarmé, as read by Derrida, sets up a scene in which *there is* miming, but in which no thing is mimed. Derrida's description, with subordinate demonstrations spread over several pages, is as follows:

> Il n'y a pas d'imitation. Le mime n'imite rien. Et d'abord il n'imite pas. Il n'y a rien avant l'écriture de ses gestes. Rien ne lui est prescrit. Aucun présent n'aura précédé ni surveillé le tracement de son écriture. Ses mouvements forment une figure que ne prévient ni n'accompagne aucune parole . . . Le mime n'est assujetti à l'autorité d'aucun livre . . . Au commencement de ce mime n'était ni l'acte, ni la parole. Il est prescrit . . . au Mime de ne rien se laisser prescrire que son écriture . . . Le Mime doit seulement s'écrire sur une page blanche qu'il est . . . Mallarmé . . .écrit sur une page blanche à partir d'un texte qu'il lit et dans lequel il est écrit qu'il faut écrire sur une page blanche. (221–5)

> (There is no imitation. The mime imitates nothing. And first of all he does not imitate. There is nothing before the writing of his gestures. Nothing is prescribed to him. No present will have preceded or supervised the tracing of his writing. His movements form a figure which no speech foreshadows or accompanies . . . The mime is subject to the authority of no book . . . At the beginning of this mime was neither the act nor the word. It is prescribed to the Mime to allow nothing to be prescribed to him other than his writing . . . The Mime must only write himself on a blank page that he is . . . Mallarmé . . . writes on a blank page on the basis of a text he reads and in which it is written that one must write on a blank page.)

And faced with the possible objection that the text Mallarmé is reporting on in 'Mimique', the *livret* for the performance of the mime, however complex that text may in turn be in its own structure[5]—faced with the possible objection that this text would nonetheless be the final referent of Mallarmé's (thereby still mimetic) writing, Derrida complicates the analysis in a way which will help us to understand the sense we can give to the 'double mark' we quoted earlier: 'Telle écriture qui ne renvoie qu'à elle-même nous reporte *à la fois*, indéfiniment et systématiquement, à une autre écriture. A la fois: c'est ce dont il faut rendre compte.' ('A writing referring only to itself *simultaneously* refers us, indefinitely and simultaneously, to another writing. Simultaneously: that is what we have to account for.') (229) This seems to be the difficult point to grasp: Derrida is not getting excited in a general way about the discovery of what was at the time of 'La double séance' being taken up enthusiastically, by for example Barthes and Kristeva, under the name of 'intertextuality': the point is not (as might seem to be the case in some of Barthes's work, for example) to celebrate self-conscious intertextuality *in general*, but to stress the *singularity* (this will lead us to the *exemplarity*) of *each* referral. Whence a difficult and perhaps rather awkward *enchaînement*:

> Une écriture qui ne renvoie qu'à elle-même et une écriture qui renvoie indéfiniment à une autre écriture, cela peut paraître non-contradictoire: l'écran réfléchissant ne capte jamais que de l'écriture, sans arrêt, indéfiniment, et le renvoi nous confine dans l'élément du renvoi. Certes. Mais la difficulté tient au rapport entre le médium de l'écriture et la détermination de chaque unité textuelle. Il faut que chaque fois renvoyant à un autre texte, à un autre système textuel, chaque organisme ne renvoie qu'à lui-même comme structure déterminée: *à la fois* ouverte et fermée. (230)

> (A writing referring only to itself and a writing referring indefinitely to another writing—that might appear non-contradictory: the reflecting screen only ever captures writing, endlessly, indefinitely, and referral confines us in the element of referral. Of course. But the difficulty resides in the relation between the medium of writing and the determination of each textual unit. Each time referring to another text, another textual

system, each organism must refer only to itself as a determinate structure: *simultaneously* open and closed.)

This 'en même temps' and 'à la fois' of the open and the closed (this simultaneity or undecidability being just what Derrida will attempt to formulate with the word 'hymen' a little later, bespeaking both the maintenance of a distinction and its transgression) constitutes the double mark, or the re-mark we are trying to understand: just as a vague sense of intertextuality will not make Derrida's point, so it is not enough to invoke a vague sense of *self-referentiality* whereby writing refers to itself as writing by referring in general to writing in an indeterminate way. The point is that *this* singular writing here both refers to itself as this singular writing here *and in so doing* refers itself to other writing too.[6]

This demonstration is part of a more general Derridean claim about identity in general: the self-referential 'ceci' in the sentence from *Les Mots anglais* ('Lecteur, vous avez sous les yeux ceci, un écrit . . .' ('Reader, you have before you this, a writing . . .')) confirms the identity of the 'écrit', or at least of the word 'ceci' itself, only by *getting outside itself* to point to itself from the position of the other, the reader explicitly addressed by the sentence apparently referring only to itself. The mark ('ceci') is re-marked as itself ("ceci") by a ghostly doubling whereby the mark marks itself as marking, refers to itself referring to itself, only by the fact of separating itself enough from itself to open the gap across which reference can function: but the 'end' of that reference, the referent to which that reference is supposed to refer, is nothing other than the fact of reference or referring itself.[7] This 'miming' of reference (without which no reference at all could take place, for want of sufficient self-identity in the mark doing the referring) is the principle according to which mimesis's referral to truth will never quite be successful.[8]

What the 'official'[9] Platonic doctrine of *mimesis* cannot contain, then, is this simultaneity of reference (be it thought of as reference to 'reality' or simply to other texts) and self-reference. 'Se donnant à lire pour elle-même et se passant de tout prétexte extérieur, *Mimique* est aussi hantée par le fantôme ou entée sur l'arborescence d'un autre texte.' ('Giving itself to be read for itself and doing without any external pretext, *Mimique* is also haunted by the ghost or grafted onto the aborescence of another text.') (230) More importantly, Mallarmé's text is not only structured in this way (it only takes a moment's reflection to realize that any text must *a priori* be so structured), but it writes that fact into itself: 'Mimique' is not only a growth grafted on to the complex branching structure of the history of Pierrot, but a grafted growth which 'remarks' the fact of that grafting:

> L'investigation bibliographique, la recherche des sources, l'archéologie des Pierrots serait à la fois interminable et inutile, du moins pour ce qui nous intéresse ici, puisque le processus de renvoi et de greffe est *remarqué dans* le texte de Mallarmé, qui n'a donc pas plus de dedans qu'il n'est proprement de Mallarmé. (233)[10]

> (Bibliographical investigations, the search for sources, the archaeology of Pierrots, all this would be interminable and futile, at least for what we are concerned with here, since the process of reference and grafting is *remarked within* Mallarmé's text, which therefore has no more an interior than it is properly Mallarmé's.)

So Mallarmé's text refers to a performance which is apparently to be a pure production with no prior text determining its acts,[11] but does so by referring itself to another text (Paul Margueritte's *livret* with its complex internal structure and endless referrals to the tradition of the *commedia dell'arte*), and yet folds back onto itself insofar as it refers to its own gestures of referral. Derrida's contention is that this structure cannot be described either by the official Platonic doctrine of *mimesis* as adequation, or by the associated view that this would therefore be the pure production of truth itself as an inaugural unveiling (truth as *aletheia*). The point is that the Mime *mimes*, but mimes nothing, no-thing: this is what Derrida calls a 'reference without referent',[12] whereby the apparent structure of *mimesis* is maintained, and indeed generalized, so that what we have is an imitation without a model, a ghost which is there from the start, the ghost of no once living (and now dead) thing. This *generalized mimesis*, obtained by the re-marking in the text of the referral of the text to another text (by the apparently reflexive re-marking, then, of the failure of the text to achieve closure and self-identity) is here presented as powerful enough to suspend the subordination of literature to truth, insofar at least as that truth is secured by an ontology or a dialectics.[13]

But it follows directly from this suspension of the ontological referent ('being') that it will be impossible to maintain the structure used so far to establish a contrast between a Platonic doctrine and a Mallarmean contestation of that doctrine: generalized *mimesis* will be general only if this type of structure is itself complicated or disrupted too. Derrida's prose presents this consequence as a sort of theoretical narrative within a paragraph we may ourselves take as provisionally *exemplary* of the deconstructive manner:

> Mallarmé maintient ainsi la structure différentielle de la mimique ou de la *mimesis*, mais sans l'interprétation platonicienne ou métaphysique, qui implique que quelque part l'être d'un étant soit imité. Mallarmé maintient même (se maintient dans) la structure du *phantasme*, telle que la définit Platon: simulacre comme copie de copie. A ceci près qu'il n'y a plus de modèle, c'est-à-dire de copie et que cette structure (qui comprend aussi le texte de Platon, y compris la sortie qu'il y tente) n'est plus référée à une ontologie, voire à une dialectique. A vouloir renverser le mimétologisme ou à prétendre lui échapper d'un coup, en sautant simplement *à pieds joints*, on retombe sûrement et immédiatement dans son système: on supprime le double ou on le dialectise et on retrouve la perception de la chose même, la production de sa présence, sa vérité, comme idée, forme ou matière. Par rapport à l'idéalisme platonicien ou hegelien, le déplacement que nous nommons ici par convention 'mallarméen', est plus subtil et plus patient, discret et efficient. C'est un simulacre de platonisme ou de hegelianisme qui n'est séparé de ce qu'il simule que par un voile à peine perceptible, dont on peut tout aussi bien dire qu'il passe déjà—inaperçu—entre le platonisme et lui-même, entre le hegelianisme et lui-même. Il n'est donc pas simplement faux de dire que Mallarmé est platonicien ou hegelien. Mais ce n'est surtout pas vrai.
>
> Et réciproquement. (235)

(Mallarmé thus maintains the differential structure of mimicry or *mimesis*, but without the Platonic or metaphysical interpretation, which implies that somewhere the being of an entity be imitated. Mallarmé even maintains (maintains himself in) the structure of the *phantasm*, as Plato defines it: the simulacrum as copy of a copy. Except that there is no model left, and therefore no copy and this structure (which also comprehends Plato's text, including his attempted escape from it) is no longer referred to an ontology, nor even to a dialectic. Wanting to overturn mimetologism or claiming to escape from it in one go, simply jumping *with both feet*, one falls back certainly and immediately into its system: one suppresses the double or one dialectizes it and one gets back to the perception of the thing itself, the production of its presence, its truth, as idea, form or matter. Compared to Platonic or Hegelian idealism, the displacement we are here, conventionally, calling 'Mallarmean', is more subtle and patient, discreet and efficient. It is a simulacrum of Platonism or Hegelianism which is separated from what it is simulating only by a scarcely perceptible veil, a veil one can just as well describe as already passing—unperceived—between Platonism and itself, between Hegelianism and itself. Between Mallarmé's text and itself. So it is not simply false to say that Mallarmé is Platonic or Hegelian. But it is above all not true. And reciprocally.)

In accordance with what Derrida means by deconstruction more generally, apparent escape from the closure of metaphysics leads inevitably to a fall back into it: the apparently greater difference falls back into no difference, in-difference, sameness.[14] A more radical difference, then, is made by making an apparently smaller difference, an apparently minor displacement, or even what may look like a re-doubling confirmation. Mallarmé *looks just like* a Platonism or a Hegelianism, but just because of that insistence on mimetic doubling, that insistence on looking just like itself, Mallarmé makes a bigger (because 'more subtle and patient') difference. Mimesis is exceeded by a mimesis of mimesis, a second-order mimesis, a miming of mimesis, that takes as its reference the act of reference of first-order mimesis (which has a referent as *its* reference). But bringing out the 'truth' of mimesis in this way displaces the truth: at what it can only be a provisional convenience to call this second level, mimesis is shown to have no truth other than the referring movement itself whereby it always might *not* be truthful. And this must be just as true of first-order mimesis too, so that in Plato, too, there is a doubling up of mimesis, so that the most official examples of it always might be just mimicry or false imitations.

At which point there is a possibility and a danger. The *possibility* (of which Mallarmé would, then, be *exemplary*) is that *there be* some sort of 'escape' from philosophy (metaphysics), here showing up as the generalization of mimesis and therefore of 'literature'. This possibility is the more alluring in that it looks as though its necessary *generalization* means simply that *there is no philosophy*, so that Plato, too, would turn out to be just another instance of what is now a general literature. The *danger* is that just this alluring possibility pitches the analysis back into the very problem Derrida has just been praising Mallarmé for avoiding (by keeping the mime in mimesis) and leads simply to a sameness in which all differences are lost. To avoid this consequence, or rather to face up to this danger, Derrida appeals to a notion of *strategy*, and this will lead to a reintroduction of something like history into the account, which appeared earlier to be bracketing history out in the name of a transcendental structure of the re-mark. The danger would consist in declaring *straight-forwardly* that all texts necessarily escape metaphysics, which could then simply be forgotten in the name of something like a general literature or textuality in which we could henceforth triumphantly or blissfully install ourselves, with Mallarmé our hero. Such a declaration would have at least the heuristic advantage of dramatizing a 'performative contradiction': the thetic form of a metaphysical proposition would have been borrowed just long enough to declare the subsequent (and antecedent) invalidity of any such thetic metaphysical statement. The only valid metaphysical statement would be the eminently metaphysical statement that all metaphysical statements are invalid. Deconstruction is the ongoing and necessarily interminable demonstration (or enactment) of the over-hastiness of this consequence, the perpetual holding back short of this apparent *telos* of its arguments. Whence the need for a long footnote about this notion of strategy, appended to the paragraph we have just quoted:

> Comme le motif de la *neutralité*, dans sa forme négative, ouvre le champ aux tentatives de réappropriation les plus classiques et les plus suspectes, il serait imprudent d'annuler les couples d'opposition métaphysiques, d'en *démarquer* simplement tout texte (à supposer que cela soit possible). L'analyse stratégique doit être constamment réajustée. Par exemple, la déconstruction des couples d'opposition métaphysiques pourrait désamorcer, neutraliser le texte de Mallarmé et servir les intérêts investis

dans son interpétation traditionnelle et dominante, c'est-à-dire, jusqu'ici, massivement idéaliste. C'est dans ce contexte, contre lui, qu'on peut et doit souligner le 'matérialisme de l'idée'. Nous empruntons cette définition à Jean Hyppolite ('il imagine dans ce matérialisme de l'idée les diverses possiblitiés de lire le texte' ('Le coup de dés de Stéphane Mallarmé et le message', in *Les études philosophiques*, 1958, No. 4)). C'est là un exemple de cette *dissymétrie stratégique* qui doit sans cesse contrôler les moments neutralisants de toute déconstruction. Cette dissymétrie doit être minutieusement calculée, compte tenu de toutes les différences analysables dans la topographie du champ où elle opère. On constatera d'ailleurs que la 'logique de l'hymen' que nous déchiffrerons ici n'est pas une logique de la neutralité négative, ni même de la neutralité tout court. Soulignons aussi que 'matérialisme de l'idée' ne désigne pas l'éventuel contenu d'une doctrine 'philosophique' de Mallarmé (nous sommes en train de déterminer en quoi il n'y a pas de 'philosophie' dans son texte ou plutôt que celui-ci se calcule pour n'être plus *dans* la philosophie), mais bien la forme de ce qui se met en jeu dans l'opération d'écrire et de 'Lire—Cette pratique—', dans l'inscription des 'diverses possibilités de lire le texte'. (235, n. 18)

(As the motif of *neutrality*, in its negative form, opens the way for the most classical and suspect attempts at reappropriation, it would be imprudent to cancel the metaphysical oppositional couples, simply to *distinguish* every text from them (supposing that to be possible). The strategic analysis must constantly be readjusted. For example, the deconstruction of the metaphysical oppositional couples could defuse and neutralize Mallarmé's text and serve the interests invested in its traditional and dominant interpretation, which has been, until now, massively idealist. It is in this context, against it, that one can and must emphasize the 'materialism of the idea'. We borrow this definition from Jean Hyppolite ('he imagines in this materialism of the idea the various ways of reading the text' ('Le coup de dés de Stéphane Mallarmé et le message', in *Les études philosophiques*, 1958, No. 4)). This is an example of the *strategic dissymmetry* which must constantly check the neutralizing moments of any deconstruction. This dissymmetry must be minutely calculated, taking account of all the analysable differences in the topography of the field where it is operating. It will moreover be noted that the 'logic of the hymen' we shall be deciphering here is not a logic of negative neutrality, nor even of neutrality *tout court*. Let us also stress that 'materialism of the idea' does not designate the possible content of a 'philosophical' doctrine of Mallarmé's (we are in the process of determining how there is no 'philosophy' in his text or rather that it is calculated no longer to be *in* philosophy), but instead the form of what is put in play in the operation of writing and 'Reading—That practice—', in the inscription of the 'various ways of reading the text.')

This notion of strategy or calculation is of course itself not simple.[15] But it leads to a thought that each textual occasion is *singular*, and of course just this was the point Derrida was making about the generalizing *reference* he was also describing in Mallarmé's text. This singularity of textual occasions opens the field of 'strategic calculation' as to the best example on a *given* occasion: we may then want to say that it is no accident that Derrida is choosing to read Mallarmé in 1969, in the context not only of the 'massively idealist' reception of Mallarmé, but also of a Tel Quel 'textual materialism' he is also discretely and patiently displacing.

The same configurations can be seen at work in the second part of the text, in the critique of Jean-Pierre Richard. The argument here is that Richard's two exemplary 'themes', *blanc* and *pli*, cannot in fact satisfactorily be thought of as themes, on the one hand because, as Richard himself recognizes, they are, like all 'themes', defined diacritically rather than substantively, but on the other, more importantly, because these are 'themes' only to the extent that they *also* say something about the possibility of all other 'themes', or the possibility of anything like 'themes' in general. Let us rehearse briefly this argument, which relies on the structure of what it has become commonplace to call 'quasi-transcendentality' in Derrida's thought.

The point here is that, whatever thematic series or perspective Richard sees fits to insert *blanc* into (the *Tableau* text suggests 'neige, froid, mort, marbre, etc.; cygne, aile, éventail, etc.; virginité, pureté, hymen, etc.; page, toile, voile, gaze, lait, semence, voie lactée, étoile, etc.' ('snow, cold, death, marble, etc.; swan, wing, fan, etc.; virginity, purity, hymen, etc.; page, canvas, veil, gauze, milk, semen, milky way, star, etc.') (372)), all the terms in that series or perspective are separated from each other by blanks or gaps. A thematic series can only be recognized as a series if its members are articulated among themselves, and the minimal condition of such an articulation is that they be at least relatively separable, to be recognized as the terms that they are: this separability entails that there be a gap or space, however construed, between them. It will follow that any thematic term which can be thought to refer to just that space or gap will have a privilege over other such terms, and just this is the case with *blanc*. *Blanc* is of course a common 'theme' in Mallarmé, and can convincingly be placed in a series or perspective with other *blanc*-related terms, but it also, in an apparently transcendental manner, refers to the gapping or spacing that is a condition of possibility of that series in which it is also only one member or term. *Blanc* is to be found on the same level as all the other textual signifiers identifiable as themes in Mallarmé, but, still occurring in the text, provides the 'supplementary re-mark' of the spacing or gapping which is a condition for all textual signifiers to take their place in the text at all.

Now this double or duplicitous position of *blanc* is the same as that of Mallarmé himself as exemplary of a certain excess of Platonic *mimesis*: Mallarmé is, on the one hand, merely a sample of that excess, one of a series insofar as any text at all might be taken more or less clearly to show that excess, insofar as it just is a necessary condition of textuality. But Mallarmé is a good, perhaps the best, example, because his text brings out that condition in an unusually salient way, making it difficult to avoid. Similarly, it can in principle be shown on the basis of any theme at all how themes work and that in fact *there is no theme* (no atomic thematic unity identifiable as such outside the network of other 'thematic' 'unities'),[16] but *blanc* is a better example than others from this point of view, because it quite literally refers, beyond the figural richness Mallarmé's text invests it with, to the spacing that is the condition and undoing of themes in general. As always in Derrida, the quasi-transcendental gives us conditions both of possibility (there can be no theme without a spacing or gapping of themes) and of impossibility (just that spacing disallows atomic thematic identity to any theme whatsoever). But it also generates an undecidability on each occasion of *blanc* (but by extension, too, of all the words that might be its figural substitutes), insofar as each such occasion refers the reader both to the 'theme' in question *and* to its condition of (im)possibility. Further, this undecidability is not just a modish way of referring to an additional semantic resource in the text, because *blanc* as condition of any meaning at all is itself *meaningless*, not a meaning at all, but the spacing that Derrida here consistently refers to as a *syntactic* excess over any semantics.[17] As such, it cannot become the Great Transcendental Blank it might be tempting to see as the final—nihilistic—signified of Mallarmé's work, because all it does is to refer *back down* into the actually occurring signifiers in the text. After all, *blanc* is still just one term among many, Mallarmé still only an example among others.

Just this double or duplicitous structure of the *blanc*, the rising and falling movement or *rhythm*[18] of the quasi-transcendental, make it possible to argue that it is already, from the start, affected by a *pli*. *Blanc* is constantly folded back into the text whose (im)possibility it also indicates while more or less exuberantly confirming that text's 'figural' movement, moving us down the 'thematic' axis of *blanc* and *pli* to *éventail* and soon to *page, plume* and so on:

> Le blanc se plie, est (marqué d'un) pli. Il ne s'expose jamais à plate couture. Car le pli n'est pas plus un thème (signifié) que le blanc et si l'on tient compte des effets de chaîne et de rupture qu'ils propagent dans le texte, rien n'a plus simplement la valeur d'un thème.
>
> Il y a plus. Le 'blanc' supplémentaire n'intervient pas seulement dans la série polysémique des 'blancs' mais aussi *entre* les sèmes de *toute* série comme *entre toutes* les séries sémantiques. Il empêche ainsi toute sérialité sémantique de se constituer, de se fermer ou de s'ouvrir simplement. Non qu'il y fasse obstacle: c'est encore lui qui libère des effets de série, *fait prendre*, en se démarquant, des agglomérats—pour des substances. Si le thématisme ne peut en rendre compte, c'est qu'il surévalue le *mot* et confine le *latéral*. (285)

> *Blanc* folds itself, is (marked with a) fold. It never exposes itself flat out. For the fold is no more a (signified) theme than the *blanc* and if one takes into account the chain reactions and ruptures they propagate in the text, nothing has any longer simply the value of a theme.
>
> There is more. The supplementary *blanc* does not only intervene in the polysemic series of *blancs* but also *between* the semes of *every* series and *between all* the semantic series. It thus prevents any semantic seriality from constituting itself, from simply closing or opening itself. Not that it puts up an obstacle to that:

it is still it which liberates series-effects, makes agglomerates take, distinguishing itself from them, and makes them be taken for substances. If thematism cannot account for this, it is because it overestimates the *word* and restricts the *lateral*.)

It remains to show how this leads necessarily to the reading of sub-lexical features of the text. The logic here is as follows: once it is recognized in this way that themes have no identity outside the textual—syntactic—system in which they are at work, then 'themes' are no longer essentially to do with meaning at all. In the *Tableau* text, Derrida says quite straightforwardly that critical and rhetorical reading methods have always relied on the determinability of meaning (however much they may celebrate semantic wealth, complexity or polyvalence): but once the operation of the re-mark obliges the reader to attend to the failing structure of thematics in general, then it will follow that the traditional structure of the sign (textual signifiers name signifieds which we organize thematically) can no longer be relied upon. A first consequence is that syncategorematic terms (which resist nominalization) can come to the fore in a way thematic criticism would find difficult to read[19]. But this functioning in Mallarmé is further complicated by exploitation of possible play between different syntactic values of the 'same' word, or words sounding the same (the *Tableau* looks briefly at *elle/aile* (she/wing), *lit/lis/lys* (bed/read/lily), and, like 'La double séance' itself, *or* (gold/thus)), and this leads inexorably to a break-up of the unity of words which thematic criticism must presuppose, so that, for example, 'or' appears not only as a word which might be a noun or a conjunction, but *within* other words such as 'dehors, fantasmagoriques, trésor', ('outside, fantas- magorical, treasure') etc., and in complicated plays with *son or, sonore*, (his gold, sonorous) and even the *English* word 'or'. And this leads further still to an insistence on the letter 'o' or 'i', so that Mallarmé's texts become in some sense ('ceci, un écrit') *about* the disposition on the page of letters which in and of themselves have no meaning whatsoever, still less a *thematic* value.[20]

Again, Mallarmé is *exemplary* in this respect. No text can function to generate effects of meaning, however literal, without disposing pre-semantic marks on the page. In principle, any text, including the texts of Plato himself, can show this, however much the meaning- effects they generate may seem dedicated to repressing it (but that's metaphysics, and most of literature). But despite the best efforts of idealistic thematic critics, Mallarmé, whose texts cannot of course *prevent* themselves from being read thematically, dialectically and metaphysically, provide ample material to make the accomplishment of such readings difficult to maintain.

How, finally, are we to understand the relationship between Derrida's writing and Mallarmé's? Given the progressive suspension by Derrida of all the usual critical *points de repère*, it is difficult to believe that the categories of commentary, interpretation or analysis[21] will suffice to describe that relationship. It seems more plausible to suggest that Derrida's text has a relationship to Mallarmé's which is somewhat of the order of the relationship he describes as holding between Mallarmé's text and Margueritte's *livret*, or more generally of the order of what Mallarmé's text calls 'mimique'. It would not be difficult to find evidence in Derrida's text of a more or less marked mimicry of Mallarmé. This does not of course mean that Derrida is somehow simply repeating Mallarmé or doing no more than quoting Mallarmé against, say, Plato. But it follows from everything we have seen that, while being concerned to stress an exemplary singularity of Mallarmé, Derrida is also committed, among other things just through the careful reading of Mallarmé, to the disappearance of anything as easily identifiable as 'Mallarmé' or 'Derrida'. If one of the paradoxes of Mallarmé is that he signs and affirms the 'disparition élocutoire' of the poet, then we might think we can read 'Mallarmé' wherever such a disappearance leaves its trace. This is why Derrida suggests that we cannot think of Mallarmé straightforwardly as an 'event' befalling Platonism. And by extending and generalizing that structure, Derrida would on this account be usurpatorily signing all the texts he reads just as he withdraws from them and puts them before us in their incontrovertible and shocking literality. Or, which we will have tried, still, here to do, to him.

Drosophila Ludens
Oulipian Designs on Mallarmé

Burhan Tufail

comme on voit, les sonnets de Mallarmé sont un matériel de choix,
comme la drosophile en genetique
(as we can see, Mallarmé's sonnets are very high-grade material,
like the fruit-fly in genetics)[1]

A Workshop of Potential Literature

In the 1960s, alongside the monumental study by Jean-Pierre
Richard, *L'univers imaginaire de Mallarmé,* and the various attentions
of *Tel Quel,* an altogether more strange encounter with the poet was
taking place, hidden for the most part, during this decade, from public
view. Less concerned with detailed critical analysis or with the
elaboration of philosophical and theoretical responses, this encounter
with the Oulipo was unashamedly literary, and was directed, in very
specific ways, towards exploring how certain literary traditions might
inform the working practices of contemporary writers.[2] Although by
no means specifically or exclusively focused on Stéphane Mallarmé,
the Oulipo on occasion approached his work by means of creative
transformation and rule-governed play, in the creative laboratory
they devoted to the exploration of formal constraint. In various forms,
Mallarmé would appear as an iconic symbol of the writer, as
proto-modernist, as proto-Oulipian, and as a theorist of the relationship between literature and chance. His writing served both as model
for literary production and as 'raw material' which could be submitted
to transformatory procedures, prefiguring the contemporary attention
to the materiality of language and to the work of writing, and

foregrounding the problematics of referentiality and language. For the writers of the Oulipo, the engagement with such illustrious forbears as Mallarmé provided firstly a tradition, a justificatory structure, within which they might locate themselves, and secondly a body of texts upon which to practise their art. The interplay of these activities produced a complex dialogue in which the possibilities of literature, of invention, and of the 'new' in art were to be articulated.

Founded in 1960 by Raymond Queneau and François Le Lionnais, the Oulipo, or *Ouvroir de Littérature Potentielle*, a group comprising both writers and mathematicians, has from its inception dedicated itself to the invention and exploration of formal constraints in the production of texts.[3] The Oulipian return to a kind of formalism has been argued, by Marjorie Perloff, to be a logical response to the limiting quality of much 'free' writing and the predominance of aleatory or chance-generated procedures in many fields of artistic production:

> As the speech-based poetics of mid-century has given way, more and more, to the foregrounding of the materiality of the written sign itself, a prosody based on intonational contours has become increasingly problematic. The emphasis on the moment of enunciation (at best variable and transitory) now seems a questionable procedure, whether for the poet or the reader. For such 'momentary' or 'instantaneous' rhythm suggests that there is first an experience, something lived and felt out there, and only then and secondarily its verbal rendering.[4]

Perloff, citing Derrida's critique of the concept of an originary speech prior to writing, suggests two possible directions forward for ' "writerly" prosodic form': on the one hand, the parodic treatment of existing metrical structures, and on the other, the development of techniques of constraint and procedurality which are concerned with 'language as a site of paragrammatic play, of the sedimentation of verbal, phonemic, and graphemic traces in interaction'.[5] Although Perloff quite rightly discusses the Oulipo as an instance of the second of these possibilities, she stresses that for them the constraint is primarily generative, and opposes the notion of constraint to that of the 'rule', which may be exemplified by any inherited fixed metrical structure such as the sonnet. Perloff argues that traditional forms set up certain expectations in the audience who will quickly grasp the formal patterning of, say, a sonnet or ottava rima. This distinction, useful as it is, somewhat simplifies the complexity of the Oulipo's position vis-à-vis such traditional literary forms, and their reverence for the Provençal troubadours, the Grands Rhétoriqueurs, and more modern figures such as Mallarmé or Raymond Roussel. At one their earliest meetings, Le Lionnais outlined the two branches of Oulipian research:

> Il y a deux Lipos: une analytique et une synthétique. La lipo analytique recherche des possibilités qui se trouvent chez certains auteurs sans qu'ils y aient pensé. La lipo synthétique constitue la grande mission de l'Oulipo, il s'agit d'ouvrir de nouvelles possibilités inconnues des anciens auteurs.

> (There are two Lipos: an analytic and a synthetic. Analytic lipo seeks possibilities existing in the work of certain authors unbeknownst to them. Synthetic lipo constitutes the principal mission of the Oulipo; it's a question of opening new possibilities previously unknown to authors.)[6]

Anoulipism, as defined above, was oriented towards uncovering the hidden potentiality in writing both past and contemporary, but in addition broadly included another project, the as yet uncompleted *Histoire des littératures expérimentales*—an activity which 'indicated the desire to inscribe the Oulipo within a history'.[7] Typical of many avant-garde movements in France, the most obvious being the Surrealists,[8] the Oulipo felt the need to create an alternative literary canon, a genealogy which located the group as only the most contemporary manifestation of a literature that had always existed but which had heretofore been viewed as a marginal or perverse activity. This history identified the researches of the Oulipo as recuperative of formal and rhetorical aspects of writing previously ignored in favour of content, theme, inspiration, and so on.[9] *Synthoulipism*, on the other hand, explored the literary potential of newly devised constraints—either through the application of procedures to already existing material, or through the elaboration of structures within which the creative or inventive act might occur.

Mallarmé as Model

How does Mallarmé figure in the Oulipian canon? Firstly, an inherited 'Mallarmé' might be seen as an iconic name, a revered image of the absolute poet, a figure who is part of a shared literary universe. Historically, the Oulipo might be thought to be predisposed towards him for the simple reason of its origins as an offshoot of the *Collège de 'pataphysique*: the Collège, acknowledging the legacy of Alfred Jarry, would have been mindful of Jarry's relationship to Mallarmé, and of Jarry's inclusion of the poet in the library of Faustroll.[10] This concept of a 'portable library' of canonical texts—including, for the Oulipo, Jarry, Mallarmé and Raymond Roussel—is common to many avant-garde movements: to include Mallarmé in their family tree might simply be seen as necessary and justificatory cultural baggage for the Oulipian pataphysicians. Certainly some of the uses the Oulipo make of Mallarmé depend, in the first instance, on the reader making an immediate identification of the poet and of his writing: that is, many Oulipian transformations of iconic texts in part depend on the reader being familiar with and recognizing the traces of those texts in the treated versions.

In works by Oulipo members published outside of the group itself, as well as the poet being treated as critical object in texts by Ross Chambers and Jacques Roubaud,[11] Mallarmé also appears in this iconic guise. Harry Mathews, for example, in his transformatory sequence *Trial Impressions*, which develops Oulipian variants on a source poem by John Dowland, includes a Mallarméan pastiche entitled 'L'Homme Mal Armé'—playing on the obvious puns of the poet's name. The first few lines run thus:

> I and my pens disgorged by the finger in the fold
> Of thick literal leaves? or what if fabled art bunts
> From a racked best brim violation of brass that shunts
> The phoenix peering, defenestrated, through cold[12]

The title of one of his stories, a meditation on the question of translation, 'Le dialecte de la tribu/The Dialect of the Tribe', is a quotation from Mallarmé's 'Le Tombeau d'Edgar Poe'. Mathews writes:

> How can you translate a process? You'd have to render not only
> words but the spaces between them—like snap-shooting the
> invisible air under the beating wings of flight. An impossibility.
> All that can be done is describe, suggest, record impressions and
> effects.[13]

The allusion to the white spaces of *Un coup de dés* is clear. For
Mathews, it seems, Mallarmé had already anticipated the apprehension of the literary text as, to return to Marjorie Perloff's phrase,
'verbal, phonemic, and graphemic traces in interaction'—as a pro-
cessual rather than a static activity. If, as Mathews suggests, all
literature is an act of translation, it is also, after Mallarmé, an 'envol
tacite d'abstraction' ('silent flight of abstraction')[14] which follows that
poet's desire to 'peindre non la chose mais l'effet qu'elle produit'
('paint, not the object, but the effect it produces').[15]

In Georges Perec's case, apart from a version of 'Brise marine'
discussed below, there was a plan, sadly unrealized at the time of his
death, to translate into French the *hörspiel* (a German radio play)
he had written in collaboration with Eugen Helmle. *Die Maschine*
was based on a series of transformations of a well-known poem by
Goethe. Perec's French version was to have substituted the Goethe
text with one by Mallarmé: an interesting choice given the cultural
centrality of the Goethe text in Germany.[16] With Perec, however,
the greatest isomorphisms perhaps lie with the *vers de circonstance*
and with the cryptonomy of the name.[17] Perec composed several texts
that linked 'hommage personnel, écrit de circonstance, contrainte
littéraire: trois grandes traditions de la poésie occidentale' ('personal
tribute, occasional writing, literary constraint: the three great traditions of western poetry').[18] For Perec, the compositional method
centred on the names of the recipients: if Mallarmé played lexical
games with names, Perec's addresses were composed at the level of
the letter. The *Belles Absentes* permitted the use of all letters of the
alphabet except those in the addressee's name, the *Beaux Présents*
permitted the use of only those letters which occurred in the name,
and, in his 'Epithalamia', Perec mingled the letters of the couple's
names, joining them materially on the page. This series of poems
combines the Mallarméan address with a cabbalistic interest in the
signification of the letter—an onomastic dedication.

As advocates of the value of formal structure in writing, the Oulipo valorized Mallarmé as a virtuoso of metrical forms, as a poet of constraint, tight structures, and deliberately imposed rhymes, rather than reading him for expressive or symbolic content. They identified as a precursor the author who declared himself 'profondément et scrupuleusement syntaxier' ('I am deeply and scrupulously a syntaxer')[19] and for whom syntax was a 'guarantee' ('Quel pivot, j'entends, dans ces contrastes, à l'intelligibilité? il faut une garantie—La Syntaxe'), ('What fulcrum is there, I mean, for intelligibility in these contrasts? A guarantee is necessary—Syntax')[20]; the poet who was above all a follower of a rule-driven poetics, stating in the preface to *Un coup de dés* that 'je ne transgresse cette mesure, seulement la disperse' ('I do not transgress this measure, only disperse it').[21] Here is a Mallarmé who fetishizes the mystery of the combinatorial alchemy of the alphabet, and explicitly opposes the 'mathematical' to the random in his attention not only to the poem, but to the arrangement of poems in a volume:

> un livre qui soit un livre, architectural et prémédité, et non un recueil des inspirations de hasard fussent-elles merveilleuses

> (a book which is a book, architectural and premeditated, and not a miscellany of chance inspirations, however marvellous they may be)[22]

> Un miracle prime ce bienfait, au sens haut ou les mots, originellement, se réduisent à l'emploi, doué d'infinité jusqu'à sacrer une langue, des quelque vingt lettres—leur devenir, tout y rentre pour tantôt sourdre, principe—approchant d'un rite la composition typographique.

> (But that advantage is secondary to a miracle, in the highest sense of the word: words led back to their origin, which is the twenty-four letters of the alphabet, so gifted with infinity that they will finally consecrate Language. Everything is caught up in their endless variations and then rises out of them in the form of the Principle. Thus typography becomes a rite).[23]

Three years before the founding of the Oulipo, Jacques Scherer discussed the possible form of 'Le Livre' (The Book), Mallarmé's speculative great work, and proposed a combinatorial structure based on permutations of pages.[24] Such critical work might easily have contributed to the conceptual groundwork for the Oulipo's permutational version of the poet.

The author of *Un coup de dés* is also applauded for producing a work which breaks linearity to produce a poetics of simultaneity and spatial organization. In Le Lionnais's words: 'il s'agit de ne pas écrire des poèmes linéaires, mais de les écrire avec une dimension de plus. Ou de les écrire dans des directions différentes, de façon à obtenir un ensemble' ('it is a question of not writing poems in a linear way, but of writing them with an additional dimension. Or writing them in different directions, so as to obtain a group').[25] Or again, the poet for whom the ideal literary language did not depend on a one-to-one correspondence with the world, but rather depended on effect, evocation, and the realization that language itself is an object to be worked and studied, is reflected by Le Lionnais with approval, in his citation of Valéry's assessment of Mallarmé's work: 'Il a cependant atteint profondément la littérature empirique' ('He has, however, profoundly affected empirical literature').[26] The 'empiric' here gestures towards the scientific cast of Oulipian activity, to the terminology of the laboratory or experiment (the quotation from Valéry likens Mallarmé's literary production to chemistry), and to the curious amalgam of impersonality and expression that characterizes the theorizing and production of writing under constraint. The Oulipo reject the automatic writing of the Surrealists because, under the guise of a supposed freedom, one nevertheless betrays the existence of psychic, linguistic and cultural constraints on the process of literary production—far better to impose rules which paradoxically allow a more unfettered expression precisely in their observance. Raymond Roussel would be a *prima facie* case of the psychic liberation of artificial constraint,[27] and similarly Mallarmé, attempting to rethink the orthodoxies inherent in codified and inherited metrical schema, can state: 'je connais qu'un jeu, séduisant, se mène avec les fragments de l'ancien vers reconaissables' ('I know that a seductive game can be played with the recognizable fragments of the old line')[28]—likewise, for the Oulipo, the game consists not of rigid obeisance to an unexamined law but of the inventive recontextualizing of form. The aim is to play with and make play an individual machine of writing:

concurrement aux grandes orgues générales et séculaires, où s'exalte, d'après un latent clavier, l'orthodoxie, quiconque avec son jeu et son ouïe individuels se peut composer un instrument, dès qu'il souffle, le frôle ou frappe avec science; en user à part et le dédier aussi à la Langue.

(along with the general and traditional great organ of orthodox verse which finds its ecstacy on an ever-ready keyboard, any poet with an individual technique and ear can build his own instrument, so long as his fluting, bowing, or drumming are accomplished—play that instrument and dedicate it to Language.)[29]

What results, from neither absolute laxity nor calcified observance, is 'une haute liberté' ('a lofty freedom')[30] which neither fetishizes novelty, nor obliterates the inventions of the past.

One might in addition draw parallels between the Mallarméan and Oulipian focus on writing at the level of the word, the phoneme, or the letter: the use of devices such as complex rhymes and homophonic transformation, of puns and acrostics, of encryption, exceed what might be seen as natural in the text.[31] The element of gaming, of play, disrupts the normal circuitry of 'seriousness': the large body of work termed the *vers de circonstance*, and the extended use of multi-syllabic rhymes challenge the categories and genres of writing and the uneasy taxonomies of the limits of form. An impropriety breaks in where the words are not pretending to be transparent conduits to referents but rather are constantly pointing to the fact of being marks on paper, patterned and doing things. The polysyllabic *rimes léonines* and *rimes équivoques* of 'Prose (pour des Esseintes)' tend towards the excessive artifice which the Oulipians have often favoured, especially in their group publications and the demonstrative pamphlets of the *Bibliothèque oulipienne*. Malcolm Bowie notes that:

although the brilliance of [Mallarmé's] rhyming in 'Prose' has not gone unrecognized, it has often failed to win critical approval: it has been presented as an irresponsible flirtation with an archaic mode, as the thrusting of a fading ornamental style upon an otherwise austere and strong-minded argument.[32]

Bowie points out that this 'rhyming tradition' harks back to the *grands rhétoriqueurs* (also much beloved of the Oulipo), and that 'Prose' may be placed 'marginally but firmly within the traditions of elegant artifice and learned wit'.[33] This is the genealogy in which Georges Perec places the work of the Oulipo. In his 'History of the Lipogram', an essay attacking that strain of literary history which affects deliberately to 'ignorer l'écriture comme pratique, comme travail, comme jeu' ('ignore writing as practice, as work, as play'), Perec also notes the tendency to marginalize such aberrant work by means of the formation of literary taxonomies of 'curiosities'—'où les "exploits" rhétoriques sont décrits avec une complaisance suspecte, une surenchère inutile, et une ignorance crétine' ('where rhetorical "exploits" are described with suspect complaisance, useless exaggeration, and cretinous ignorance'). Perec does not insist that 'les artifices systématiques se confondent avec l'écriture, mais seulement qu'ils en constituent une dimension non négligeable' ('systematic artifices are identical to writing, but only that they constitute a dimension of writing which must not be ignored').[34]

What both writers question is the boundary condition of the literary device—that such devices are only to be permitted if they exhibit a certain modesty and do not flaunt themselves: too much, and the work becomes excessive, pathological. The rhymes in 'Prose' short-circuit conventional signification, play on the ear, eye and mouth. Famously, Mallarmé links 'de visions/ devisions', 'se para/ sépara', 'désir, idées/ des iridées', 'par chemins/ parchemins', and so on, a torrent of homophonic transformations that stress the visual and material plasticity of words.

A century later, the Oulipo extend the homophonic rhyme in many directions, from the 'exercises' of the booklet 'La Cantatrice sauve', which puns repeatedly on the name of Monserrat Caballé ('Mon Chirac a baîllé' being one of more outrageous examples), to the chapter in Perec's *La Vie mode d'emploi* which homophonically encodes the names of the members of the group ('Joseph d'Arimathie ou Zarathoustra' hiding the name of Perec's close friend Harry Mathews, and so on).

The earlier quotation from Malcolm Bowie raises the issues of definition: literature seen as either natural or monstrous. What is at stake in terming such literary devices as 'irresponsible', what is the moral infraction here? Why is one not to elaborate upon a 'strong-minded argument'? What is 'proper' to literature and what is not? Until recently, the *vers de circonstance* were, on the whole, ignored in favour of the 'major' works, but much interesting recent work has been done to amplify not only their charm, but also their linguistic inventiveness. If they do not now occupy the central place in Mallarmé's œuvre, and there is no reason that they should except by virtue of being numerous, they can certainly be seen to elaborate certain fundamental poetic principles of Mallarmé's literary procedures. The Oulipo's systematic investigations of constraints in writing were concurrent with the theoretical demolition of an arbitrary separation of form and content—even if this was something writers had been doing for centuries (Rabelais, Dante, Sterne, Joyce, Queneau spring to mind)—and from the 1960s onwards it became a commonplace observation.

Alongside the Oulipo's fascination with verbal play lies an interest in the application of mathematical structures to the production of literary texts, and here, too, Mallarmé can be seen to have made some preliminary experiments. There is, prefiguring the Oulipian interest in combinatorial structures, an example of a permutational poem hidden among the *vers de circonstance*: poem VIII of the *Œufs de Pâques* series can be multiply configured. The note to the section in the *Œuvres complètes* states that:

> Chaque vers était écrit à l'encre d'or sur un œuf rouge et précédé d'un numéro de manière à reconstituer le quatrain.—Une seule fois, le numérotage put être omis, et, en intervertissant les œufs, l'ensemble lu ainsi plusieurs fois de façon différente.

> (Each verse was written in gold ink upon a red egg and preceded by a number allowing one to reconstitute the quatrain. Only in one case was the numbering omitted, and, in inverting the eggs, the ensemble could thus be read several times each in a different way).[35]

Four possible permutations are given. The 'Rondels' also provide semi-permutational structures of repetition and recurrence. Permutation and recombination become devices for breaking linearity—the linguistic kaleidoscope shuffles set elements into new relationships, grammatical and lexical items are shifted to a state of potentiality, comprising a set of possibilities rather than being fixed in a particular configuration.

Mallarmé as Material

Marcel Bénabou's article 'Rule and Constraint' usefully provides a taxonomy of elementary Oulipian constraints in the form of a table of objects and transformations. Down the left-hand side of the table are listed 'Linguistic Objects' (Letter, Phoneme, Syllable, Word, Syntagm, Sentence, Paragraph), and across the top are listed 'Operations' (Displacement, Substitution, Addition, Subtraction, Multiplication or Repetition, Division, Deduction, Contraction): Oulipian procedures are categorized according to the conjunction of these various elements. For example, a constraint which alters the consonants of a text while leaving the vowels unchanged (homo- or iso-vocalism) is a substitution at the level of the letter, whereas a constraint which takes only the final words of the lines of a poem (haikuization) would be a deduction at the level of the word. The initial work of the group tended to focus on exploring these transformations: more complex rule-generated work tended to occur later, especially in the work of individual writers producing longer texts, although Perec's *La Disparition* is an example of a simple constraint (the rule being simple, not the execution of it) applied to a whole novel.

Very early in the group's history,[36] Queneau presented a study of 'Redundancy in Mallarmé' (a seemingly perverse notion given the general acknowledgement of the density and complexity of Mallarmé's verse). By applying the method of 'haikuization' (as mentioned above, the elimination of all words from a poem except the rhyming elements), Queneau produces texts which serve both as new 'poems' created out of found materials, and as critical commentaries on the original poems by Mallarmé:

> Pour employer un langage mathématique, je vais considérer une restriction de ce poème à ses sections rimantes. (Je me permettrai d'y ajouter une ponctuation subjective.)

> Aujourd'hui
> Ivre,
> le givre
> pas fui!

Lui
se délivre . . .
où vivre?
L'ennui . . .

Agonie
le nie,
pris,

assigne
mépris,
le Cygne.

Quel intérêt? Primo, j'obtiens un nouveau poème qui, ma foi,
n'est pas mal et il ne faut jamais se plaindre si l'on vous offre de
beaux poèmes. Secundo on a l'impression qu'il y a presque autant
dans la restriction que dans le poème entier: c'est pourquoi j'ai
parlé de redondance. Tertio: sans aller jusqu'à cette limite
sacrilège, on peut au moins dire que cette restriction éclaire le
poème primitif: elle n'est pas dépourvue de valeur exégétique et
peut contribuer à son interprétation.[37]

(To use mathematical language, I shall consider a restriction of
this poem to its rhyming sections. (I shall permit myself to add
subjective punctuation):
    Drunk, | frost | not flown! | He | is delivered . . . | where to
    live? | Boredom . . . | Agony | denies him, | caught, | assigns
    | contempt, | the Swan.
What is the point of this? *Primo*, I obtain a new poem which,
upon my word, is not bad, and one should never complain if one
finds beautiful poems. *Secundo*, one has the impression that there
is almost as much in the restriction as in the entire poem; that
is why I spoke of redundancy. *Tertio*: without going to the far
limits of sacrilege, one can at least say that this restriction sheds
light on the original poem; it is not wholly without exegetical
value and may contribute to interpretation.)

Queneau's sly exercise compounds multiple activities—the 'haikuization' which gestures towards a twentieth-century post-Imagist
genealogy, drawing on the brevity, density and direct perception of
the Japanese verse form (for Ezra Pound, 'dichten = condensare'),

154

and suggests parallels which might be drawn with the mesostics of John Cage;[38] the invoking of the tradition of the 'found poem'; the defamiliarization that accompanies the recontextualization of famous texts; the critical–literary activity which demonstrates richness and complexity even in the consideration of a highly restricted zone of enquiry; and the application of an artistic procedure to the inter-pretative moment. The process of constraint-driven work is one of active and complex production, not trivial simplification. The application of the same method to the 'Sonnet en -yx' ('ses purs ongles . . .') gives rise to Queneau's observation that 'le septuor', in this haikuized context, invites the possible reading of 'les septs rimes rares du sonnet' ('the seven rare rhymes of the sonnet'), a reading recently echoed by Graham Robb.[39] In addition, such a self-reflexive reading (of the poem as referring to its own construction) might, looking ahead from 1961, confirm this Mallarmé as an Oulipian before-the-fact—one of the later-formulated Oulipian *dicta* being that a text written under constraint must refer to that constraint—for, in addition to the critical commonplaces about Mallarmé's verse dramatizing its own creation, the poem refers to the difficult constraints under which it has been composed. The 'Sonnet allégori-que de lui-même' ('Sonnet allegorical of itself') is self-referential both in terms of sense and compositional process: the poem's meaning, 's'il en a un . . . est évoqué par un mirage interne des mots mêmes' ('if there is one . . . it is evoked by an internal mirage created by the words themselves'), and shifts from the referential to the alchemical, or the cabalistic ('on éprouve une sensation assez cabalistique' ('you get a fairly cabbalistic sensation')).[40]

Queneau doesn't labour the point—his mode is one of rapidity and lightness, without the lumber of dense explication—and he goes on to note that not all poets are conducive to this treatment: Racine (for the most part), Molière, Hugo, do not give such good results. The implication is that there is 'something else' in Mallarmé which admits such productive mutilation. In the case of haikuization, he offers a short remark on the nature of Mallarmé's poetics: 'chez Mallarmé . . . chaque vers est un petit monde, une unité dont le sens vient en quelque sorte s'accumuler dans la section rimante' ('in Mallarmé . . . each line is a little world, a unity whose meaning accumulates, as it were, in the rhyming section').[41] In a longer version of the demonstration to be found in *La Littérature potentielle: Créations*, *re-créations, récréations,* Queneau renders haikuizations of eight of Mallarmé's sonnets, and claims that one composes new poems 'qui, loin de laisse échapper le sens de l'original, en donneront au contraire, semble-t-il, un lumineux élixir' ('which, far from allowing the original meaning to disappear, give them, on the contrary, it seems, a luminous elixir')—a justification that itself nods to the poet.[42] But the *matériel de choix* (as he later terms it) is elusive, alchemical, always potential—it has a quality which only reveals itself through being subjected to constraint and transformation, and, moreover, one which remains stubbornly recognizable. The procedure paradoxically hinges on the idiosyncrasy and identifiability of the source text. A poem which begins 'Onyx?/ Lampadophore . . . / Phénix?/ Amphore . . .' is proprietorially stamped S.M. even in its reduced state.

Other transformative procedures include Queneau's isovocalic version of 'Le vierge, le vivace et le bel aujourd'hui . . .'[43] (which becomes 'Le liège, le titane et le sel aujourd'hui . . .')—here the vowel sequence of the original is kept intact, but the consonants are freely altered. In this example, Queneau preserves the final word 'le Cygne', 'comme rappel du texte primitif' ('to recall the original text'), to mirror early Cubist *trompe l'œil*—a disjunctive reminder which jumps between planes of perception and orders of representation. Elsewhere, as Allen Thiher has pointed out, Queneau, in his poem sequence *Morale élémentaire*, plays on the homophony of 'Cygne' and 'signe', in an invented verse form that owes something to the non-linearity first explored in *Un coup de dés*.[44] Georges Perec, in *La Disparition*, a 300-page novel which excludes the letter 'E' (a lipogram —subtraction at the level of the letter), produces a selection of iconic poems 'translated' so as to exclude the banned vowel. Among them we find 'Brise marine' which has become 'Bris Marin' by 'Mallarmus', and begins 'Las, la chair s'attristait. J'avais lu tous folios . . .' (instead of 'La chair est triste, hélas! et j'ai lu tous les livres'). The poem, placed amongst a gallery of greats, obviously depends for its effect on the reader 'hearing' the original alongside it, but it also directs a new attention towards the linguistic detail of the poem. In a reduced, etiolated language which forswears any word containing the most often-occurring letter in French, what remains possible? What can one write, and what is one forbidden to write? The author is forced to consider every aspect of expression: 'being unable to say what you normally would, you must say what you normally wouldn't. Without [the letter] e, what has become unsayable and what remains to be said?'[45] This, in the case of what amounts to an intralinguistic translation of a poem, results in an active critical re-production of the text in which every substitution, every change accesses the machinery of the vocabulary or rhythm or metre. A way of reading as well as writing, which is active rather than passive, and which stresses production rather than consumption.

If the above procedures retain a noticeable echo of the source text, there are others where the source becomes impossible to identify. Jacques Bens, in an exercise entitled 'Inclusions'[46] where 'un texte est lisible dans un texte plus vaste' ('a readable text is included in a vaster one'), uses one of Mallarmé's 'Eventail' poems as the scaffolding for a longer text. 'Là-bas de quelque vaste aurore . . .' (*Eventails* VII) is expanded to '*Là-bas* du côté *de* Clichy-sous-Bois, où s'élève *quelque* cité, sinistre et *vaste* ensemble, chaque matin pointe une *aurore* . . .'

In addition to Oulipian procedures based on linguistic formulae, there exist mathematically-based exploratory tools. Combinatorial or permutational techniques based on, for example, the manipulation of elements arranged in matrices (single letters, words, phrases, sentences, or larger linguistic units) provide a critico-mathematical route for the analysis of texts. Harry Mathews' essay 'Mathews' Algorithm' gives an account of such matrix-based activity. In its English version it uses Shakespearean sonnets as its primary literary resource—the French text of course uses Mallarmé. The operation of the algorithm at the level of the word, using the initial lines from four sonnets to provide the verbal elements of the combinatorial matrix, produces new verses such as:

> Du roc dédiant la fatale éternité . . .
> La pure loi telle que ses ongles la roulent . . .
> Lui-même courroucé que l'onyx menaça . . .[47]

At the level of the line, Mathews produces a text using a permutation of lines from fourteen sonnets (e.g. line 1 from sonnet 1, line 2 from sonnet 2 etc.):

> Yeux, lacs, avec ma simple ivresse de renaître
> La rose qui cruelle ou déchirée et lasse

A quelque baume rare émané par mensonge
Que se dévêt pli selon pli la pierre veuve[48]

To give just the first stanza. Mathews comments that 'it is perhaps at this point that the analytic potential of the algorithm clearly manifests itself. This new poem throws light on the structure and movement of the Mallarmean sonnet.'[49] (As with Queneau's haikui-zations, Mathews prefers to suggest rather than make explicit the critical dimension of such procedures.) Another type of defamiliari-zation is occurring here, in which recombination allows the preservation of the line, but throws it into strange juxtapositions—one might detect here a writer's urge to apprehend structure, a dis-articulation aimed at yielding up an extralinguistic patterning or logic, rather than a structuralist's atomizing analysis. The Oulipo, mindful of this, have described themselves as 'structurElist' rather than 'structuralist' in a light parody of the written, visually demarcated Derridean paragram (in the printing rather than Saussurian sense) of 'différance'. As a corollary, however, it should be noted that even in the 1960s, the Oulipo were exploring the possibilities of computer analysis for the study of sonnets, Mallarmé again being one of the sources of poetic data: unfortunately there is no easily available documentation on the outcome of these early analyses.[50]

In Conclusion

Transformative procedures, therefore, both play on the reader's ability to recognize the source text and treat the same text as raw linguistic material to be shaped by the application of constraint. The Work of Literature as object becomes the *work* of literature as process—at the same time the identity of the Work remains, is appealed to, for it is not just any sonnet that we can deform, but this particular one, the trace of which will attest to the process, will mark the origin of the game: a continual oscillation between reverence and iconoclasm. The problematics inherent in the Oulipian approach might be seen in this very tension, for the questions raised are never fully answered: what is literature, and what is it about certain texts that lead to pleasing results after being subjected to transformation? Is there a covert appeal to the transcendent in literature? Or does, perhaps, the Oulipian approach simply point to the fact that any definition of literature is inevitably flawed and open to criticism, and that such definitions invariably exclude certain categories of writing, especially those which valorize a notion of balance between outmoded categories of style and content? Oulipo's repeated invocation of the figure of Mallarmé might seem to gesture precisely in this direction, and thus, after all, there may be an unavoidable sympathy with the interpretative issues confronted by critics as diverse as Richard and the members of *Tel Quel*. After all, the Oulipian fascination with mathematical organization and with the language of process and production is echoed in the vocabulary of *Tel Quel*, whatever the differences between the two groups might have been, and the writings of Scherer and Richard both nod towards combinatorial and numerical speculation. The Oulipo might then be seen as one response to a commonly felt set of theoretical problems at a certain moment in time.

Nevertheless, it is perhaps in the very specific encounter with Mallarmé as a practising writer where the relationship of the Oulipo to Mallarmé might begin to be made clear: not as a literary genealogy, although it would be easy enough to draw one up, and not necessarily as a critical position firmly opposed to others, although the case has been made, but through an occasional convergence, a mirroring, an echo, or, finally, through the inscription of Mallarmé in the Oulipo's own image. As Raymond Queneau stated: 'Mais je crois que notre bon Mallarmé est parfaitement potentiel.' ('But I think good old Mallarmé is truly potential.').[51]

9

On the Side of Poetry and Chaos
Mallarmean *Hasard* and Twentieth-Century Music

Kate van Orden

Musical theatre and *Un coup de dés*

When confronted by the overwhelming enthusiasm for Wagner's music-dramas among avant-garde writers and intellectuals in France and asked by Édouard Dujardin to comment on Wagner in the first issue of the *Revue wagnérienne* (1885), Mallarmé wrote that the art work of the future must shine forth from 'the literary principle'.[1] Wagnerian music-drama, he suggested, ill-suited the French, for the Gallic mind was 'strictly imaginative and abstract, and thus poetic' and required not a *Gesamtkunstwerk*, but an *art* based on a French poetic genre, the ode. The French theatre should be reformed under the influence of poetry and employ a variety of myth that projects no narratives, has no heroes, and instead expresses the

> sens latent en le concours de tous, [la Fable] inscrite sur la page des Cieux et dont l'Histoire même n'est que l'interprétation, vaine, c'est-à-dire, un Poème, l'Ode. Quoi! le siècle ou notre pays, qui l'exalte, ont dissous par la pensée les Mythes, pour en refaire! Le Théâtre les appelle, non! pas de fixes, ni de séculaires et de notoires, mais un, dégagé de personnalité . . .[2]

> (meaning latent in the concourse of all, the Fable inscribed on the page of the Heavens and of which History itself is merely a shadowy interpretation, namely, a Poem, the Ode. Could it be that the age, or our country, which exalts it, have dissolved Myths through thought, only to forge new ones! These are what

the Theatre calls for, not myths which are fixed, or venerable or famed, but one, stripped of all personality . . .)[3]

Thus in the essay 'Richard Wagner, rêverie d'un poëte français', Mallarmé proposes to strip both the music and the drama (read: narrative and characters) from Wagner's music-drama and transpose the whole effort into a theatrical miracle that features no set or actors or music, yet reveals the divine in silent poetic contemplation.[4] Even Wagner's *côterie littéraire* concurred, for they believed that music-drama was evolving toward a perfect state, free of sets, costumes, and lights, where the drama would unfold in the minds of ideal spectators who would be able to recreate the work 'without any need of electrical or musical gadgetry, but by merely reading and exerting the will'.[5] More an ideological topos than a musical reality, Wagner's œuvre signified a symbolist theatre of the imagination upon whose illusory stage 'les parfums, les couleurs et les sons se répondent'[6] ('perfumes, colours, and sounds correspond') and represented the first step toward the ideal of an internalized theatre celebrating 'the sovereign pageantry of Poetry'.[7]

The passage from Mallarmé's 'Rêverie' cited above presages the themes of his last work, *Un coup de dés*, suggesting that to some extent his typographical poem of 1897 realizes the potential he ascribed to French lyric poetry twelve years earlier. The images of a poem inscribed on the page of the heavens and the poem as a fixed constellation expressing the meaning latent in celestial gyrations or eternal truths are featured in *Un coup de dés*, where the look of the poem on the page is itself intended to be a negative reflection in black letters on the white page of the possibility that a text might be able to signify mysteries and point beyond itself to a heavenly realm where stars are scattered across the black expanse of the night sky. *Un coup de dés* rises to the challenge Wagner posed to poets and meets it with a musical theatre of words on the page:

Un solitaire tacite concert se donne, par la lecture . . . [A]ucun moyen mental exaltant la symphonie, ne manquera, raréfié et c'est tout—du fait de la pensée. La Poésie, proche l'idée, est Musique, par excellence—ne consent pas d'infériorité.[8]

(A solitary silent concert is given, by the act of reading . . . [N]o mental means exalting the symphony will be missing, it's rarefied and that's all—because of thought. Poetry, close to the idea, is Music, par excellence—does not recognize any inferiority.)

The reading of a poem is musical in its mode of signification. Mallarmé tends not to stress the mechanical connections between music and poetry such as poetic meters and rhyme as the site of poetry's musicality—though his preference for traditional lyric verse forms is meaningful in this regard—but inclines instead to draw out the semiology of pure music and the way it signifies an ideal plane. That is to say, Mallarmé likens poetry to 'absolute' or 'pure' music.[9] Usually understood to be instrumental music such as the symphony, nineteenth-century critics believed that pure, untexted music could awaken the sense of infinite truths in the listener. By rejecting the portrayal of narratives, emotions, and characters outside itself, music could take as its subject the infinite, and owing to music's in-determinate character, it could transport the listener to a tran-scendental realm beyond the reach of the intellect.[10] To use Hegel's terminology, music was a special 'language of the soul'. For our purposes, it is crucial to note that poets valued music's ability to signify metaphysical truths in an indeterminate language that circum-vented the intellect and spoke directly to the soul. Free of the bonds linking things to thoughts and words, the semiology of absolute music involved a type of *hasard* that made its signs impossible to decode in rational terms, since they referred to the inexplicable and infinite but immensely powerful tools of the Ideal.

Mallarmé presumed to recuperate the poetic from music by employing music's non-discursive codes, to transpose the symphony —that genre of absolute music par excellence—into a poem or book (*le Livre*).[11] *Un coup de dés* can be understood as a seminal example of what Mallarmé's projected *Livre* might have included, since it addresses fundamental questions about poetry and announces its unprecedented union of free verse and the prose poem as one effected under the influence 'of Music, as it is heard at a concert'.[12] *Un coup de dés* is a new genre like a 'symphony' or 'personal song' for dealing with 'subjects of pure and complex imagination or intellect'.[13] As we have seen in Mallarmé's other writings, music here figures an inner concert of the thoughts. But elsewhere in the poem's preface, instructions prescribe the reading or performance of the poem in literal musical terms that equate the poem to a symphony replete with a first theme (in the largest type):

Un coup de dés jamais n'abolira le hasard

(A throw of the dice will never abolish chance)

second theme (in smaller block letters):

rien n'aura eu lieu que le lieu excepté peut-être une constellation

(nothing will have taken place but the place except perhaps a constellation)

and ornamental developments (in smaller and/or italic type) such as:

Toute Pensée émet un Coup de Dés

(All Thought emits a Throw of the Dice)

The first theme, or 'fil conducteur latent' (latent guiding thread), is woven through the poem like a Wagnerian leitmotiv that ebbs against the white spaces of the pages and swells in the reader's intonations. The rising and falling vocalise that Mallarmé recommends clothes the theme in musical timbres analogous to the invisible folds of chordal fabric Wagner used to mantle his heroes. Its fractured presentation also contributes to Mallarmé's aesthetic of the theatrical, for the typographical effect creates 'subdivisions prismatiques de l'Idée . . . dans quelque mise en scène spirituelle exacte' ('prismatic subdivisions of the Idea . . . in some exact mental setting').[14] The poem's symbols play upon the stage of the reader's poetic dream-world, revealing its Idea through the suggestive magic of words.

If *Un coup de dés* can be linked to musical–poetic ideals that coalesced as symbolism and Wagnerism in France, the musical performance implied by the poem is not the only point of contact. Equally important are the poem's attempt to create a pure poetic language and its concern with an inner theatre. The dice throw that initiates the poem scatters the words across the pages and fixes them there in graphic constellations charged with semantic attractions, collisions, and repulsions that produce its rhythmic pulse and prosody. Nothing external to the poem fully accounts for the multiple and unforeseen meanings created in this way: words resonate spatially as well as syntactically in the poem's unique grammar. The referential meanings assigned to words by arbitrary convention or 'chance' seem to have been 'vaincu[s] mot par mot' ('vanquished word by word') in this work governed by its own internal laws.[15] The poem thus represents a structure for reflection that incorporates semantic probabilities but no definite meaning:

> comme cela se groupe et se construit à la manière des architectures mobiles musicales, toutes les probabililtés que contient une riche substance de rêve tour à tour s'érigeant, illuminant et souriant[16]

> (as it comes together and constructs itself in the manner of musical mobile architectures, with all the probabilities contained by a rich dream-substance alternately emerging, illuminating and smiling)

Behind the prefatory performance instructions that introduce *Un coup de dés* lies the wreckage of theatrical plans for two other works, 'Hérodiade' and 'L'Après-midi d'un faune', both of which were destined early on for the Théâtre-Français, and quite possibly conceived for the theatre under the spell of Wagnerian music-drama.[17] In both of those works the lyric mode subverts any possibility of dramatic narrative, but even though they are not playable on the stage, Mallarmé said of 'Faune' that it 'needed' the stage.[18] *Un coup de dés* surpasses the theatricality of 'Hérodiade' and 'Faune' by abandoning the scenic imagery of those poems and casting the poem in the form of a musical score that enlists the reader as a performer. Mallarmé's theatrical metaphors invite the reader into a space of reflection where the poetic Idea will be played out with the transcendent force associated in his day with the experience of Bayreuth. The poem becomes an illusory theatre

> qui montre seulement une représentation, pour ceux n'ayant point à voir les choses à même! de la pièce écrite au folio du ciel et mimée avec le geste de ses passions par l'Homme.[19]

(which only shows a representation—for those not needing to see things up close!—of the play written on the folio of the sky and mimed with the gesture of his passions by Man.)

Acting now as an interpreter, the reader participates in an open-ended process of reflexive play between poet and audience that invests reading with the creation of meaning. And *Un coup de dés*, more so than any of Mallarmé's poems, persistently refers to its own performance. As Mary Lewis Shaw argues in her *Performance in the Texts of Mallarmé*, the withdrawal of the poetic self dramatized in the poem leaves 'the carefully structured yet highly flexible empty space of the Ideal, metaphysical Self that every human subject must be allowed, paradoxically, to enter and fill'.[20] Yet the final disappearance of the poet that permits the poem's transposition onto an ideal plane cannot take place until the poetic text finds its own reflection in a theatrical performance. *Un coup de dés* treats the death of the Poet or lyric Self in mythological terms, reversing the personifying poetics of myth in order to create a poem that is the identical contrary of myth. Shaw explains that for Mallarmé, 'all mythology (or poetic fiction), . . . is ultimately a *personification* of the infinite, irresolvable conflict of contraries that both creates and destroys the natural world'.[21] In contrast, *Un coup de dés* operates at the level of myth and uses mythic modes, but with modern aesthetic goals: 'just as the ancient personifying myths necessarily authenticated themselves through ritual gestures, so must this modern, abstract, depersonalized myth find its own ideal consecration in a modern, abstract, depersonalized performance.'[22] Mallarmé's poetics of myth, I believe, explains why in the 'Rêverie' on Wagner he insists upon the ode as a more perfect counterpart to the mythology of Wagnerian music-drama. *Un coup de dés* is that Fable or Poem, the Ode: theatre with no actors, no stage, and no narrative, stripped of all personality, strictly imaginative and abstract.

I have lingered over *Un coup de dés* at some length because it generated such a stunning constellation of artistic responses in the twentieth century. While its thematization of chance and a pure poetic language was born in part of nineteenth-century debates on absolute music, its abstract qualities appealed to twentieth-century sensibilities as well. In addition to its effacement of the self, the poem enacts the crisis of modern art that occurred when poets, musicians, and painters turned away from conventional lyric, harmonic, and representational forms. Like cubist paintings, *Un coup de dés* risks unintelligibility in order to reveal what standard poetics left cast in syntax so clear that it refused the magic potency of words. Many modern movements and artists were influenced by Mallarmé's typographical poem: Futurist Filippo Tommaso Marinetti, Dadaists Man Ray and Marcel Duchamp, and composers of 'chance' music such as Pierre Boulez and John Cage.[23] The backward-looking idealism of the poem-cum-constellation, 'veillant, doutant, roulant, brillant et méditant avant de s'arrêter à quelque point dernier qui le sacre' ('keeping vigil, doubting, rolling, shining and meditating before coming to a halt at some terminus that sanctifies it') never refuses the *hasard* modernists made their touchstone.[24] In the musical arts, Mallarmean thought was received and reformulated during the 1950s in two general musical strains. The first, initiated by Pierre Boulez, grew from Mallarmé's dialectic of referential and pure language and seems linked back through them to French Wagnerism. The second strain, developed by John Cage, both refers to and denies Boulez's reading of Mallarmé and expands the Mallarmean notion of a musical theatre for the imagination.

Pierre Boulez and Mallarmé

The twentieth-century composer most evidently influenced by Mallarmé is Pierre Boulez (b. 1925), who has set several of Mallarmé's texts and has written on Mallarmé in his essays.[25] Boulez's compositions based on Mallarmé include an unfinished setting of *Un coup de dés* for large orchestra and chorus (begun circa 1950), the *Troisième Sonate pour piano* (1957), and *Pli selon pli* for soprano, small ensemble, and orchestra (published 1958–82).[26] *Pli selon pli* includes as its central movements three *Improvisations sur Mallarmé* which set, respectively, 'Le vierge, le vivace et le bel aujourd'hui', 'Une dentelle s'abolit', and 'A la nue accablante tu', while the framing movements allude to 'Don du poëme' and 'Tombeau (de Verlaine)'.

Boulez turned to Mallarmé early on in his career at a time when, shortly after World War II, many composers had reached an artistic impasse. The serial techniques developed from Arnold Schoenberg's twelve-tone experiments largely discarded the tonal and harmonic language of Western music's 'common practice' period, a language that had been current for some 350 years and that depended on a gravitational hierarchy of pitches theorized according to mathematically demonstrable consonances and dissonances. Serialism equalized each of the twelve chromatic pitches by organizing them in a series or 'row' that ensured their equal occurrence in a composition and shattered the triadic structures based on local and overarching tonal centres that governed earlier compositions. The syntax of tonal music was in this way unhinged, to be reassembled according to infinitely variable grammars, for each new composition required a new row that would ensure its uniqueness. In other words, tonal musical rhetoric dissolved as chromaticism broke apart the harmonic structures upon which it was based.

Boulez believed twelve-tone or serial composition to be an absolute necessity and even went so far as to claim that any musician who did not cry out for dodecaphonic language was 'USELESS'.[27] And in 1950 most composers might have agreed, for the torch of chromaticism handed on to the post-war generation by Schoenberg had earlier passed through Wagner's hands as well; thereby, serial techniques seemed to have the force of historical progress behind them. Yet a problem emerged as serialism exhausted its own promise with frightening rapidity: the rows organizing pitch were extended to control register, dynamic, duration (rhythm), and attack, and the entire fabric of some musical compositions came to be determined by rows. Composing hence reached an impasse even as it achieved a perfect non-referential purity, for the creative musical act had rigidified into the mechanical composing-out of multiple rows. Total serialism controlled the choices composers made by subverting the hierarchy of pitches and structures in which tonality revelled, and collapsed in upon itself with each new development, leaving fewer and fewer options to the composer. Boulez came to refer to total serialism variously as 'schematization', 'a statistical display', and 'a fetishism of numbers which leads to pure and simple bankruptcy'.[28]

For this reason, Boulez turned to Mallarmean *hasard* as a means to 're-open' the score and bring serialism into a new phase. (This sort of teleological strategizing is writ large in the way Boulez aligned himself not just with Mallarmé, but with Wagner as well.)[29] Boulez issued a manifesto on his aesthetic of chance in the *Nouvelle revue française* in 1957 which coincided with the publication of his *Troisième Sonate pour piano*, his first 'chance' composition. The *Troisième Sonate* bears superficial formal likeness to Mallarmé's *Un coup de dés*—the movements may be performed in variable sequences around a central movement entitled 'Constellation'; the score of 'Constellation' is printed in fragments scattered across nine large pages through which the performer can choose multiple paths; and the movement is organized along a series of axes mirroring the median axis dividing *Un coup de dés*—and, combined with the essay 'Aléa' in the *Nouvelle revue française*, Boulez summarily co-opted Mallarmean chance and assimilated it to his works. His musical score evinces mobility and multi-directionality: the *formants* (movements) circulated around the central 'Constellation', and the 'Constellation' also exists in a retrograde version called the 'Constellation-miroir'. So, in another obvious allusion to Mallarmé and *Un coup de dés*, Boulez named these chance procedures *musique aléatoire* after the Latin word for dice and explained the whole of it in 'Aléa'.

From the outset, however, Boulez's admittance of chance into the work of art was highly qualified. Indeed, his denial of 'inadvertent chance' in which 'the [musical or sound] event arrives as it can, uncontrolled, but inside a certain established network of probable events' actually precludes chance altogether.[30] Compositions like the Mallarmé *Improvisations* and the 'Constellation' movement of the *Troisième Sonate* merely left certain formal aspects unfixed and mobile, the order of their unfolding left to the performer. In the *Trois Improvisations sur Mallarmé*, the best example of freedom laid in the hands of the performers occurs in the second *Improvisation* where the soprano soloist can alter the pace of her declamation during sections marked 'senza tempo' while the director co-ordinates the instrumental accompaniment. The rest of the *Trois Improvisations* consists of music that is composed to sound improvised with a classical allowance for rubato within measures in certain places. Chance procedures determined nothing in these compositions. For example, the notes were not chosen by throwing dice. Rather, the scores contain indeterminate features, most of which, like rubato, had been standards of interpretive licence for centuries.[31]

Of course, the text of *Un coup de dés* was not composed with dice throws, and in this respect the indeterminate features Boulez created in·the scores of the *Trois Improvisations sur Mallarmé* and 'Constellation' are analogous to Mallarmé's writing processes. Likewise, in *Un coup de dés*, Mallarmé precisely determined every detail of the poem's layout and content. What distinguishes Mallarmé's poetics of chance from Boulez's said adoption of it is the way in which chance is introduced into the work of art. In poetry, language itself embodies chance in its references to things outside itself. The typographically exploded grammar of Un coup de dés might aspire to vanquish hasard word by word through the poem's careful construction, but the poem is still written in words and hence fraught with the hasard inherent in referential materials, a referentiality that Mallarmé at once multiplies and confounds by embracing chance in the poem's layout. Language bound the poet in a dialectic confrontation with chance on the field of referential language, where hermetic poetry confronted its referentiality, amplifying the meanings of words, heightening and increasing their significations. Poetry would always have content, because words have meanings, but it was a content that would be cast off as the poem transcended its own language. Or, in Mallarmé's words from his oft-quoted letter to Cazalis, 'le vers ne doit donc pas, là, se composer de mots; mais d'intentions, et toutes les paroles s'effacer devant la sensation' ('verse should be composed not out of words but out of intentions, and every utterance should be effaced before its corresponding sensation').[32] Thus the work of l'universel reportage that burdened language in its ordinary usage might be shed, not by circumventing language altogether, but by reinventing it to serve transcendent Ideas. Un coup de dés still refers to something outside itself which is then regulated or abolished within, and it is the transformation of references within the poem that establishes Mallarmé's hermetic fold. In contrast, the serial language Boulez employs in his musical compositions is even more highly hermetic than the late nineteenth-century tonal music Mallarmé envied for its rarefaction: by negating the web of meanings a listener brings to music through a system of entirely self-referential structures, serial language evacuates Mallarmean chance from music and erases its aesthetic function. The musical analogue to linguistic semantics is the tonal discourse that serialism eradicates. Serial structures free the composer 'from all melody, all harmony and all counterpoint, since serial structure has caused all these essentially modal and tonal notions to disappear'.[33]

Perhaps Boulez realized the incompatibility of serial music with Mallarmé's poetics, for his projected setting of Un coup de dés has never been completed. The piece, for large orchestra and choir, was to be a totally serialized composition employing microtones such as eighteenth- and twenty-fourth-tones, making it the first of its kind and so difficult that ordinary instrumentalists would not be able to perform it. In a letter to John Cage from 1953, Boulez relates his plans to build a special instrument to produce the microtonal passage at the end of the piece. He then goes on to suggest that when machines replaced instrumentalists, serial music might be able to progress unhindered:

> I think that with the mechanical recording-means (the 'tape-recorder' in particular) we shall be able to realize structures that no longer depend on instrumental difficulties and we shall be able to work with any frequencies, using the serial method of generation. And thus each work will have its own structure and its own mode of generation on all levels.[34]

This aesthetic aim reads Mallarmé's wish for an entirely self-referential poetry at face value without accounting for the human subject who enters into the work—at least in *Un coup de dés* and in the projected *Livre*—in a process that both effaces the poet and permits the work's signification in a mode of ritual transcendence. Boulez's unwillingness to open his scores to performers eventually led him to eradicate indeterminate elements from the Mallarmé *Improvisations*, confessing 'where you have thirty or forty people and you give them all some choice, you may be sure that there will be very many mistakes. Really, it's not worth the game'.[35]

John Cage, Marcel Duchamp, and Mallarmé

Boulez was not the only musical heritor of Mallarmean chance, and significantly so. His continual invocation of Mallarmé during the 1950s seemed partially designed to enlist French modernism as an authentication of his inventions. American and German composers were developing indeterminate music, and Boulez was anxious to dismiss the 'chance music' of his one-time friend John Cage. Indeed, the relationship between Boulez and Cage—documented in their correspondence between 1949 and 1954—turned acrimonious over precisely the issue of chance in art and the legacy of Mallarmé.[36] According to Cage, Boulez rejected outright any acceptance of the idea of chance. That wasn't a part of his views. Later came Mallarmé's posthumous *Book*, which could have brought us together again, since in the end Mallarmé too accorded primacy to chance. In fact, Boulez in turn threw himself into chance operations. But for him, chance served as a pretext for inventing the term *aleatory*. I believe he established its present musical definition. Well, he used that word only to describe appropriate and correct chance operations, as opposed to those which seemed to him inappropriate or incorrect—mine![37]

In the early 1950s, Cage had begun to compose using aggregate sounds of the sort one might achieve in a totally serialized composition. He arranged them not in rows, but in charts through which he might 'move' as across a chessboard. In composing the last movement of his 'Concerto for Prepared Piano and Orchestra', it occurred to Cage to use the Chinese *I Ching* to determine the moves through the charts, throwing coins to produce numbered hexagrams and translating them into moves on the charts. He described the process in a letter to Boulez in May 1951, saying that this method of composing freed him 'from what I had thought to be freedom, and which actually was only the accretion of habits and tastes'.[38] This nondirected composing is what Boulez decried as 'inadvertent chance' in his polemic 'Aléa', dismissing Cage's methods as 'a philosophy dyed with Orientalism and masking a fundamental weakness in the technique of composition'.[39] In other words, Boulez denied the appropriateness of the chance operations Cage drew from the *I Ching* and attacked Cage's craftsmanship.

Cage relied heavily on the texts and philosophies of Eastern thought while developing the techniques of chance and indeterminate composition, and when he explicitly referred to sources and influences, he generally named Buddhism and Taoism, or the Indian aesthetics concerning the place of the artist in the process of creation put forth by Ananda Coomaraswamy.[40] At the same time, however, Mallarmé was very much on his horizon.[41] Boulez corresponded with Cage about his setting of *Un coup de dés*, and in a letter on chance composition from May 1951, Cage replied:

You can see from my present activity how interested I was when you wrote of the Coup de Dés of Mallarmé.

And I have been reading a great deal of Artaud. (This because of you and through Tudor who read Artaud because of
you.)[42]

Even at this early stage, Cage equated his experimental use of the *I
Ching* with Boulez's interest in Mallarmé's chance poem. In 1953,
Cage was asked to compose music for a reading of *Un coup de dés*, a
prospect that clearly interested him, but he declined in light of
Boulez's work-in-progress.[43] Cage was fluent in French and certainly
knew much of Mallarmé, particularly since Boulez sent Cage a copy
of Mallarmé's *Œuvres complètes* in 1953.[44] He also owned a copy of
Jacques Scherer's 1957 publication of Mallarmé's notes for the
Livre.[45] Cage took the projected *Livre* as firm evidence that Mallarmé
'accorded primacy to chance' in the same way he did, while Boulez's
reading of the notes confirmed his aleatoric ideals, which 'were
identical with those that Mallarmé had pursued and formulated but
never had time to explore to the full'.[46] Each composer claimed
Mallarmean chance for their own, though upon radically different
premises.

Neither composer ever set *Un coup de dés*, but as I have argued
elsewhere, Cage's _____, _____ *Circus on* _____: *means for
translating a book into a performance without actors, a performance which
is both literary and musical or one or the other* is a musico-poetic
performance of literature that takes *Un coup de dés* and *Le livre* as its
point of departure.[47] The translation of the book into performance
involves two operations: in the first, the name of the author or title
of the book becomes the subject of a series of mesostics (a variety of
acrostic) that rework the text into a poem, and in the second,
operation, tape-recordings are made of all the sounds and at all the
places mentioned in the text and played concurrently with the read
mesostics. Cage's realization of the piece was based on James Joyce's
Finnegans Wake and entitled *Roaratorio: An Irish Circus on Finnegans
Wake*.[48] The thickly layered sounds result in a musical 'circus' that
celebrates the mystery of 'poetry and chaos', a decentered three-ring
circus overflowing with aural side-shows, monstrosities, and diver-
sions.[49] The notion of a circus is doubly important in the way it
relates to the Mallarmean notion of a ritualistic theatre—also taken
up by Artaud—and for the non-narrative circularity it implies. Both
Finnegans Wake and *Un coup de dés* end with a movement that leads

back to the beginning: the sentence fragment that Joyce ends with is completed by the first line of the book, whereas in Mallarmé, the last phrase is also the first. The circularity enacted by these false endings cause the reader to question the meaning of the text and where s/he is in it. This rich confusion of time and direction that turns back upon itself is also evident in *L'Après-midi d'un faune*, where the narrative proposed in the italicized passages is interrupted, reflected upon, and abandoned to inebriated dreaming in a counter-point that presages the more radical use of typography in *Un coup de dés*.[50] Much of the 'musicality' of Mallarmé's verse arises from its refusal of the linear and narrative, just as its most radical implications —the coexistence of chance and art—depend on its adoption of open, recursive, and even potentially chaotic structures. Cage embraces the endlessness of *Finnegans Wake* and the non-directed reading it invites: 'just go into any one word, like that word "laughtears" and then move out from it as though you'd become a pebble tossed into this ocean . . . This attitude is more akin to music, where experience becomes more to the point than understanding.'[51] One can go out through the text from any point in any direction. This aesthetic of undirected time, it is important to note, is one Boulez staunchly refused to adopt in his compositions, which develop in a unidirectional musical discourse.[52] Even the 'Constellation' of the *Troisième Sonate*, which appears fragmented on the page, seems to have been conceived as a linear whole before being broken into sections, while the retrograde 'mirror' version of the piece betrays the progressive logic governing it. Boulez's structural incorporation of chance never disrupts the music's aesthetic essentialism, whereas Cage's 'musicircus' allows chance and indeterminacy to undercut discursive logic, authoriality, and artistic closure.

Apart from Cage's association with Boulez in the early 1950s, another genealogy of artistic influence helps explain Cage's interest in Mallarmé: his friendship with Marcel Duchamp, a friendship that lasted from 1943 to 1968 and produced a rich array of compositions. In an interview conducted shortly before his death, Cage articulated precisely this French inheritance when asked about his own influence on others:

> I am not really interested in the notion of influence, nor by that of leaders, consciousness of an era . . . but only grateful when

someone has a new idea. This is why I will always be grateful to artists such as Duchamp, Satie, Mallarmé . . .[53]

Duchamp's interest in Mallarmé is well known, and Cage elsewhere paired the Dada artist and symbolist poet in one of his 'statements re Duchamp' entitled 'Duchamp Mallarmé?'[54] Indeed, Duchamp particularly favoured *Un coup de dés* and Mallarmé's poetics of chance.[55] Like Mallarmé, Duchamp believed that a work of art could convey meanings that defied rational explanations (in Mallarmé's lexicon, the ineffable mystery expressed by poetry and non-linguistic media such as music, dance, or mime). While later twentieth-century modern aesthetics replaced the aim of expressing any transcendental Ideal with that of exposing the subconscious, the emphasis on an expressive metalanguage remained intact. According to Duchamp, works of art could not be understood by the intellect any more than their effect could be described in words; rather, art required an emotional precondition in the viewer analogous to 'a religious faith or a sexual attraction—an aesthetic echo'.[56] In this emotional state, 'the "victim" of an aesthetic echo is in a position comparable to that of a man in love or a believer . . . when touched by aesthetic revelation, the same man in an almost ecstatic mood, becomes receptive and humble'.[57] The 'auditor' of an aesthetic echo not only communes with the work of art, he or she is a necessary component of the creative process, for since the artist, too, was incapable of rationally directing the creation of the art-work, a gap remained between 'the unexpressed but intended and the unintentionally expressed'.[58] Just as Mallarmé created in *Un coup de dés* a stage upon which the reader's thoughts came into play, so Duchamp's 'intentional gap' required the participation of a sensitive listener temporarily to complete the process set in motion by the artist. 'To all appearances', Duchamp said, 'the artist acts like a mediumistic being who, from the labyrinth beyond time and space, seeks his way out to a clearing.'[59] By relinquishing half of the creative process to the aesthetic 'auditor'—and no doubt Duchamp prizes hearing among the senses for the ineffability that made absolute music pre-eminent among the Romantic arts— Duchamp effaces the omniscient artist's control in the same way that Mallarmé 'died' in creating his new poetics and staged the disappearance of his poetic Self from *Un coup de dés*. By enlarging the 'intentional gap' and drawing the reader/spectator/auditor into the creative process, chance enters into dialogue with the art-work. It is important to note, however, that neither Duchamp nor Cage believed that chance negated artistic expression. Rather, chance enhanced expression by freeing the materials of art from the artist's intention. As Duchamp said:

> Your chance is not the same as mine, is it? If I make a throw of the dice, it will never be the same as your throw. And so an act like throwing dice is a marvelous expression of your sub-conscious.[60]

Duchamp believed that both the artist and the recipient of the aesthetic echo must suppress taste—governed as it is by rational likes and dislikes—in order to clear the space for an aesthetic experience of art. Extending this gloss on Mallarmé's notion of depersonalized intuition, Duchamp introduced chance into his methods as a way of keeping intention at bay. We see this in his earliest works, one of which was a chance composition in music. In it, he took the dictionary definition of *imprimeur* as lyrics which he set as a three-part song by drawing musical notes at random from a hat. The song was entitled *Erratum musical* (John Cage owned a more extensive chance composition by Duchamp named for *Large Glass* and subtitled *Erratum musical*) and Duchamp later included it in *The Green Box*.[61] Also from 1913 came a visual work composed by chance, the *3 Stoppages Étalon*, in which he let three lengths of white thread fall against a canvas and affixed them as they lay.

Cage met Duchamp just weeks after arriving in New York in 1943, and by 1944 had produced a piece dedicated to the artist for a show at the Julien Levy Gallery that took Duchamp's interest in chess as its theme. *Chess Pieces* is as much a visual as a musical composition, a score for one or two pianos rendered as a chessboard.[62] Against a grey background, the music is divided visually into sixty-four 'black' and 'white' squares by notation printed in black and white ink upon the grey surface. Although the systems can be read horizontally, their extension off the right edge of the page (as well as top and bottom) and the absence of logical musical continuity from system to system makes the piece unperformable in a traditional sense, leaving us to wonder whether one might instead perform it by moving from square to square or whether the wondering was the performance itself.[63]

The multidirectional reading encoded in *Chess Pieces* produces non-centred activity across its entire surface like that Cage later cultivated using the *I Ching* to move through the charts he had drawn up for the *Concerto for Prepared Piano*. Not only does *Chess Pieces* in this way suggest chance composition before the fact, its references to Marcel Duchamp's chess-as-art philosophy make it an early indicator of Cage's coming 'emancipation of sound', an expansion of music to include noise recalling Mallarmé's statement that 'tout, au monde, existe pour aboutir à un livre' ('everything in the world exists to end up in a book').[64] As artists broke down the barriers between art and life, dynamic and perpetually unfolding forms that could contain and express the processes of undirected doing became increasingly important.

Cage wrote at least three other pieces for Duchamp: *Music for Marcel Duchamp* (1947), *Reunion* (1968), and *Sculptures Musicales* (1989).[65] *Reunion* was a musical 'event' composed by Cage and staged in Toronto in February of 1968. In it, Cage and Duchamp played chess on a board rigged with contact microphones that set off a series of electronically amplified sounds and oscilloscopic images on television screens whenever a piece was moved. (See Figure 1).

It commemorates Cage's friendship with the artist, with whom he studied chess in the course of their socializing, and turns their chess matches into a musical performance, making a musical theatre out of their gestures and amplifying them as sound and images of sound. In *Silence*, Cage maintains that theatre takes place all the time, whereas art simply persuades us to see it.[66] *Reunion*, like the chess game it features, stresses process over outcome. And as a performance piece—importantly one played by Cage and Duchamp—it emphasizes the experiences of the artist through which art unfolds. Nothing happens in the piece ('rien n'aura eu lieu que le lieu') except, perhaps, the offering up of life's reflection for contemplation.

Reunion reverses, to some extent, Mallarmé's goal of expressing an Ideal by abandoning the attempt to symbolize a transcendent reality in favour of embodying the flux of the natural world. We see the alternatives play themselves out musically along the oppositions of closed (fixed) and open (indeterminate) form, serial music (hermetic language) and *musique concrète* (referential language), and the possibility of performing music as 'concert' or 'theatre'.[67] The open theatre implied by Mallarmé's *Un coup de dés* and his ideas for *Le*

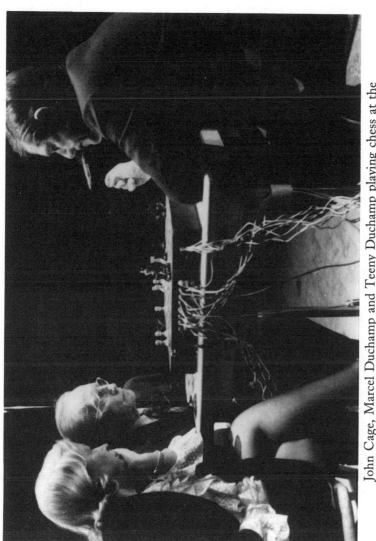

John Cage, Marcel Duchamp and Teeny Duchamp playing chess at the 'Reunion' concert in Toronto in 1968 (courtesy of the photographer, Shigeko Kubota, and the John Cage Trust).

livre created an artistic trajectory that the poet, too, understood might transform art as he knew it: in the preface to *Un coup de dés* he characterized the future that will emerge from the poem as 'rien ou presque un art'[68] ('nothing or almost an art'). The challenge to classical, fixed forms initiated by the nineteenth-century desire for a symbolist poetics of the metaphysical, when carried to its extremes by Duchamp and Cage, made the Book into life rather than making life into the Book.

Echo

John Cage died unexpectedly in his New York apartment on August 12, 1992, leaving a silence even more profound than the revolutionary one he had staged in a concert hall in 1951. In the following days, the Belgian composer Henri Pousseur cast a piece for solo piano into the stillness, a memorial entitled *Coups de dés en echos pour ponctuer au piano le silence de John Cage*.[69] Pousseur utilized two four-sided dice to compose the piece, one bearing numbers representing J-O-H-N and the other numbers representing C-A-G-E. In this way, Pousseur transformed the name into musical pitches, adding the pitch D ('Dé') to the aggregate from which the entire composition is generated. The 'dice note' (D) forms a point of orientation for the piece and is used both as a symmetrical axis around which the other pitches are deployed and in a 'manière plus secrète' in the refrains. The letters of 'Cage' are all the names of musical notes: they are used in brief refrains that recur four times in the piece to create a circular structure of return to the chord E-G-A-C which ends the piece, an ironically tonal sonority given Cage's irreverence toward Western music (it spells a minor seventh chord on A in second inversion). Pousseur also includes an *Episode 'volant'* featuring the dice note and consisting of twelve sets of four notes on which the performer can improvise at will. This can be inserted at any of three spots in the second part of the piece. Pousseur pays tribute to Cage's indeterminate music in the loose parameters set up by the flying *Episode*, and honours his chance compositions by making his name into dice that are thrown to produce the material of the piece. The emphasis on C-A-G-E in the refrains and on 'Dé' as a central pitch are Pousseur's own determinations that musically link Cage with Mallarmé's symbol of chance.

Pousseur's *Coups de dés en echos* does not just punctuate the silence left by Cage's death, but also inflects the silence created by Cage's 'silent piece' of 1951, *4'33'*, in which a pianist sat quietly on stage before the instrument for the duration of the piece while the audience listened to the sounds that occurred unbidden in the concert hall. *4'33'* was ground zero, a clearing of the mind and effacement of the composer's ego that marked a turning point for an entire artistic community and permitted the discovery that silence could open the doors to music.[70] Pousseur tosses the dice into *that* silence, a silence as vast as the *blancs* (blanks or white spaces) of *Un coup de dés.* For Mallarmé, lyric versification required the whiteness of the page as a surrounding silence,[71] and his late poem featured that white silence as the realm into which acts of thought are cast, a dynamic realm at turns unforgiving:

l'Abîme blanchi étale furieux[72]

(the Abyss blanched calm furious)[73]

and turbulent:

Une insinuation simple au silence enroulée avec ironie ou le mystère précipité hurlé dans quelque proche tourbillon d'hilarité et d'horreur[74]

(A simple insinuation in the silence enrolled with irony or the mystery hurled howled in some nearby whirlpool of hilarity and horror).[75]

Pousseur's dice-throws punctuate a silence in which Mallarmé believed we might hear the infinite and in which John Cage believed life itself resounded. The material act of 'throwing the dice' or composing is an empty one and, indeed, we hear only echos of it. But behind Pousseur's *Coups de dés* for John Cage is a spiritual determination that casts the work into that other realm, a spiritual determination with which Mallarmé and Cage pursued chaos into the white margins, silence, and the musical theatre of life.

10

Revolution in Poetic Language?
Kristeva and Mallarmé

Patrick ffrench

Julia Kristeva is predominantly known as the author of a complex and seductive theory of subjectivity and symbolic activity which offers an account of the interplay of the system of human discourse and the pulsional psychic and corporeal forces that come to disrupt and punctuate it. The work of Mallarmé offers Kristeva an exemplary reflection of that process and of its consequences. A discussion of the critical relation between Kristeva and Mallarmé has therefore to deal with the nature of this reflection and with the status of this exemplarity. The opening lines of Mallarmé's 'Prose', for example, dramatize the emergence of the poetic act 'Hyperbole' from the depths of memory:

> Hyperbole! de ma mémoire
> Triomphalement ne sais-tu
> Te lever, aujourd'hui grimoire
> Dans un livre de fer vêtu:
>
> (Hyperbole! From my memory
> Can you not triumphantly arise,
> Today like an occult language
> Copied into a book bound in iron.)[1]

To translate this into Kristeva's terms: the symbolic act of naming emerges against the backdrop of an unconscious, pre-linguistic undercurrent. This is evidently a quite specific form of translation; Kristeva's reading of Mallarmé is a markedly interested one (interested in its own reflection), and while it may be that this *interestedness* is a characteristic of criticism this possibility can be investigated via the specific critical relation of Kristeva and Mallarmé. The nature of this critical relation involves a recognition that just as there exists an anxiety of influence between literary texts, there exists a similar tension, which I might call an anxiety of exemplarity, between literary texts and their critics. Moreover, the stakes are high, for Kristeva's major work on Mallarmé is titled *Revolution in Poetic Language*.[2] There is a deliberate political meaning attached to the first word of this title. A major question, through which we can approach the others, is imposed: in what sense is Mallarmé revolutionary? I discuss this question firstly through a discussion of the psychoanalytical and ethical dimensions of Kristeva's work, followed by a consideration of its historical dimension, linking *cure* to *revolution* through an analysis of the notion of negativity crucial to Kristeva's work, then to conclude with a discussion of the implications of Kristeva's theoretical framework for the image of Mallarmé which arises from her reading of his texts.

In a discussion of Philippe Sollers's novel *H*, Julia Kristeva evokes Mallarmé's name.[3] This text, 'The Novel as Polylogue', is among the first in which Kristeva moves away from the highly theoretical language she has adopted up to this point to adopt a confessional or even autobiographical tone. To a psychoanalytically informed critic, however, the personal is always tied up with the political; her confession has a political and historical resonance. The narrative runs as follows: because of Yalta she has had to marry in order to obtain a French passport. She has had to ' "marry" the violence which has tormented [her] ever since' ('à cause de Yalta j'ai désiré me "marier" avec la violence qui me ronge depuis').[4] And she realizes that the happy community which ignores this violence is a lie, and in truth depends on the exclusion of violence. So violence appears in elements 'outside' the discourse of the community. Kristeva gives the example of the televised image of a young girl reading the five-year plan; her attention is attracted to the timbre of the voice, the vivid colour of the background. Language, then, can incorporate the violence in its rhythms, its colour, its poetry; but because of historical circumstance, because of Yalta, this was not possible in Bulgaria. The French language becomes for Kristeva the scene upon which violence plays itself out. And here three names are evoked: Robespierre, Sade, Mallarmé.

Mallarmé is thus positioned in a perverse canon which reflects a historical and political narrative: if Robespierre's Terror is premised on the absolute effacement of the past and the absolute authority of the Law, Sade's rhetoric is a knowing incorporation of violence within language. By the time of the Third Republic, however, Mallarmé offers the recognition that 'un coup de dés n'abolira jamais le hasard'. No political decision, no symbolic event or law can annul the violence which runs underneath the social bond. Mallarmé's place in the trilogy of names suggests that he occupies a provisionally final place: chance is not excluded by a revolution which effaces the past and installs an immutable Law, the Terror; chance finds its way into poetic language and is provisionally mastered in a poetry which nevertheless recognizes the irreducibility of chance. However, Mallarmé's position in relation to the State and to the politics of revolt (the Commune) is disconnected. In the historical narrative suggested by Kristeva, poetic language takes on the burden of the violence whose exclusion the social bond depends upon. Having resided in the sacred, poetry takes violence upon itself, at the expense of becoming disconnected from the discourse of politics and from the flow of history. In this account, the displacement from 'le hasard' to 'violence' suggests the tenor of Kristeva's approach to Mallarmé and the inflection she gives her reading.

This inflection is determined by a theoretical, dynamic model which underlies much of Kristeva's thinking. It proposes the notion of the pre-Oedipal, pre-discursive 'semiotic', a space which, while pre-linguistic, is rhythmically organized around the pulsions of the body. The semiotic, though, is not so much a space as a *force*, which comes to produce effects in what is termed the Symbolic—the space of discourse, language as denotation and communication, ruled by the Oedipal structure of the family. The Symbolic itself is installed by a *thetic* moment, the positioning or fixing of an object, or a form, or the positioning of a place or a structure which is subsequently affected by the forces outside the structure, whose exclusion the structure rests upon.[5] The work of art is a process (*procès*—the word also signifies 'trial')[6] or a traversal (*traversée*)[7] of Symbolic space by semiotic pulsions. It produces a '*dispositif*',[8] an arrangement of semiotic, pulsional rhythms within the work. Either side of this difficult and risky process, this crossing, lie the Scylla and Charybdis of *psychosis* (no protection from violence), and *fetishism* (over-investment in the object, the product, without mobility). Kristeva develops this dynamic model of subjectivity and of culture from the mid-1960s onwards. It is elaborated in different terms through readings of the work of a canon of 'limit texts', prominent among them the texts of Artaud, Bataille, Lautréamont, and Mallarmé.

For Kristeva, the shattering of language is a shattering of the body, but the ability to master this, to fix, position and represent this shattering is both art and cure. It is a movement beyond psychosis in its mastery of the shattered, schizoid body. Mallarmé's 'Un coup de dés n'abolira jamais le hasard' ('A dice throw will never abolish chance'), the one text by him which operates as a constant reference throughout Kristeva's work, functions as a crucial example. It is exemplary both in its visual form and in its fragmentary significations, the meanings that can be derived from it. A number of its key phrases are used by Kristeva to illustrate and legitimate the semiotic/Symbolic model, and they can be heard behind her prose in many instances. A rather crude process of translation could illustrate this: 'Un coup de dés n'abolira jamais le hasard' signifies, as we have proposed, that no symbolic event of political act can annul the violence of chance whose exclusion the social bond depends upon; 'rien n'aura eu lieu que le lieu' ('nothing will have taken place but the place')[9] suggests that without the thetic moment, the positioning or placing of the subject, 'nothing' takes place, negativity rules; 'excepté peut-être une constellation' ('except perhaps a constellation')[10] suggests that the effects of chance, of semiotic pulsions upon symbolic space produce a constellation-like figure, a shattering, a dispersal and a dis-unification, of sense; 'pas tant qu'elle n'énumère sur quelque surface vacante et supérieure le heurt successif sidéralement d'un compte total en formation' ('not so much that it does not number on some empty and upper surface the successive shock after the manner of stars of a total addition in formation')[11] suggests that the semiotic is enumerated, dispersed, disseminated on the page and gives rise to an oblique series of successive blows or shocks—this is the work in progress. The last phrase alone, which is particularly productive of different theoretical translations, can be heard behind Kristeva's difficult language, particularly in the following example, where 'les coordonnées 0–1' signifies unity and linearity:

Là où ce fonctionnement signifiant [le langage poétique], cette *opération*, a lieu, les coordonnées 0–1 ne sont qu'un frein lointain, un rappel rigoureux mais éclipsé contre le hasard du non-sens, une vigie qui contrôle la pluralité de ce 'chaos' inattendu de signifiants qui produisent le *nouveau* sens.[12]

(Where this signifying practice [poetic language], this *operation*, takes place, the co-ordinates 0–1 are only a distant brake, a rigorous but eclipsed appeal against the chance of non-sense, a vigil which checks the plurality of this unexpected 'chaos' of signifiers, which produce the *new* meaning.)

or again: 'le sujet se dissout dans cette autre scène et c'est le heurt de signifiants s'annulant l'un l'autre qui s'instaure' ('the subject dissolves in this other scene and it is the shock of signifiers annihilating each other which is installed').[13]

To illustrate the specific way in which Mallarmé functions as example, I will take an example from Kristeva's recent work. Her book on Proust, *Le temps sensible*, literally shatters a sentence from the *Recherche*, using *Un coup de dés* as exemplary of this artistic and critical strategy. A sentence is dispersed across the page with vertical arrows and lines indicating non-linear patterns of syntactic relation.[14] Different typefaces—bold and italic—indicate different grammatical functions. Each unit of sense is given one line and surrounded by white space. Kristeva reads the Proustian sentence *through* Mallarmé's typographic shattering. She uncharacteristically cites Gide as an authority for this operation:

J'imagine une phrase de *Guermantes* imprimée à la manière du 'Coup de dés' de Mallarmé; ma voix donne aux mots-soutiens leur relief; j'orchestre à ma façon les incidentes, je les nuance, tempérant ou précipitant mon débit; et je vous prouve que rien n'est superflu dans cette phrase.[15]

(I imagine a sentence from *Guermantes* printed in the manner of Mallarmé's 'Coup de dés'; my voice gives to the support-words their relief; I orchestrate the incidental clauses in my own way, I nuance them, slowing or accelerating my delivery; and I show you that nothing is superfluous in this phrase.)

This suggests that *Un coup de dés* operates as Ur-text, example, and source of legitimation for Kristeva's reading of other texts. An important conclusion can be drawn from this: the visual appearance of Kristeva's retranscription 'à la coup de dés' (as she puts it) suggests two aspects of the effect of poetic language: the shattering of the body of language and the superimposition upon it of a constellation of relations, a *dispositif* deriving from semiotic rhythms. In my reading of Kristeva, these two aspects, shattering and starring, correspond to the two key elements of Mallarmé's poetic language: the transformation of syntax and musicalization by way of work on the phonemic level.

Kristeva argues that Proust's sentences ultimately retain grammatical coherence, while Mallarmé's syntax is 'indécidable' and 'lacunaire',[16] since 'le hasard' and the 'compte total en formation' are transposed by Proust onto the level of narrative, in the novel. Proust, therefore, judges Mallarmé's formalist investigation of the materiality of language to be too obscure, and, as Kristeva proposes, he deduces the music of language 'spontaneously'.[17] This inflection suggests an ambiguity in Kristeva's vision of Mallarmé: if the representation of the shattered body of language in *Un coup de dés* is a mastery of psychosis, it is also a fetishization, an investment in the object itself, in poetic form or in the poetic word at the expense of process and production. The negative connotations of the vision of the poem as fetish suggest also that the enjoyment of form is negative in relation to a process of transcendence or sublation. The constant relaunching of the process through this dialectic process seems more suited to narrative, in Kristeva's terms. The opposition that seems to be in play here is between a process of cure and a fetishistic indulgence in form. Kristeva's curative ethic seems at odds with the sensory pleasure of an indulgence in the poem as object.

But, as a psychoanalyst, Kristeva is aware of the problematics of the fetish, and specifically addresses them. In the Third Republic, she proposes, the State itself is a fetish, divested of authority and masking the reality of economic relations. The text, which is part of such a socio-economic formation, reproduces this fetishistic logic. It is a product masking the process of production which has produced it. The process results in objects (books, words or products) which are like the commodities resulting from work, exchanged as fetishes in the economy: 'cette pratique signifiante, dans l'absence de perspective historique immédiate, limite son action à l'exploration des ressources logiques et idéologiques du fétichisme' ('this signifying practice, in the absence of any immediate historical perspective, limits its action to the exploration of the logical and ideological resources of fetishism').[18] Moreover, it seems that for Kristeva it might be *poetry itself* which is fetishistic, through its proposition of: 'le matériau même du langage poétique comme object prédominant du plaisir' ('the very material of language as the predominant object of pleasure').[19] Poetry evidently involves a certain indulgence in the *orality* of language. For Kristeva, as a psychoanalyst, this is a stage which the subject needs to move beyond; the poet (Mallarmé, Artaud) is a sick patient in need of cure. What saves the text, though, from fetishism is *signification, meaning*: 'il (le texte) est tout autre qu'un fétiche parce qu'il signifie, c'est à dire qu'il n'est pas un substitut mais un *signe*' ('The text is completely different from a fetish because it *signifies*: in other words, it is not a *substitute* but a *sign*').[20]

Mallarmé's poetry, in Kristeva's assessment of it, seems not so much fetishistic as tending towards fetishism. But in this view, poetry in general would tend towards fetishism as it inevitably invests more in the pleasure of language as object than in the production of sense—and Mallarmé's poetry in particular, without losing its hold on sense, moves towards that indulgence in oral pleasure which Kristeva connotes negatively as fetishism.

This indulgence, which might lead to a consideration of Mallarmé's less serious, less theoretically highlighted texts, the *Vers de circonstance*, for example, or of the particular sensory qualities of Mallarmé's *univers imaginaire*, analysed by Jean-Pierre Richard,[21] seems belittled by Kristeva, despite her emphasis on laughter.[22] The laughter she affirms is more of a Lautréamontian or Bataillean order. It contrasts with Mallarmé's *smile*. Indulgence loses favour in relation to the higher, more sublime aims of the process, of cure. Kristeva's analysis of the materiality of signifiers in Mallarmé's writing, posed against Richard's postulation of an imaginary space, seems to denigrate the materiality of signifiers, if not that of signifieds, through the proposition of their determination by the transcendent theoretical space of the semiotic, the drive, and the ideal of the process. This is to simplify matters, of course: Kristeva's readings insist on the materiality of both signifier *and* signified; poetry is both matter and sense. My suggestion is, however, that there is a severity and an ethical rigour in Kristeva's mode of criticism which denies us indulgence in the pleasures of the poetic object.

This apparent tension between what I have called *indulgence* and *process* can be illuminated through a discussion of narcissism. For Kristeva, in *Histoires d'amour*, modernity is haunted by the figure of Narcissus. As a link to the previous discussion we can propose that the positioning of the fetish against the shattering of the body, against the violence of the semiotic, can also be articulated as a closure, a reflexivity in an enclosed space. Mallarmé also holds a pivotal, if less explicit position in this genealogy. The prose poem 'Le nénuphar blanc' ('The White Water-Lily') is read as a version of the myth of Narcissus.[23] If Narcissus haunts modernity, Kristeva argues, Mallarmé's Narcissus is empty, hollow, 'vide': 'Comme toute la modernité, Mallarmé a hérité de l'espace psychique narcissien, mais cet espace est désormais vide; "rien n'aura eu lieu que le lieu" ' ('Like all our contemporaries, Mallarmé inherited the Narcissan psychic space. But this space is henceforth empty. "Nothing will have taken place but the place" ').[24] This vacancy is contrasted to the auto-erotic plenitude in Gidean Narcissism, which amounts to a religion of the self.

If we look at the text itself of 'Le nénuphar blanc' we can agree that Mallarmé's Narcissus, a flower which envelops in its hollow whiteness 'un rien fait de songes intacts, du bonheur qui n'aura pas lieu' ('a nameless nothingness made of unbroken reveries, a happiness never to be'),[25] an imaginary trophy 'qui ne se gonfle d'autre chose sinon de la conscience exquise de soi' ('which bursts only with that exquisite absence of self')[26] is an empty place, found by the poet as 'maraudeur aquatique' ('watery prowler')[27] in the 'canaux labyrinthiques et embourbés d'une navigation indécidable' ('the labyrinthine and muddy canals of an undecideable sailing').[28] That 'l'espace psychique narcissien' is an empty space inhabited only by its taking place provides another powerful example for Kristeva. The shattering and the constellation of language arise from an *espace psychique vide* (*empty psychic space*) which is not sterile but explosive, a negativity both violent and productive. (The previous displacement from the apparently banal 'le hasard' to violence is echoed by this sense of threat and the terror of 'le vide' behind the serenity of the colour white.) So the example that Mallarmé's Narcissus offers modernity, and Kristeva's theorization of Mallarmé, is of an explosive, shattering negativity frozen in a form—word, poem, or flower—(Rimbaud's 'explosante fixe') which is constantly threatened by the possibility of explosion or implosion into the black hole of its own emptiness. Nothing takes place but the place, and this place is purely symbolic. The poet as explorer of this underground or underwater also risks the implosion of identity, and Kristeva's reading of Artaud explores this eventuality. Again, however, Mallarmé's position in Kristeva's schema appears ambiguously unproductive in relation to this explosive negativity. In contrast to Bataille's laugh or Artaud's scream, Kristeva interprets Mallarmé's smile as 'cette énigme qui conjoint l'ironie du professeur fin de siècle et le désabusement métaphysique devant la vacuité des symboles' ('an enigma that links the irony of a turn-of-the-century professor with the metaphysical disillusionment faced with the emptiness of symbols').[29] The same gesture occurs in Kristeva's book on abjection, *Pouvoirs de l'horreur*: as counterpoint to the joy in abjection of Céline, Mallarmé offers her 'la beauté blanche, sereine et nostalgique, toujours déjà désuète' ('the stainless, serene, nostalgic beauty, always already antiquated').[30] While the poem is an 'arabesque', a 'tracé elliptique' ('an elliptical marking')[31] which, like the flower, holds nothing and comes from nothing, the form of the poem is curiously sterile, always already defunct. Form as such, or form conceived as structure and solidity rather than process, is a dead thing, and the attention of the critic is drawn rather to the more seductive empty chamber of explosive negativity from which poetic form derives. In this light, Kristeva may inherit a lot from Blanchot: the absolute tension of form always pointing to the absence that is both within it and behind it recalls Blanchot's stress on the 'absence de Livre' and the *silence* of Mallarmé. Poetic form itself is 'merely' the provisional place necessary for its own destruction.

The fact that for Kristeva this negativity seems explosive and violent seems also to point back to a rhetoric of *political* terror with which Blanchot's career, but also that of Bataille, is entangled.[32] Reminding ourselves of Jean Paulhan's opposition between Rhetoric and Terror, in *Les fleurs de Tarbes*,[33] may suggest, however, that the version of revolution suggested by Kristeva is more on the side of Rhetoric than Terror, more on the side of a constant process of integration of violence through the mechanisms of sense, than the effacement of all *topoi*. Two models of revolution are offered: Cure or Terror, and key in this distinction is the role played by the negative.

Negativity dominates the early period of Kristeva's analyses of poetic language up to the moment when it becomes psychoanalytically redefined as the 'semiotic'. A key text in this regard is Kristeva's 'Poésie et négativité'.[34] Following Hegel, Kristeva describes negativity as 'absolute difference', 'exclusive of identity and of itself'. Moreover, negation remains the fundamental operation (*démarche*) of signification, since to pose the existence of something is to differentiate it from another thing: 'L'opération logique *négation* qui semble être à la base de toute activité symbolique (dans la mesure où elle est à la base de la *différence* et de la *différenciation*, comme le remarque Hegel), est le point névralgique où s'articule le fonctionnement symbolique' ('The logical operation of negation which seems to be at the base of all symbolic activity (to the extent that it is at the base of difference and differentiation, as Hegel remarks), is the nerve centre around which the symbolic function is articulated').[35] Kristeva undertakes a detailed reading of Plato to show that while symbolism and judgement depend on negation conceived as differentiation, the negative itself is excluded from the domain of speech and judgement. The negated object is banished 'hors discours' ('outside discourse') and appears only as something essentially other and excluded, as falsity, death, fiction or madness.

Poetry, then, is a fundamentally negative operation. The operation of intertextuality, the series De Quincey–Poe–Baudelaire–Mallarmé, for example, consists in the negation of the anterior textual corpus and the affirmation of this negation. Negativity is also operative in the refusal of denotative sense and linear syntax and the absorption of this negation in the affirmative enunciation of a *volume* of sense. It operates in a negation of linear and monovalent meaning and the pluralization and infinitization of meaning.

Kristeva points to Poe's 'Nevermore' as inauguration of this operation in modern poetry: 'Le premier dans la modernité à fonder son texte sur la négation . . . est peut-être Poe avec le "never more" du *Corbeau*, ce "jamais plus" jamais égal à lui-même' ('Perhaps the first writer in the modern era to have founded his text on negation . . . is Poe with the "Nevermore" of "The Raven", a refrain which is never the same as itself').[36] Kristeva insists, however, that Mallarmé 'était un des premiers à comprendre' ('was one of the first to understand'),[37] and 'le premier [qui] en a fait la théorie de même que la pratique' ('and was the first to have formulated its theory as well as its practice').[38] *Igitur* and *Un coup de dés* are 'drames écrits qui mettent en scène le processus même de la production du texte littéraire' ('written performances which dramatize the very process of production of the literary text').[39] *Igitur* is a submission to the Law and the abolition of 'le hasard', while *Un coup de dés* negates *Igitur* (the Law) and elaborates the new laws of 'le hasard'—resulting in an 'entrelacement déroutant du positif et du négatif' ('a disturbing interweaving of the positive and the negative').[40] Mallarmé's letters, especially around the 'crise' are also glossed as a struggle with negativity. Thought thinks itself, negates itself, and what results is the impersonal play of negation as 'la démarche fondamentale de la signification' ('the fundamental movement of signification').[41] Mallarmé's poetry is ruled by negativity, as the affirmation of negation, at various levels, on the level of sense, or intertexuality, on the level of the relation of one text to another (*Igitur—Un coup de dés*) and on the level of the subject's struggle with 'le Néant'.

On this basis, we can propose a definition of Mallarmé's revolution in poetic language as Kristeva theorizes, and tie together some of the strands of argument established thus far. The pure violence of negativity, of non-Being, without mediation through discourse, is inconceivable; this is what defines it as violence. The refusal of this mediation of negativity through discourse leads to the installation of an immutable, absolutely static Law: Robespierre and the Terror. Revolution in Kristeva's sense implies the absorption of the negative into the affirmative, the affirmation of the negation. The Law absorbs the explosive negativity which shatters discourse, fixes this shattering, relaunches the process, fixes and masters again the negative, and so on. It corresponds to the mechanism of the sublime, in the sense that it operates through a representation of an unrepresentable terror or violence against thought.[42] Kristeva's *revolution*, premised on the Bataillean model of transgression, itself premised ambiguously on a Hegelian dialectical process, appears strangely dedicated to the conservation of order rather than to its destruction, and it is easy in this light to see how the rhetoric of revolution in Kristeva's work of the mid-70s shifts to the rhetoric of cure, in the late 70s, 80s and 90s. Poetic language, like theory, operates through a sublation of negativity which does not for all that lead to the end of history or to Absolute Spirit, but to the fragile maintenance of the symbol. Opposed to Terror, Rhetoric is able to master explosive negativity and to introduce mobility into the fixity of form. Mallarmé's poem/flower is able, in this sense, to evade the terror of absolutely empty fixity through the sense it produces in its reading.

Kristeva's reading of Mallarmé imbricates the meaning of 'revolution in poetic language' with the political realities of '*the* Revolution' through itself being tied in to its context: the journal and group *Tel Quel*.[43] The 1974 statement from 'The Novel as Polylogue' about marrying the violence that gnaws within is also an encoded reference to her marriage in 1968 to Philippe Sollers, the subject of the essay and ostensible director of the *Tel Quel* group. Another autobiographical essay, 'Mémoire'[44] recalls that a topic of lively discussion among intellectuals on her arrival in France in 1965 was a talk Sollers had recently given on Mallarmé at Roland Barthes's seminar. The name Mallarmé is tied in to her arrival in France and her becoming French; she 'marries' Mallarmé, a Mallarmé whose name is also intrinsic to the revolution proposed in *Tel Quel*.

The moment of this juncture, between Mallarmé and a revolutionary project, is Sollers's 'Littérature et totalité',[45] the essay on Mallarmé which prefaces Kristeva's arrival in France and which will exert a powerful influence on her own version of Mallarmé. Echoing Blanchot, Sollers writes of a 'nouvel *espace littéraire*' ('a new literary space'),[46] in which Mallarmé's position is pivotal, since his experience of literature is the most explicit. Rejecting the image of Mallarmé as symbolist ('évoquant un aspect désuet, renfermé, idéalisant, littéraire dans le plus mauvais sens du mot' ('evoking the literary in the worst sense of the word: an obsolete, constricting, idealizing element, an aesthetic decadentism'),[47] and as poet, Sollers cites Blanchot's transgressive vision of the 'espace littéraire' for which genres are limits to be broken. The image of literature as *project*, which seems inherited from Blanchot, also determines the futural temporality in which Sollers positions Mallarmé's work. In a statement which programmes Kristeva's notion of the 'future anterior' (which I discuss later) Sollers writes:

> La 'question Mallarmé' désigne aujourd'hui un passé et un avenir ou plutôt ce point du temps où la distinction passé—avenir se dissipe, où le passé semble accessible de toutes parts et l'avenir paraît refluer vers nous; ce point, ce tournant de l'histoire qui se donne comme fin de l'histoire; ce *commencement du retour* dont

nous ne sommes encore qu'à déchiffrer . . . les effets im-
prévisibles.[48]

(Today, the 'Mallarmé question' designates both a past and a
future, or rather this point in time where the past–future
distinction dissolves, where the past seems accessible from every
direction and the future appears to flow back toward us; this
historical turning point that presents itself as the end of history;
this *beginning of the return* whose unforeseeable effects . . . we
are only beginning to decipher.)

The Mallarmé question is positioned at the point at which the past
returns *as a future*, in other words, on the revolutionary horizon where
the past will catch up with itself. The *projective* nature of the literary
project (for *Tel Quel*), which empties itself out of itself (such that it
leaves the name 'literature' behind) and throws itself into the future,
is also determined, according to Sollers, by the idea that 'literature
is much more than literature'.[49] It exceeds itself and in so doing
denies itself. But the step that makes this exposition more than simply
parallel to versions of political revolution, but entangled with them,
is that this excessive emptying out of literature into the future, the
projective nature of literature attains a totality, such that it concerns
not *just* literature but *everything*: 'Révolution considérable, donc, et
qui place chacun devant sa propre responsabilité en vue d'une pratique
qui doit, non plus métaphoriquement (les belles-lettres cachaient la
littérature, la rhétorique cachait l'écriture) mais littéralement "tout
recréer"' ('A major revolution, then, and one that confronts each of
us with our responsibility toward a practice that must, no longer
metaphorically (*belles-lettres* were hiding literature, rhetoric was
hiding writing) but literally, "recreate everything"').[50] In other words,
the revolution turns us all into readers, and the world into a text.
The ethical imperative of assuming responsibility for life as a writing
or as a *creative practice* has an almost Sartrean resonance: the subject
is a project, a process always in view of a resolution in the future.
The project of literature is moreover an action 'qui s'adresse au
contraire délibérément et lucidement au futur par une opération
radicale' ('that deliberately and lucidly addresses itself to the future
by means of a radical operation').[51] The present is nothing more than
an illusion, but there remains the necessity to live in it. Sollers closes

his essay with a consideration of this necessity, citing Mallarmé's phrase: 'l'interrègne' ('the interregnum').[52] The poet whose life has disappeared into the impersonality of the project—to write—can only live the present as an inconvenience. But, Sollers argues, because of the disdain for any attachments to the present in terms of property 'il découvre aussi une coïncidence imprévue avec l'individu le plus aliéné: le prolétaire . . . Par une circularité étrange, l'homme qui n'*est* rien et celui qui n'*a* rien sont donc en profonde solidarité' ('he discovers an unforeseen coincidence with the most alienated individual, the proletarian . . . By virtue of a strange circularity, the man who *is* nothing and the one who *has* nothing are thus profoundly joined').[53] Literature, then, like revolution, belongs to the future: 'La littérature appartient à l'avenir . . .'.[54] Mallarmé is revolutionary because of the futural dimension of his work.

It is in the extensive volume *Révolution du langage poétique* that Kristeva endeavours to tie the dimension of the revolutionary project into an analysis of Mallarmé's texts. She does this essentially through a focus on the shattering and the constellation of language, the two effects referred to earlier as intrinsic to the Mallarmean operation as Kristeva theorizes it. These operations are effected at the level of *syntax* and at the level of the *phoneme*; Mallarmé operates a transformation of syntax and a musicalization of language through work at the phonemic level.

In the middle section of *Revolution du langage poétique*[55] Kristeva proposes that Mallarmé's poetry and prose operate through a transformation of a linear syntax which, at certain moments, introduces elements of undecidability. The difficulty of Mallarmé's syntax is not a result of a 'simple', quantitative complexity, but of an element of undecidability such that the recovery of linear sentences with subject, verb and object is disallowed. But this does not mean that the texts are ungrammatical. The Mallarmean phrase is not lacking in syntax but overburdened with it, in a manner which recalls Freud's condensation. The reading of the poem does not produce denotative sense from sentences centred on the action of a subject upon an object, but produces what Kristeva refers to as a *volume* of meaning, which we might translate as *evocation*, or *effect*. We can recall Mallarmé's statement: 'Peindre, non la chose, mais l'effet qu'elle produit' ('To paint, not the thing itself, but the effect that it produces'). Whence, for Kristeva, the disappearance of the subject, 'disparition illocutoire du poète' ('the illocutory disappearance of the poet')(cited in several instances by Kristeva), the elision of the verb, for example in much of *Un coup de dés*,[56] whose title itself Kristeva reads as a transformation into an impersonal form of 'Il lança les dés', and the destruction of the object, in favour of its evocation, the suggestion of its absence. Kristeva's model of *negativity*—the affirmation of the negation—corresponds to each of these levels: disappearance of the subject, for example, affirmed in an impersonal, intransitive writing whose motto is '*ça s'écrit*' ('It writes . . .'). Kristeva's theorization, and her analysis of Mallarmé, do give a convincing picture of the evocation, the impersonality, the syntactic irreducibility of the poet—and Mallarmé's 'theoretical' writings also seem to justify, *avant la lettre*, the theory of the text which Kristeva proposes.

At the phonemic level, Kristeva's description gives the image of a fine network of rhythm, alliteration, assonance, repetition, stretched across the typographic lozenge of the poem, a 'constellation' which in Mallarmé's terms is *literalized* with *Un coup de dés*. This is a 'musicalization' of language, which will be continued in the next century by Joyce. Syntactic transformation is supplemented by a further level of organization, not confined or limited by the word but using the phoneme as minimal unit, creating a supplementary meaning from effects of rhythm and repetition *and* from semantic associations of particular phonemes, even letters. Kristeva's major authority in this proposition is Saussure's 'Anagrammes', which read encoded signifiers dispersed across the text of Latin poems.[57] She invents the neologism 'paragram' to account for the dispersion of sense *across* the poem, but Barthes's 'starred' text,[58] and Derrida's *dissemination*[59] also refer to this effect in different ways. The phoneme, then, is not simply an element of the word, but a signifier in itself, which can thus be read in terms of its pulsional significance, or its semantic associations. In analysing the former aspect—the pulsional significance of the phoneme—Kristeva refers as an authority to the work of Ivan Fónagy on the 'pulsional bases of phonation',[60] and in analysing the latter aspect—the semantic associations of phonemes or letters—she has recourse to Mallarmé's *Les Mots anglais*.[61]

Kristeva reads Mallarmé's poem 'Prose' for the 'differential of signifiers' that it carries—the constellation of sense at the phonemic level and the pulsional signification which it produces. In doing so she refers to the work of Robert Greer Cohn, whose analysis she describes as untheorized and empirical 'faute de justifier théoriquement et linguistiquement le principle de sa lecture' ('for not having theoretically or linguistically justified the principles of his reading').[62] The pulsional signification of phonemes is, however, deduced 'intuitively', while in referring to Mallarmé's *Les Mots anglais* Kristeva unwittingly enters into a debate of which she is apparently ignorant, around the use-value of this text, which Mallarmé had dismissed as a 'besogne dont il sied de ne pas parler' ('textbook which it would be well not to mention').[63] The obvious question about the use-value of a text on the significance of English words, over which Gérard Genette and Greer Cohn disagree,[64] is minor, however, in comparison with the question of the critical strategy Kristeva adopts in referring to this text. It is a strategy, moreover, which characterizes her whole approach to Mallarmé: a text in which Mallarmé is evidently *indulging* his pleasure in language is sublated into the theoretical cornerstone of his work. He thus appears as not only theorizing his own poetic production *at the time*, but also founding the theory which will, *après coup*, be used as the basis of an analysis of his poetic production. Greer Cohn's analysis remains *untheorized* and *empirical* precisely to the extent that it *indulges* Mallarmé's pleasure in language without transcendentalizing it as theoretical foundation.

This difference, between *indulgence* and *theorization* is also a difference concerning temporality which has implications at the *political* level. Our distinction between the two levels at which the 'revolution in poetic language' could be discussed (the image of 'revolution' and the transformation of language by poetry) leaves out a major factor—that the two levels are, or should be, linked. This 'should be' is the ethical and political thrust of *Tel Quel* and of Kristeva's work—the revolution in poetic language *should* coincide with a 'cultural revolution', given the right circumstances. 'The right circumstances' do not, however, arrive, and, while politics and culture limp behind constrained by the bounds of power and by the economic relations of production, poetry is forced to repeat itself in what Kristeva refers to as the 'future anterior'. It projects itself onto the utopian horizon from where it announces: 'the revolution will have happened'. There is no essential difference between the rhetoric of revolution and Kristeva's later ethical mode, where she also seems to imply 'at the end you will have been cured'.

The Mallarmé who is used as example by *Tel Quel* and Kristeva is thus the one who postulates a future for literature which does not yet exist. The image of Mallarmé which *Tel Quel* and Kristeva offer us is thus a Mallarmé who 'will have been'. The works which are most consistently appealed to are those of Mallarmé's writings which are either not works as such but constructed as works after the event ('Hérodiade', 'Le tombeau d'Anatole'), or projects for works (the *Livre*). Mallarmé is in the same position as the working class in postulating a revolutionary horizon and experiencing the present as *project*.

There is certainly this element in Mallarmé's concerns. In the text 'Autobiographie' he writes:

> Au fond je considère l'époque contemporaine comme un interrègne pour le poète qui n'a point à s'y mêler: elle est trop en désuétude et en effervescence préparatoire pour qu'il ait autre chose à faire qu'à travailler avec mystère en vue de plus tard ou de jamais et de temps en temps à envoyer aux vivants sa carte de visite, stances ou sonnet, pour n'être point lapidé d'eux, s'ils le soupçonnent de savoir qu'ils n'ont pas lieu.[65]

> (Essentially, I feel that our time is an interregnum for the poet; he should stay out of it; it is at once too obsolete and too seething with preparation; all he can do is work in mystery with an eye to the future or to eternity, and occasionally send his visiting card, a few stanzas, or a sonnet to the 'living', so that they won't stone him should they suspect him of realizing that they do not exist).

This is a *topos* of poetry, of course, of which Baudelaire's 'Albatros' is another example, but it also lends fuel to a vision of Mallarmé as producing a mystery whose sense will only be revealed in the future. The present is an 'interrègne', but Mallarmé's description of his time as 'trop en désuétude et en effervescence préparatoire' could as much apply to a vision of a Symbolist, 'fin de siècle' Mallarmé disdaining any politics of revolt ('effervescence') arising from 'la foule', as it does to a Mallarmé projecting a revolutionary future onto the horizon. The present is an intermediary space in which 'des contemporains ne savent pas lire' ('my contemporaries don't know how to read'),[66] but the present is also the time in which the poet sends his 'cartes de visite' to the living. The present is the time of the 'vers de circonstance', poems written 'aux loisirs de la poste', poems written on Easter eggs—concessions to the necessities and pleasures of the moment.

To the future anterior is opposed *circonstance*, then, and to revolution and cure an indulgence in the pleasures of the moment, in the pleasures of the poem as fetishistic object, for example. Like many other modern readers of Mallarmé, Kristeva concentrates on works which barely attain that status and point to the absence of work: the fragments of the *Livre*, 'Hérodiade', 'Le tombeau d'Anatole', or works such as *Un coup de dés* and *Igitur*, which are proposed to constitute the kernel of Mallarmé's œuvre. Most significant is the use of the prose pieces not as poetic material but as example and legitimation, foundation of a theory. The exceptions to this are Kristeva's reading of 'Prose' in terms of its 'differential of signifiers', and her later fairly fragmentary comments on 'Le nénuphar blanc'. In *Tel Quel*, Sollers takes most of his material from 'Crayonné au théâtre', and Pierre Rottenberg analyses *Igitur*. The major omission is the *verse* of Mallarmé, so that we are offered an image of Mallarmé as theorist of poetry and author of one canonical, exemplary text (*Un coup de dés*), rather than as poet. The Blanchotian movement, whereby the work points to its own absence, seems to operate also in the *Tel Quel* image of Mallarmé. The postulation of a future in revolution or cure tends to reduce the investment in the work itself—especially the poetry, which is thereby denied in favour of the work which negates itself in favour of its transcendental horizon.

The image that this reading of Mallarmé in Kristeva and *Tel Quel* gives is of a criticism which is also a performance. In its relation to the object it studies, this mode of criticism tends to deny the value of the object if it fails to offer a legitimation of the theoretical assumptions of the critic. The image offered is thus of a curiously circular operation whereby Mallarmé offers Kristeva an opportunity to legitimate and found the theory she uses to read Mallarmé, or other writers. This may be the shape of theory itself, or of reading itself, which must always involve a *participation* in the text read. If criticism necessarily involves an element of *reflexivity* then the critical relation will always tell us less about the literary object than the critic. It is the nature of this reflexivity and this participation which are the basic features of the critical relation. Participation in the literary object necessarily complicates the notion of a pure reflection. Reading, as participation, throws a spanner in the works of a theory which calls for a strict, allegorical reflection of itself. Kristeva and *Tel Quel*'s version of Mallarmé is certainly not of the order of this pure reflection, as the theory they offer is one which bases itself on the practice of reading and writing. Participation, or reading, as a pure enjoyment in form, is problematized, nevertheless, by the element of reflexivity involved. Indulgence in reading 'for its own sake' is disallowed, since the reflection which is demanded is one devoted to a higher, transcendent ideal. In conclusion I would offer the proposal that the critical relation involves a conflict between the demands of theory (reflection and legitimation) and those of reading (participation and indulgence).

11

The Mirage of Critical Distance
The Mallarmé of Yves Bonnefoy

Clive Scott

1. A preliminary confrontation

> Je te voyais courir sur des terrasses,
> Je te voyais lutter contre le vent,
> Le froid saignait sur tes lèvres.
>
> Et je t'ai vue te rompre et jouir d'être morte ô plus belle
> Que la foudre, quand elle tache les vitres blanches de ton sang.
>
> (I saw you running on the terraces, / I saw you fight against the
> wind, / The coldness bled on your lips. / And I have seen you
> break and rejoice at being dead—O more beautiful / Than the
> lightning, when it stains the white windowpanes of your blood.)

The mythic, ritual and originary significances of this, the first poem
in Bonnefoy's *Du mouvement et de l'immobilité de Douve* (1953), have
been admirably analysed by Thélot.[1] But what, faced with these lines,
would come to the mind of a reader of Mallarmé's verse?

The poem opens with two decasyllables, a verse-line Mallarmé
never turned to. For Bonnefoy, the decasyllable, at least as it is found
in *Le Chanson de Roland*, 'y draine l'obscur, de son rythme double
(quatre pieds comme l'éternel, six comme le temps) étendant sa paix
sur la terre' ('drains darkness away, with its twofold rhythm (four
syllables for the eternal, six for time) spreading peace over the earth');[2]
as he makes clear elsewhere[3] the decasyllable admits human time by
'un acte de sympathie' ('an act of sympathy'), only to re-absorb it into
the eternal. Bonnefoy finds other metrical means of installing this

blend of the stable and the contingent, of the absolute and the random, but the decasyllable, particularly in a 6//4 form which symbolically releases him from the classical 4//6 model,[4] remains an important pattern of utterance.

But in order to speak of these first two lines as metrical decasyllables, rather than as nonce lines which happen to be ten syllables each, we really need the evidence of isosyllabism as a structural principle: it is the lineal context which defines the line as verse-line (rather than as a line of verse).[5] Without this support, the measure, a rhythmic *constituent* of the line, begins to take precedence over the line itself as the rhythmic determinant. The measure, with its new autonomy, makes the line a product of episodes, incidents, encounters, something componential. In the fourth line here, we may argue that an alexandrine—

Et je t'ai vue te rompre et jouir d'être morte 4+2+3+3

—becomes a fifteen-syllable line thanks to the addition of an apostrophe ('ô plus belle'), attached seamlessly to the line by a positive act of non-punctuation. Bonnefoy's lines may strike us as the temporary products of processes of *montage* and *démontage*. In Mallarmé's verse, the line maintains its transcendental authority, its intransitive design, its preordained field of rhythmic possibility; he proposes a version of the alexandrine which transforms it from a *vers composé* (i.e. composed of two hexasyllabic sub-units) to a *vers simple* (integrated dodecasyllable), without structural 'interruptions'.[6] Bonnefoy would consider this as part of the Mallarmean line's drive towards formal closedness, towards acoustic self-absorption, as it severs its contacts with the world.

The poem begins, too, with a syntactical repetition, alien to Mallarmé's verse where language seems to be given to the divagatory and self-distracting, which poetic form ultimately surprises with a destination. Repetition, in Bonnefoy, is part of a tireless re-centring of language, a liturgical movement, an or(atoric)al movement of *ressaisissement de soi* (recovery of self), controlling, harnessing. Origins are constantly returned to, and responsibility assumed.

The poem's last line, on the other hand, will remind us that, for Bonnefoy, the mute e is a crucial resource of verse. He taxes Valéry with not having understood its true value, as a point of leakage in formal closure, a fault which undoes conceptual complacency: 'cette faille entre les concepts, cette intuition de la substance, cette chance extraordinaire du français' ('this fissure between concepts, this intuition of matter, this extraordinary opportunity for French') (*L'Improbable*, 105). Elsewhere (*Poétique d'Yves Bonnefoy*, 32, 41 and 255) he indicates that the mute e has the capacity to express fruitful hesitation, the sense of the poem's blind field, or, indeed, 'l'équilibre ou la tension qui existe entre le réel et l'esprit' ('the balance or tension which exists between reality and spirit'). Rather, then, than being a syllable of facilitation, of liaison and elastication, the e, for Bonnefoy, is a gap, something which lets in finitude; it is mortality made palpable, like the snowflakes of which he writes:

On dirait beaucoup d'e//muets dans une phrase. 3+3//2+4

(You would say it was many mute e's in a phrase)

Here the caesura creates the very hesitation that the e is. I have tried to demonstrate elsewhere[7] that the e, for Mallarmé too, is an agent of formal equivocation, a moment of existential fragility; he himself writes that formal regularity can only be tolerated thanks to the unstable nature of the e's perceptibility:

J'ai toujours pensé que l'*e* muet était un moyen fondamental du vers et même j'en tirais cette conclusion en faveur du vers régulier, que cette syllabe à volonté, omise ou perçue, autorisait l'apparence du nombre fixe, lequel frappé uniformément et réel devient insupportable autrement que dans les grandes occasions.[8]

(I have always thought that the mute e was a fundamental resource of verse and I even concluded, in favour of regular verse, that this optional syllable, either omitted or perceived, justified an apparently fixed syllabic quota, which, if made real and consistently counted out, becomes intolerable on all but grand occasions.)

How hermetic is Mallarmean closure? His emphasis on verbal transitions, on the acoustic continuity of the line, in no way precludes the vagaries of readerly perception and of paralinguistic input. At all events, Bonnefoy's last line here is a feast of articulated e's, occurring at a moment of revelatory instantaneousness ('la foudre') when a death-affiliated writing ('sang') becomes possible ('tache les vitres blanches').

One might expect that part of the project of turning poetry outwards, of opening it to its blind field, would be a preference for tense (external time) over modality (attitudinal or inner time). Although in this poem we may suspect the unfolding of a drama or rite which takes us from a relatively stable past to a violent, sacrificial present, these tenses have a high degree of ambiguity (Is the imperfect durative or iterative? Is the present punctual, iterative or omnitemporal?) which inevitably engages modal values: the sense of pacification and clear-sightedness in the imperfect, perhaps; the sense of responsibility accepted in the perfect; the sense of apprehensive urgency in the present. Conversely, one might expect that, in all of Mallarmé's tense usage, external time is absorbed into modality or the temporal perspective of inner fictions. But from time to time, one feels the irresistible beckonings of a contact externally located (as in 'Sonnet', *Œuvres complètes*, 60):

Comme un éventail frais dans la chambre s'étonne
A raviver du peu qu'il faut ici d'émoi
Toute notre native amitié monotone.

(As a fresh fan in the room surprises itself / By reviving with the little emotion here required / All our monotonous native friendship.)

One might have expected, too, that Bonnefoy's verse would not draw attention to its acoustic play. Although, in speaking of verse, he underlines the materiality with which it is endowed by rhyme, alliteration, assonance, he has nothing to say about the acoustic resourcefulness of the poets and poems he cites. A strange silence? For Bonnefoy, acoustic effects are part of the way in which a poem's autonomous textuality, its liberation into its own field of signifying play, its liberation from its author, are exacerbated. Bonnefoy regrets the attitudes to text developed by structuralism and post-structuralism. But this poem has all the acoustic scintillation of a Mallarmean text. Since the poem seems to be about the acquisition of a voice, through a sacrificial spilling of blood, through the orgasm of death, then we are bound to find that voice in perceptual cognition—the /vwa/ which is in 'voyais'—and, voicelessly, in the blood's other source /fRwa/ (the air whose bite is as powerful as the fire of 'foudre'). The achievement of voice seems to derive from a reciprocity: the /ã/ of 'ton sang' is already in the 'vitres blanches', but is also in the 'vent', where the voiced consonant also is. And the cold which bled has taken the place of 'Je' as subject, perhaps *is* the 'Je' (/ʒə/) looking for a consummation in a kiss, and then in 'jouir'; the cold bleeds on the lips which will speak, just as you bleed on the white sheets which will speak (their writing). Even the /Rə/ ending creates a suggestive constellation: 'lèvres' joins with 'vitres' through the mediation of 'rompre', 'être' and 'foudre'.[9]

Finally one might mention determiners. Mallarmé's necessary journey, from the accidental to the essential, from the indefinite article to the definite article, from the common noun to the proper noun (as, in 'Le vierge, le vivace et le bel aujourd'hui', 'un cygne' becomes 'le Cygne') is one shared by Bonnefoy, but the same terms, in his critical idiom, have a rather different weight. Bonnefoy's definite article is a guarantor of presence, of the density of being, and of committed spectation; the indefinite article, on the other hand, is a casual and non-penetrative interest. Of course, the definite article in French has a second, threatening dimension: it genericizes and conceptualizes, the last thing Bonnefoy wants of it; as he himself points out (*Poétique d'Yves Bonnefoy*, 260): 'Il y a en somme *concurrence* de l'article défini de la pensée conceptuelle et de l'article défini de la pensée poétique' ('In short, there is *contention* between the definite article of conceptual thought and the definite article of poetic thought'). This poem describes a movement from an indefinite article ('des terrasses') to definite ones ('la foudre', 'les vitres blanches'). And perhaps the syntactical ambiguity of 'de ton sang' (adverb of instrument or noun complement of 'les vitres blanches') tells us something about the relation of the definite article to the possessive adjective: the definite article is both established as being *other* than the possessive, by superseding the possessive, and, on condition of that supersession, is also possessed by it. The same dialectical reciprocity is to be found, for example, at the close of Mallarmé's 'Petit Air I':

> . . . si plonge
> Exultatrice à côté

Dans l'onde toi devenue
Ta jubilation nue.

(If into the wave become you | Exultingly alongside | Your naked jubilation dives.)

The definite article is a performative of placing, naming, the already there. The apostrophe, no less important to Bonnefoy, shifts naming to the exclamatory and responsive mode; as it designates, it invests with aura, with intensity. Mallarmé's apostrophes are equally moments of epiphany, of transfigured, because mere, being. Bonnefoy would argue that Mallarmean apostrophe is pure invocation, a corridor into absence, a way of putting stars into the night sky, of hyperbolic interiorization. But for both poets, at any rate, apostrophe is a pretext for substantivization—here, momentarily, of an adjective. Neither Mallarmé nor Bonnefoy allow the verb any privileges. And, like the e mute, the apostrophe is an optional element, an *available* syllable; in other words, from a metrical point of view, both mute e and apostrophe are *chevilles* (elements of padding, to make up syllabic number),[10] able to turn a *vers pair* (line with an even number of syllables) into a *vers impair* (line with an odd number of syllables), and vice versa. According to Bonnefoy (*L'Improbable*, 117): 'elles sont pourtant la seule réponse valable à l'ancienne prosodie close' ('they [*chevilles*] are, however, the only valid response to the traditional, closed prosody'). The apostrophe, splendidly, is both the lyricism of lyricism, a summit of relating, and also 'l'imperfection [qui] est la cime' ('the imperfection [which] is the summit').

2. Voices

First, there was the voice that Valéry listened to as it initiated him into the mysteries of *Un coup de dés*:

> Sur sa table de bois très sombre, carrée, aux jambes torses, il disposa le manuscrit de son poème; et il se mit à lire d'une voix basse, égale, sans le moindre 'effet', presque à soi-même.[11]

(He laid out the manuscript of his poem on his square table, with its very dark wood and twisted legs; and he began reading in a low, even voice, without the hint of an 'effect', almost to himself.)

This voice without artifice, this voice 'si belle intérieurement, et prise au plus près de sa source' ('so inwardly beautiful, tapped almost at its very source'), refuses to interpret, to show off the goods, to intervene between words and listener. This cannot but remind us of Bonnefoy's own reading voice, a voice whose echo he found in Seferis:

> C'est dans cet octobre déjà d'une poésie qui soit moins une formule qu'un acte, moins quelque bien qu'un désir, que Séféris a trouvé sa grandeur propre. Je n'en veux pour preuve que sa voix quand il lit, si magnifiquement, ses poèmes: voix sourde, retirée au profond de soi, monotone; voix qui consume l'objet pour y délivrer la présence; voix non possessive à jamais, comme la navigation d'île en île, comme le chant grégorien (*L'Improbable*, 244)

> (It is in this October light of a poetry less turn of phrase than act, less possession than desire, that Seferis found his inimitable greatness. As proof I need only his voice, reading his poems so magnificently: a muted voice, withdrawn to the depths of his being, monotoned; a voice which consumes the object only to liberate its presence; a forever non-possessive voice, like navigation from island to island, like Gregorian chant).

This is the 'voix unie' ('even/unified voice'), reading 'uniment' ('smoothly/unifiedly'), searching out the One in its imperturbable unfolding.

But part of Bonnefoy's diagnosis of the present predicament of the poetic voice is to be found in comments he makes about a letter written by Mallarmé to Lefébure 27 May 1867, in which Mallarmé recounts a walk in the fields and an encounter with a cricket:

> Je ne connaissais que le grillon anglais, doux et caricaturiste: hier seulement parmi les jeunes blés j'ai entendu cette voix sacrée de la terre ingénue, moins décomposée déjà que celle de l'oiseau, fils des arbres parmi de la nuit solaire, et qui a quelque chose des étoiles et de la lune, et un peu de mort;—mais combien plus

une surtout que celle d'une femme, qui marchait et chantait devant moi, et dont la voix semblait transparente de mille morts dans lesquelles elle vibrait—et pénétrée de Néant! Tout le bonheur qu'a la terre de ne pas être décomposée en matière et en esprit était dans ce son *unique* du grillon! (*Correspondance*, 355)

(I knew only the English cricket, a soft-toned caricaturist: it was not until yesterday, in the young corn, that I heard the sacred voice of the artless earth, son of the trees amid the solar night, with something of the stars and moon about it, and something of death; but how much more *one* it was than the voice of a woman who was walking and singing some steps in front of me; *her* voice seemed transparent with the thousand deaths in which it vibrated—and permeated with Nothingness! All the pleasure the earth takes in not being split up into matter and spirit was gathered in this cricket's *inalienable* sound).

Bonnefoy reads this passage with the error of the Mondor/Richard edition (1959): 'transparente de mille *mots*' rather than 'de mille morts'. Little matter. For him, it represents Mallarmé's poignant registration of the fact that language has irreversibly dispossessed us of a world with which we might, and indeed frequently do, coincide. We have the voice necessary to the task, 'aux sonorités nombreuses, maîtrisables' ('with its numerous and controllable sonorities'),[12] and the consciousness, but our language is invested with the 'néant' of words, which the cricket's cry is not. Bonnefoy returns to this Mallarmean passage in his preface to the poems of Marceline Desbordes-Valmore: 'La terre est *une*, les mots sont multiples, la parole en risque de rester, même chez un poète qui veut mourir à tout sauf l'esprit, subjective, "décomposé". Autrement dit le grillon prend figure ici d'inaccessible limite' ('The earth is *one*, words are multiple, and consequently language risks remaining, even in the hands of a poet ready to die to everything but the spirit, subjective and "split up". In other words, the cricket here represents an inaccessible limit').[13]

And yet Valéry's description of Mallarmé's reading will remind us perhaps of what Barthes calls 'le grain de la voix' ('the grain of the voice'), or 'l'écriture à haute voix' ('writing aloud'): 'son objectif n'est pas la clarté des messages, le théâtre des émotions; ce qu'elle cherche

... ce sont les incidents pulsionnels, c'est le langage tapissé de peau, un texte où l'on puisse entendre le grain du gosier, la patine des consonnes, la volupté des voyelles, toute une stéréophonie de la chair profonde' ('its aim is not the clarity of messages, the theatre of feelings; what it seeks are the pulsional incidents, language clothed in skin, a text in which can be heard the throat's grain, the patina of the consonants, the sensuousness of the vowels, a whole stereophony of deep flesh').[14] Uttering the 'douze timbres' of the alexandrine requires a sensitivity to phonemic quality, a willingness to let the language-music of text speak; but equally the reader's body affirms its presence in articulation, enunciation, as does 'toute l'âme résumée' ('all the soul summed up'). Bonnefoy's poetic voice, too, is anti-expressive; but it seeks, like the cricket, to enact through utterance the rite of being, the very presence of the 'other' in its naming. These voices share many features; the differences all hang on the site of being:

> A toute la nature apparenté et se rapprochant ainsi de l'organisme dépositaire de la vie, le Mot présente, dans ses voyelles et ses diphthongues, comme une chair; et dans ses consonnes comme une ossature délicate à disséquer (*Œuvres complètes*, 901)

> (Related to Nature in its wholeness, and thus sharing kinship with life-bearing organisms, the Word appears, in its vowels and diphthongs, as if made flesh; and, in its consonants, as if a delicate skeletal structure to be dissected).

3. The lesson of photography

How to create a verse which will embody the shifting configurations of the many becoming the One? In this enterprise, there is much to remind one of Cartier-Bresson's pursuit of the 'decisive moment'.[15] If a writer, Cartier-Bresson would have found his place 'somewhere between Mallarmé and Jules Renard or Flaubert'.[16] Bonnefoy applauds Cartier-Bresson's carelessness of film-processing, an aesthetic concern which must not assert itself at the expense of the object; and he claims that Cartier-Bresson is not subject to the photograph's 'image'-ness:

And a photograph, which is also an image, is less a reproduction
of the world than it is the point where this world effaces itself
before another world, the crossroad [sic] where we may decide
to prefer our 'self', with its myths, its poverties, its ghosts. And
it is clear, from the very first photographs by Cartier-Bresson
. . . that he is fundamentally opposed to this practice whether
it tends toward vulgar egocentricity or toward loftier creations.
(*Henri Cartier-Bresson*, 5–6)

We must suspect that certain Romantics, and then Mallarmé, lurk
in these last two noun phrases. And yet, elsewhere in this introduction, Mallarmé is referred to as 'another master of the evidence
of things', who 'also once declared himself an unconscious Buddhist'
(*Henri Cartier-Bresson*, 7).

How Bonnefoy must have envied Cartier-Bresson his medium: this
art of anticipated seeing, permanently informed by intuition, this
seeing which is split-secondly preceded by knowing, this instantly
responsive mobilization of the self, this perception unclouded by
analysis, this jumping, 'like a wild animal, on that which is in the
process of being born but also of dying' (*Henri Cartier-Bresson*, 6).
Cartier-Bresson has the spiritual readiness of a Zen monk, and
Bonnefoy moves easily on to the connection between photograph and
haiku:

What strikes me in these perceptions of the passing moment
—or, rather, in these seconds that deliver us—is that within
every gesture, movement, or sound that emerges from the
running step or the sounding voice is the same silence as in
the *haiku* or the *ukiyo-e*, those poems and prints which speak
of the universal cloud. And in it is this silence that reveals to
us what words differentiate to prompt action, or to arouse
sensations: awareness, dizziness, fear—all that is only a shadow,
the scale of the creature, with nothing of the whole trout's
quicksilver. (*Henri Cartier-Bresson*, 7)

These words reveal Bonnefoy's apprehensions about the
instrumentality of language, its insistence on a manipulative function,
its concern with achieving effects. This involves it in acts of
discrimination which undo the non-differentiatedness of unmediated
vision, the wholeness of capture. The One, the Absolute, must

breathe through the All. But these words reveal, too, strange contradictions in Bonnefoy's reading of himself and of Mallarmé.

4. Haiku, the part and the whole

Haiku, like the photograph, has no need of access to the transcendent; its whole business is to reveal the known to us, the world with its 'immanence encombrée' ('saturated immanence')[17] and its endless reciprocity. Mallarmé, Bonnefoy tells us, already has a yearning perception of these things: 'pour l'artiste oriental la dénomination, rêve-t-il, est transparence, est extase' ('for the Oriental artist designation, so he dreams, is transparency, is ecstasy') (*Entretiens*, 136). For Mallarmé, the Chinese are perhaps the only contemporary possessors of a Cratylic language. But for us, the dispossessed, who have sold our 'sens' for a mess of 'significations', who have put 'aspect' and 'essence' asunder and pursue either, but not both simultaneously, the haikuist looks like a blessed model. Through the very instantaneousness of his perception, the haikuist catches that moment, coincidence, which is both when chance participates in temporal design, and when All is also concerted co-presence. While the Occidental poet must use special means, the image, comparison, expressly to generate an inclusive and penetrative consciousness, the haikuist dazzles us with mere immediacy of presence, that mutual participation in being which is expressed by 'avec' rather than 'comme'. This spirit of the 'terre-à-terre' is beyond our courage as we look for those signs and symbols which will guarantee a transcendence.

Certainly Bonnefoy blamed Mallarmé for the death of the author and for the generation of that writerly approach to reading, of that reverence for text, which begets a ludic irresponsiblity in the critic; in 'Lever les yeux de son livre', he writes:

> Aujourd'hui, en effet, on perçoit dans la structure d'un texte, dans le rapport de ses mots entre eux, une réalité plus fiable et tangible que le sens qui court en surface, ou l'intention de l'auteur, ou l'être même de celui-ci, que problématisent jusqu'à en défaire les ambiguïtés de ses moindres phrases (*Entretiens*, 223)

(Today, in fact, we perceive in the structure of a text, in the relationship between its words, a more reliable and tangible reality than the meaning which runs across its surface, or the intention of the author, or the author's very being, which is problematized to the point of disaggregation by the ambiguities of its smallest units).

There are two factors in Bonnefoy's argument that are troubling: first, the introjection of a 'blind field' into verse, at one stroke thwarting the self-absorbed and systematic work of signification, in order to 'interrupt' it with *sens*. This view, that to look up from one's reading is to install the reader's world in the text, is at odds with that instantaneity, celebrated elsewhere, which draws parts of the world together in epiphanic revelation. How are we to reconcile instantaneity and inner duration (*temps vécu*) in Bonnefoy's thinking? Secondly, and relatedly, Bonnefoy's notion of interrupted reading lies along a line of propositions which also includes the necessary heterogeneity of the poem, and the recuperability of presence only in a fragmentary way. Mallarmé's verse, on the other hand, is devoted to the pursuit of a homogeneous unity:

> Un poème, en somme, si d'emblée il ne se limite pas à simplement quelques vers [the haiku?], n'est qu'un aggrégat où le hasard des divers moments de sa conception n'est jamais transcendé ni même aboli—de ce point de vue l'idée mallarméenne du livre, qui suppose l'écrit parfaitement homogène, et veut d'ailleurs que le lecteur s'y résorbe, me semble moins le premier principe sérieux d'une science moderne de l'écriture que le manifeste d'une certaine pensée, celle qui veut réduire un poème à des relations purement intraverbales, parce que le monde lui-même ne serait qu'une architecture d'essences intemporelles, vouées par leur naissance dans la région des Intelligibles à la dénomination par des mots aussi stables et transparents, dans leur relation mutuelle que les constellations dans le ciel. (*Entretiens*, 236)

> (A poem, in short, if it is not from the outset confined simply to a few lines [the haiku?], is only an aggregate in which the chance of the various moments of its making is never transcended or even abolished—from this point of view the Mallarmean idea of the book, which presupposes a perfectly homogeneous piece

of writing, and which moreover intends that the reader should be assimilated into it, seems to me not so much the first serious principle of a modern science of writing as the manifestness of a certain way of thinking, which would reduce a poem to purely intraverbal relationships, because the world itself would be no more than a structure of atemporal essences, destined by their birth in the realm of things intelligible to be designated by words as stable and transparent, in their reciprocal relations, as constellations in the sky.)

Perhaps what makes the haiku and the photograph so attractive to Bonnefoy is their formal paradoxicality: the complete fragment. At all events, Bonnefoy is a cultivator of the one-line anthology, whether it is lines from Yeats, or these from Marceline Desbordes-Valmore:[18]

> Jours heureux pleins de bruits que nuls bruits ne défont

> (Happy days full of sounds that no sounds undo)

> On ressemble au plaisir, sous un chapeau de fleurs.

> (We are like pleasure, beneath a flowery bonnet.)

Not surprisingly, Bonnefoy very rarely quotes *lines* from Mallarmé; instead, odd noun phrases—'salle d'ébène', 'guirlandes célèbres', 'bois oubliés', 'hiver sombre'—litter his discourse, alluding to a whole œuvre.

Bonnefoy is impatient with Saussure's arbitrariness of the sign. Ultimately he would wish this arbitrariness away, either by affirming that our relationship with words has such a history that we *do* know what we are talking about, or that verse context has a way of mitigating the effect of the arbitrariness of the single lexical sign. There would here seem to be an inconsistency. Mallarmé taxes Coppée with highlighting the individual lexical item:

> Sans qu'il y ait d'espace entre eux, et quoiqu'ils se touchent à merveille, je crois que quelquefois vos mots vivent un peu trop de leur propre vie comme les pierreries d'une mosaïque de joyaux (*Correspondance*, 330)

(Although there is no space between them, and although they
are wonderfully contiguous, I think that sometimes your words
live their own lives a little too much, like the stones in a mosaic
of jewels).

Mallarmé's own enterprise is the creation of a language in which
words 'se reflètent les uns sur les autres jusqu'à paraître ne plus avoir
leur couleur propre, mais n'être que les transitions d'une gamme'
('reflect so much one on the other that they seem to have lost
their local colour and to be no more than the transitions of a
scale') (*Correspondence*, 329–30). Bonnefoy is suspicious of Mallarmé's
aspectual and relational programme largely because it is dangerously
illusory and evasive; instead, he would install language in the
indexical—to which photography has peculiar access—would replace
signification with designation or interpellation, translation with
quotation from the world. And yet Mallarmé's strategy of outwitting
the stasis of the sign's arbitrariness with the fluidly relational is no
less shared by Bonnefoy, or at least by his verse, in its inevitable
and involving multiformity. But while Mallarmé's relational and
distributional writing aims to capture the refractions of the Idea, a
fugitive from chance which, all the same, will have its way, what is
relativized by Bonnefoy's verse is the moment of encounter with
presence which can only be seduced into existence by the intricate
web of contingency.

5. The proper noun

Despite what he writes in 'Lever les yeux de son livre' and elsewhere,
Bonnefoy does not sufficiently lay the deficiencies of language at the
door of reading habits. Concordances, our need to encompass the
whole work (rather than the whole 'author') encourage us to turn
words into themes, already a conceptualization, a verbal rather than
a preverbal design; the drive of language towards metacognitive levels
is exacerbated by the metalanguage of criticism. Are we not guilty as
readers of refusing the 'avec' relationship, and of surreptitiously
substituting for it a 'comme', replacing the co-operation of selfhoods,
their moment of meeting, with reciprocal interference, which, while
multiplying signification, does so in a way which is corrosive of 'sens'?
For, in reality, Bonnefoy has no *linguistic* solution to the 'crise

mallarméenne'; he has a diagnosis and a remedial vision, but no method. He can tell us about the true place of language on the 'threshold' between 'parole' and 'présence'. He can tell us what kind of 'wordness' he has in mind:

> Conceptuellement au plus vide, sensoriellement au plus plein, le mot *arbre* s'est retiré de ses déterminations dans le dictionnaire, dans les manuels, dans les œuvres de la littérature, pour ne viser qu'à cet indéfait qui, en retour, s'y indique, aussi impénétrable que proche. (*Entretiens*, 243)

> (Conceptually at its emptiest, sensorily at its fullest, the word *tree* has disowned definitions provided by dictionaries, by manuals, by literary works, in order to set its sights on the as yet unravelled, which, in return, manifests itself in the word, as impenetrable as it is within reach.)

He can assure us:

> Et moi qui l'emploie de cette façon, en ce bref instant, je suis sur un seuil d'où, bien qu'encore parmi les mots, j'aperçois ce qu'ils nous font perdre: et où je puis rêver différer, un moment encore, le retour à l'emploi usuel. (*Entretiens*, 243)

> (And I who use it in this fashion am, in this brief moment, on a threshold, from which, although still in the world of words, I can perceive what words deprive us of; and where, for a moment longer, I can dream of suspending its conventional use.)

But for those of little faith, what proofs, what guarantees? The photograph, ironically, is close to a mythic language, because it refuses all that is not it, that does not belong to the photograph's place, to its here and now. And its uncritical inclusiveness often surprises our selective and generalizing ways of looking, by showing us what is there and what we did not (at first) see (were not prepared to see). For Bonnefoy, words which achieve 'threshold' status, the status of pure evidentiality, become equivalent to proper nouns:

> Disons cela autrement: chacun de ces mots emplis d'un sacré est devenu un *nom propre*, au sens où Pierre ou Marie, cela ne chiffre

de l'enfant qui vient 'au monde' que la présence, sans rien retenir ou anticiper de ce qu'il est ou va être.[19]

(To put it otherwise: each of these words filled with something of the sacred has become a *proper noun*, in the sense in which Pierre or Marie designates only the presence of the child who comes 'into the world', without either fixing what he/she is, or anticipating what he/she will become.)

Bonnefoy implicitly asks us to treat the capital letter as 'appropriated' by Mallarmé—'Ma Pensée s'est pensée, et est arrivée à une Conception Pure' ('My Thought has thought itself, and has attained to a Pure Conception') (*Correspondence*, 22)—with circumspection, as a shortening of the odds or a forcing of the pace. But we should take care: Bonnefoy equally uses this device, and, for his own purposes one might argue, overworks the demonstrative adjective, often italicized. Besides, in line with what we have already said, what appeals to Mallarmé in the capital letter, in the proper noun, is not its designatory or deictic power, a willing into existence, but its capacity to provoke acts of pure semanticization. He lays much store by the 'pieuse majuscule' ('the reverent capital letter') (*Œuvres complètes*, 654) of the line of verse because it inaugurates the generation of meanings and their synthesis; the line of verse is a composite proper noun, holding together, in a single span of rhythmic perception, its chain of signifiers: 'Le vers qui de plusieurs vocables refait un mot total, neuf, étranger à la langue et comme incantatoire, achève cet isolement de la parole' ('The line of verse which, from several vocables, refashions a new word, encompassing, unknown to the language and as if incantatory, completes this isolation of utterance') (*Œuvres complètes*, 368). While then for Bonnefoy, the proper noun has all the attractions of a word transparent in its power of designation and opaque in its density of preserved being, Mallarmé is fascinated by its ability endlessly to re-constellate all the effects it produces. For Bonnefoy, such a notion confirms Mallarmé's policy of self-defence through closure; but to create circles whose circumferences enclose a perpetual and ever-changing dynamic of association is not necessarily a gesture of either exclusion or abstraction. The following definition of the proper noun by Barthes[20] serves both to underline, in its opening remarks, the fundamental difference

between the the positions of Bonnefoy and Mallarmé, and also to
show, at its close, how much that difference grows from strategic
choice of terminology:

> Le Nom propre est lui aussi un signe, et non bien entendu, un
> simple indice qui désignerait, sans signifier, comme le veut la
> conception courante, de Peirce à Russell. Comme signe, le Nom
> propre s'offre à une exploration, à un déchiffrement: il est à la
> fois un 'milieu' (au sens biologique du terme), dans lequel il faut
> se plonger, baignant indéfiniment dans toutes les rêveries qu'il
> porte, et un objet précieux, comprimé, embaumé, qu'il faut ouvrir
> comme une fleur. Autrement dit, si le Nom . . . est un signe,
> c'est un signe volumineux, un signe toujours gros d'une épaisseur
> touffue de sens, qu'aucun usage ne vient réduire, aplatir, con-
> trairement au nom commun, qui ne livre jamais qu'un de ses
> sens par syntagme

> (The proper noun is itself a sign and evidently not a simple
> index, designating without signifying, as current thinking, from
> Peirce to Russell, would have it. As a sign, the proper noun is
> susceptible of exploration, of decipherment: it is at once a
> 'habitat' (in the biological sense of the term), in which one must
> immerse oneself, bathing in all the reveries it is heir to, and a
> precious object, compressed, embalmed, which must be opened
> like a flower. In other words, if the proper noun . . . is a sign,
> it is a voluminous sign, a sign always bursting with a density
> crammed with meaning, which no use of it can reduce or flatten
> out, unlike the common noun, which only ever activates one of
> its meanings per syntagm).

6. The 'vers de circonstance'

For Bonnefoy, Mallarmé's 'vers de circonstance' were an existential
strategy, whereby he could answer the call of the here and now, fulfil
the desire to possess, but on a scale which would not endanger the
higher enterprise, the penetration to 'notions pures' achieved through
the poet's death to all but poetry. To accept Bonnefoy's diagnosis,
one needs to accept his premisses: that, for example, Mallarmé's
relational and aspectual approach to Beauty is, without possession,
doomed to entropy, because 'c'est le désir de la possession qui est à
l'origine du monde comme le langage le constitue, pour voir il faut

désirer avoir' ('it is desire for possession which generates the world as language constitutes it, to see you need to desire possession');[21] or that the desire for possession is necessarily a 'blinding' of poetry, a surrender to chance, incarnation. Bonnefoy creates a dialectical relationship between these futile 'mondanités' and the serious poems, wrought out of a tragic solitude; and it may seem that the diminution of the former is begotten of a purely argumentational logic. Of the quatrain to Élémir Bourges—

Les dames, les fleurs, les courges	5+2
Se partagent les émois	3+4
De Monsieur Élémir Bourges	6+1
En Seine-et-Marne à Samois	4+3

(Ladies, flowers, courges / Share the close attention / Of Mister Elemir Bourges / In Samois's general direction)

—Bonnefoy writes that it

> marque d'abord et surtout la primauté de la forme: l'amusement n'étant que la conséquence d'un amenuisement que la rigueur prosodique a opéré. Etre réduit à penser aux courges quand on parle d'Élémir Bourges, c'est renoncer, en effet, aux choses sérieuses, c'est dissuader l'auteur de 'Les oiseaux s'envolent et les fleurs tombent' de s'élever au lyrique ou à l'héroïque. (*Vers de circonstance*, 40)

> (underlines first and foremost the primacy of form: amusement being the natural consequence of a diminution brought about by prosodic rigour. To be reduced to thinking about marrows when speaking of Élémir Bourges is, in fact, to abandon serious matters and to discourage the author of 'Les oiseaux s'envolent et les fleurs tombent' from rising to the lyric or heroic.)

This comment seems a little too dismissive. The essence of a poem like this, as of all Mallarmé's work, is the acute sense of living dangerously, on the cusp between sense and nonsense, pathos and bathos, ingenuity and pedantry, invention and convention. Bonnefoy wants to suggest that verse itself discourages concept and intensifies evidentiality:

le vers, par l'accent qu'il met sur les articulations formelles, lesquelles concurrencent celles du sens, desserre le réseau des relations conceptuelles et permet à l'esprit de voir en son immédiateté sensorielle quoi que ce soit qui existe, serait-ce l'humble pichet de cidre. (*Vers de circonstance*, 38)

(the line of verse, by virtue of the emphasis it puts on its formal articulations, which compete with those of the sense, loosens the network of conceptual relations and allows the mind to perceive anything which exists—be it only the humble cider jar—in all its sensory immediacy.)

This sounds like wishful thinking, or a description of Bonnefoy's highly componentialized verse structures, evidentially differentiated. What a quatrain like this can do is create a wonderful meshing together of tones, aspects, experiential metamorphosis. Does the rhythm of the first line produce a complicity, through the liaison of the mute e, between 'dames' and 'fleurs', leaving 'courges' high and dry, to nurse its awkwardness? Or is there a *coupe lyrique* at 'dames' which has the effect of welcoming 'courges' into a democratic enumeration (3'+2+2)? Does the sequence of /a/'s leading out of 'dames'—'partagent', 'émois', 'Marne', 'à', 'Samois'—tell us what Bourges's real preoccupation is, and that 'courges' is merely (too obvious) a decoy? At all events, he clearly deserves his harem—'émir Bourges'—even if the Oriental ring of the *prénom* is sharply refuted by the *nom de famille*, pushed out into isolated architectural splendour by what I read as a 6+1 segmentation.

Are not these 'vers de circonstance' then very close in spirit to haiku, occasional, full of blind field, full of reversed perspective, that is to say, where there is no horizon, where the vanishing point is in the spectator and space radiates out from the spectatorial position? Bonnefoy refers to haiku in his introduction to the 'vers de circonstance', but in parenthesis and as if absent-mindedly:

Mais il n'en est pas moins remarquable que l'auteur d'*Igitur* . . . ce soit aussi celui qui sait donner à la pêche ou aux fleurs odorantes du syringa, à l'orange fraîche ou confite, à la rose réelle ou métaphorique—car des lèvres sont là présentes, dans ces vingt-huit ou trente-deux syllabes, guère plus que le haïku —l'intensité qui révèle une adhésion des plus vives, autant que des plus sereines, aux biens les plus fugitifs. (*Vers de circonstance*, 44–45)

(But it is no less remarkable that the author of *Igitur* . . . is none other than the writer who can bestow on the peach or the fragrant blooms of the syringa, on orange whether fresh or crystallized, on the rose whether real or metaphorical—because there are lips to be found in these twenty-eight or thirty-two syllables, hardly more than a haiku—that intensity which reveals the liveliest as well as the steadiest of commitments to the most fugitive things.)

This case should be made more strongly perhaps, but with a qualification: whatever the extent of Mallarmé's Sinophilia or 'japonisme', he is a firmly Occidental haikuist, in at least two ways. First, these 'loisirs de la poste' (leisures of the post) have a specific, but third-person addressee, as though letter and envelope had been fused; much of the pleasure of these texts lies in this attitudinal ambiguity, this poise between disinterested bystanding and affectionate involvement. Secondly, the verse is inhabited not by an even consciousness, the undifferentiated screen of evidential/photographic perception, but by something more mercurial and variegated, something creatively restless.

Verse has no way, however brief its being, of projecting the immediacy of the instant, designate it though it might. Being and concept, materiality of the word and materiality of a possible referent, phoneme/morpheme and line, these are among the co-ordinates that poetry operates within and swings between. Mallarmé's lines to Degas—

Rue, au 23, Ballu.	1+3+2
J'exprime	2
Sitôt Juin, à Monsieur Degas	3+5
La satisfaction qu'il rime	6+2
Avec la fleur des syringas	4+4

(At rue Ballu I point my finger / Satisfied that the flower 'syringa' / Rhymes in the month of June / With Mister Degas's nominal tune)

—provoke Bonnefoy to ask:

> A un être de cette sorte tragique, pourquoi diable parler du
> syringa, aussi odorantes en soient les fleurs? Et n'est-il pas
> déplacé de lui faire part d'une 'satisfaction' de simple rimeur?
> (*Vers de circonstance*, 41)

> (Why the devil speak of the syringa, however fragrant its flowers,
> to someone of this tragic cast? And is it not inappropriate to
> announce to him a simple rhymer's 'satisfaction'?)

Bonnefoy surmises that Mallarmé wished to take his friend's mind
off his 'recherche de l'impossible' ('search for the impossible'), to
encourage a re-charging of batteries. But perhaps Mallarmé merely
wanted Degas, no mean poet himself, to enjoy the resourcefulness of
this greeting: the way in which 'J'exprime' already *exceeds* the
hexasyllable of the address, whose last syllable (/ly/) rhymes with its
first; the way in which the choppy rhythm of the first line accedes
to the perfect balance of the last, the perfect balance of what Degas
rhymes with; the fact that 'rimer' is both transitive and intransitive,
so that Degas himself rhymes 'satisfaction' with 'la fleur des syringas',
while Mallarmé rhymes 'Degas' with 'syringas', or rather with 'la
fleur'. Here, then, rhyme is not the predictable pairing of homophonic
syllables, but the discovery of 'inner' consonances between the
phonetically dissonant. Bonnefoy might himself have noted that the
preposition with 'rimer' is not 'comme', but 'avec': rhyming is an
affirmation of contiguity before it is metaphoric relating.

7. A second encounter

Ta jambe, nuit très dense,
Tes seins, liés,
Si noirs, ai-je perdu mes yeux,
Mes nerfs d'atroce vue
Dans cette obscurité plus âpre que la pierre,
O mon amour?

Au centre de la lumière, j'abolis
D'abord ma tête crevassée par le gaz,
Mon nom ensuite avec tous pays,

Mes mains seules droites persistent.

En tête du cortège je suis tombé
Sans dieu, sans voix audible, sans péché,
Bête trinitaire criante.

(Your leg, deepest night, / Your breasts, bound, / So black, have
I lost my eyes, / My nerves of agonized seeing / In this darkness
harsher than stone, / O my love? / At the center of light, I
abolish / First my head cracked by gas, / Then my name with
all lands, / Only my straight hands persist. / At the head of the
procession / I have fallen, godless, voiceless, sinless, / A crying
trinitarian beast.)[22]

This, one of the poems entitled 'Une pierre', from *Pierre écrite* (1965),
bears out Starobinski's judgement about Bonnefoy's verse:

L'œuvre poétique indique par là son souci originel, le lieu de son
surgissement, qui est l'instant du *péril*, où tout balance entre vie
et mort, entre 'rédemption' et 'perdition'.

(The poetic work thereby makes clear its founding concern, the
site of its source, which is the moment of *danger*, when
everything is balanced between life and death, between 'redemp-
tion' and 'perdition').

While the Mallarmean dialectic operates with a polarizing
mechanism, its 'suspens vibratoire' ('vibratory suspension') intensify-
ing our sense of the gamble—and thus of any reality's hypothetical
nature—pushing further apart the metaphysical and the occasional,
the absolute and the random, the 'notional' and the sensorily
immediate, Bonnefoy's dialectic works with much narrower oscilla-
tions, between the verse-line and the line of verse, between syllabic
metre and accentual metre (iambic),[23] between continuity and in-
terruption, between the atemporal and the temporal, between essence
and chance.

We might look upon the layout of this poem, a layout shared by
the other poems entitled 'Une pierre' in this collection, as a *prise de
position*. It is not just that these words look to be hewn in stone, in
the *pierre tombale*, and thus achieve an iconicity, even indexicality,

THE MIRAGE OF CRITICAL DISTANCE

which an exploitation of the conventions of the *page* would always deny them. It is also that poems with a medial axis like this generate a centripetal energy, like the products of analytic Cubism, whereby the multiple is felt to be gravitationally related to a single centre; Mallarmé's *Un coup de dés*, for its part, may be experienced as verbal *éparpillement* (dispersal). This perhaps captures an underlying distinction that one might make between Mallarmé and Bonnefoy, a distinction which is to do with direction of trajectory. While in Mallarmé an apparent homogeneity is attempting to scatter itself, to recover, despite itself, some of its accidentality, in Bonnefoy a heterogeneity is trying to assemble itself into a compactness, a composition. A further 'directional' differentiation is indicated by the layout: poems constructed on a central axis diminish the inaugurative and terminational force of line-beginnings and line-endings. These poems—and we must remember that these are the only instances in which Bonnefoy uses the central axis—present us with a poetic consciousness whose self-possession is engaged in a process of self-relinquishment (Baudelairean 'vaporisation du moi' ('evaporation of the self')); the voice that re-initiates utterance with each line in a 'justified' poem, here drifts towards a non-differentiating inwardness. Significantly, the final stanza provides us with a hypostatized trinity of deprivation which becomes a synthesized singleness in the 'bête trinitaire', with hypostatization still echoing in the ternary rhythm (1+4+3); and ' sans voix audible' ('the externally uttered') becomes 'criante', the voiceless cry of the written stone and a reminiscence of the 'cri' of the cricket, perhaps ('trinitaire': /Ri/./i/. . . taire/terre). Mallarmé, on the other hand, returning from a death of the self, assuming an anonymity which yields the initiative to words, uses the 'justified' poem to re-install the 'singular' voice as initiator ('Il m'amuse d'élire avec le seul génie'), while the seal of rhyme acts as the signature of each completed line.

Evidence in Bonnefoy's verse of a heterogeneity seeking inward gravitation is provided by further examples of the componential nature of his verse, the sense of *montage* and *démontage*. The first stanza has lines of 6.4.8.6.12.4. syllables, which might be 're-composed' as three dodecasyllables followed by a tetrasyllable:

Ta jambe, nuit très dens(e), tes seins liés, si noirs,	3'+3+4+2
Ai-je perdu mes yeux, mes nerfs d'atroce vue	4+2+2+4

Dans cette obscurité plus âpre que la pierre, (2+4)+2+4
            O mon amour?   4

Conversely, the first two lines of the second stanza (11.11.9.8.) might be 'demontaged' thus:

Au centre de la lumière,	2+5
J'abolis d'abord ma tête	3+2+2
Crevassée par le gaz	3+3

This is a poem which descends from the *pair* line (ll. 1–6) into the *impair* (ll. 7–9, 11), to re-emerge from it (ll. 12–13). The conjunction of the *pair* and the *impair* is one of the means by which the tendency of the *pair* to court the absolute, the gnostic, the aesthetically closed, can be countered by the finite, the contingent, the time-bound. Bonnefoy's cultivation of the hendecasyllable, particularly in its 6//5 guise, is well known, as are his reasons for doing so: this hendeca-syllable begins 'like an alexandrine—that is, with these six syllables which lead in the alexandrine to their symmetrical image in the second hemistich', but it then 'ends with only five syllables and thus breaks the arrogant symmetry of the great verse of Racine and Mallarmé, with its refusal of time, of everyday life, of death'; it combines within it 'the spiritual quality of Shakespeare's verses, which are a form, a reference to the absolute' (6 syll.), and also the direct encounter with life (5 syll.).[24]

These remarks invite a twofold qualification:

(a) None of the hendecasyllables we meet in this poem are unequivocally of the 6//5 type: line 7 is 7//4 or 8'//3; line 8 is 4//7 or 5'//6; line 11 may be read as 6//5 but is more likely 7'//4. What is important in these lines is not so much whether the 6//5 configuration is affirmed or denied, but the consistent presence of an articulated mute e as the 'post-caesural' syllable, that is, at the point at which this 'faille' is structurally most disruptive and likely to persuade the reader to read it as a *césure lyrique*, pushing the hemistichs apart and opening up the verse-seams. Furthermore, in lines 7 and 11, this moment of rupture involves the first person. And this phenomenon occurs as much in lines without a caesura—line 1 (3'+3), line 10 (3+3'+2/4'+2'+2), line 13 (6'+2)—as in those with one—line 12 (7'//3). This 'post-caesural' e is the 'gaz' by which the poet's head is 'crevassée', the wound of mortality through which the presence of death within the tomb wakens us to light, erects the hands which will restore 'la voix sacrée de la terre ingénue' ('Sans Dieu . . . sans péché') to the 'bête trinitaire'. The 'faille' is the threshold which joins as much as it separates.

(b) This poem opens with a sestet of question; the second and final stanzas make declarations, in a quatrain + tercet pattern reminiscent of the sonnet. Bonnefoy may speak of the 'arrogant symmetry of the great verse of . . . Mallarmé', but as he himself points out, Mallarmé, too, explores the collision of the *pair* and the *impair* in the very structure of his many sonnets. In relation to line 9 of Mallarmé's 'Quelle soie aux baumes de temps', Bonnefoy writes:

> C'est le moment d'ailleurs où se marque, entre quatrains et tercets, ce passage du pair à l'impair qui ne peut être vécu, sauf par les versificateurs les plus sourds, que comme une incitation à la réflexion métaphysique. Le pair, c'est la symétrie interne des strophes, l'autosuffisance, l'intemporel; l'impair, c'est le temps qui recommence, et que l'un succède à l'autre, c'est l'occasion de pressentir—d'où le succès du sonnet dans le néoplatonisme—que l'âme est divisée entre le monde intelligible et le lieu terrestre. (*Vers de circonstance*, 22)

> (Furthermore, it is the moment at which is registered, between quatrains and tercets, the shift from the even to the odd which can only be experienced, by all but the deafest versifiers, as a spur to metaphysical reflection. The even embodies the internal symmetry of the stanzas, self-sufficiency, the atemporal; the odd represents time beginning again, and that the one comes after the other is the occasion to sense that the soul—hence the sonnet's success in Neoplatonism—is divided between the world made intelligible and the terrestrial locus.)

But even to tax Mallarmé with the 'arrogant symmetry' of his verse lines is hardly justifiable, not only because he occasionally uses the heptasyllable, not only because his alexandrines create unsteady musics—

Coure le froid avec ses silences de faux,   4+5+3/4+6'+2
Je n'y hululerai pas de vide nénie   7+2+3
                        ('Mes bouquins refermés . . .')

(Let the cold come with its scything silences | I shall not there
ululate an empty lament)

Sur les crédences, au salon vide: nul ptyx
                        4+5+3/5'+5'+3/4+6'+2
                        ('Ses purs ongles . . .')

(On the sideboard, in the empty room: no ptyx)

—but also because, despite what he says elsewhere, Bonnefoy can
maintain that the classical alexandrine, like other long lines, is
sufficiently self-investigative and complex to encompass the *vécu*, the
existentially volatile, the tension between order and unmediated
contact with things. In particular, the changing patterns of mute e's
and *coupes* can ensure that, within a group of lines, the individual
alexandrine is a highly relativized entity (see *Poétique d'Yves Bonnefoy*,
255).

8. Hamlet and Lear

It is tempting to imagine Bonnefoy casting Mallarmé as Hamlet ('The
readiness is all') to his own Lear ('Ripeness is all'). Certainly,
Mallarmé's characterization of Hamlet (*Œuvres complètes*, 300) as the
'*seigneur latent qui ne peut devenir*' ('*the nobleman whose latent being
cannot be*') and the play as drama in its essential state ('l'antagonisme
de rêve chez l'homme avec les fatalités à son existence départies par
le malheur' ('the struggle in man between dream and the in-
evitabilities apportioned to his life by misfortune')) coincides with
Bonnefoy's discovery of the rupture between the archaic and modern
worlds at the very heart of the play:

> La ligne de fracture qui a rompu l'horizon de l'intemporel, et
> voue l'histoire du monde à son devenir toujours plus incertain
> et précipité, passe, c'est évidemment une de ses causes, par
> *Hamlet*, et je dirais même en plein milieu de cette œuvre.[25]

(The fault line which fractured the horizon of the atemporal, and condemns the history of the world to its ever more uncertain and headlong future, passes—and it is evidently one of the play's causes—through *Hamlet*; I would go as far as to say that it runs through the very heart of the work.)

The archaic world, the Middle Ages—'c'est quand une pensée du tout, de l'unité, et de celle-ci comme vie, comme présence, réglait tous les rapports qu'on pouvait entretenir avec les réalités particulières' ('it is when a conception of the whole, of unity, and of this unity as life, as presence, governed all the relationships which could be fostered with specific realities') (*Hamlet, Le Roi Lear*, 7)—experiences a seamless continuity between the material and the transcendent, with the one, indelibly and perforce, the sign of the other. It is with descriptions of this earlier world that Bonnefoy characteristically prefaces his accounts of Mallarmé's own crisis. And Hamlet's 'readiness' is 'simplement, négativement, une technique de survie de l'âme, utile pour tout le temps où l'humanité se souvient de son espérance' ('simply, negatively, the soul's survival strategy, useful whenever humanity becomes mindful again of its hope') (*Hamlet, Le Roi Lear*, 16): it is irony, compensatory dream, a last defiant desire addressed to a God who has withdrawn from his Word. Lear's 'ripeness', on the other hand, is:

> la maturation, l'acceptation de la mort comme dans *Hamlet*, mais non plus cette fois parce qu'elle serait le signe par excellence de l'indifférence du monde, de l'insuffisance du sens,—non, comme l'occasion de s'élever à une compréhension vraiment intérieure des lois réelles de l'être, et de se délivrer des illusions, des poursuites vaines, de s'ouvrir à une pensée de la Présence qui, reflétée dans le geste, assurera à l'individu sa place vivante dans l'évidence du Tout. (*Hamlet, Le Roi Lear*, 20–1)

(maturation, acceptance of death as in *Hamlet*, but not this time because it would be the perfect sign of the world's indifference, of the insufficiency of meaning,—no, but as the opportunity to attain to a truly inward understanding of the true laws of being, and to break free from illusions, from vain pursuits, to open one's mind to the thought of Presence which, reflected in our every

act, will assure the individual of a living place in the evidence
of the All.)

But Learish 'ripeness' is as much wishful thinking as Hamlet's wishful
thinking; Bonnefoy is as aware of the hairline thickness of his
'threshold' as Mallarmé is of the fragility of his hope. Hamlet has a
profound nostalgia for Hamlet *père*, but feels more spiritual affinity
with the 'new' king, Claudius (*Hamlet, Le Roi Lear*, 11); these divided
feelings surface most poignantly in Bonnefoy's translation of the last
line of Laertes's dying speech (Act V, sc. ii, l. 326):

I can no more. The King—the King's to blame.

Je n'en peux plus. . . Le roi, le roi est coupable.   4+2+2+3

Here, Bonnefoy's 'etymon', the 6//5 hendecasyllable, finds itself at
odds with the syntactic structure—'Je n'en peux plus. . . Le roi,//le
roi est coupable'—so that the king exists both in the hexasyllable of
order and essence and form, and in the pentasyllable of disorder,
contingency, finitude. The 'rois', Hamlet *père* and Claudius, or
Hamlet *fils* (I) and Hamlet *fils* (II), struggling to find a line of true
succession, a continuity in time, are pulled apart by the verse-
structure. Mallarmé, no less than Hamlet, is the dramatized performance of Bonnefoy's 'etymon', in which Bonnefoy, in his turn,
must act out his contradictions, in the hope that their competing
terms can be dynamized in a dialectical relationship, which will allow
movements of reversal, of fruitful *choc en retour*, when beauty is
revealed: 'elle est l'unité qui soudain affleure et la surprise qui lui
répond—instant d'adhésion passionnée—avant que la nostalgie ne
reprenne' ('it is the unity which suddenly surfaces and the surprise
by which it is greeted—a moment of passionate connection—
before nostalgia resumes').[26] However much he may have struggled
with Mallarmé, as with the ghost of a father, however clearly he
may distinguish between Baudelairean (and Rimbaldian) 'other' and
Mallarmean 'absence', Bonnefoy is too much a disciple of Mallarmé
ever to transcend the struggle or to avoid walking in the ghost's
company.[27]

Notes

Chapter One

1. 'And as for him, I think he considered my astonishment, without astonishment'. The phrase is Paul Valéry's *Écrits divers sur Stéphane Mallarmé* (Paris: Gallimard, 1950), 16. It stages the problem of a memorializing 'subject' regarding a dead 'object', and presents a profound missing of minds by confronting Valéry's surprise with Mallarmé's lack of astonishment. It should perhaps be read alongside the following passage, in which Valéry appears to be mounting a typically decadentist attack on the contemporary vulgar: '*L'ère du provisoire est ouverte*: on n'y peut plus mûrir de ces objects de contemplation que l'âme trouve inépuisables et dont elle peut s'entretenir indéfiniment. *Le temps d'une surprise est notre présente unité de temps.*' ('*The age of the provisional has begun*: one can no longer cultivate those objects of contemplation which the soul finds inexhaustible and with which it may dialogue indefinitely. *The time of a surprise is our current unit of time.*') (*Écrits divers sur Stéphane Mallarmé*, 53, my emphasis). Broadly speaking, this collection will argue for a surprising, provisional, and diffuse Mallarmé.

2. This phrase is quoted by Charles D. Minahen in his essay 'Poetry's Polite Terrorist: Reading Sartre Reading Mallarmé' (see Chapter 3). Here are just a few examples of Sartre rehearsing 'the death of Mallarmé' (compare Leo Bersani's celebrated 1982 study): biographically speaking: 'Mallarmé déteste sa naissance: il écrit pour l'effacer' ('Mallarmé hates his birth: he writes in order to wipe it out') (Jean-Paul Sartre, *Mallarmé* (Paris Gallimard, 1986), 151); 'Pas un jour ne s'est écoulé sans qu'il ne fût tenté de se tuer . . . Cette mort en sursis lui donnait une sorte d'ironie charmante et destructrice' ('Not a day goes by without the temptation to kill himself . . . This suspended death-sentence gave him a kind of charming and destructive irony') (167); in literary terms: 'C'est le mouvement même du suicide qu'il faut reproduire dans le poème' ('It is the very movement of suicide that the poem must reproduce') (157);

philosophically speaking: 'Sacrifice et génocide, affirmation et négation de l'homme, [dans] le suicide de Mallarmé . . . la matière se retrouve matière' ('Sacrifice and genocide, affirmation and negation of man, [in] Mallarmé's suicide . . . matter rediscovers itself as matter') (156); and finally, mixing these various modes: 'Un poète mort à vingt-cinq ans, tué par le sentiment de son impuissance: c'est un fait divers. Un poète de cinquante-six ans qui meurt au moment où il a conquis peu à peu tous ses moyens et où il se dispose à commencer son oeuvre: c'est la *tragédie même* de l'homme. La mort de Mallarmé est une mystification mémorable' ('A poet who dies at twenty-five, killed by his feeling of impotence: that's a story in the local paper. A fifty-six-year-old poet who dies when he has little by little mastered his art and is beginning his real work: that is man's *essential tragedy*. The death of Mallarmé was a memorable mystification') (166). One might add that Sartre seems, therefore, to have had no problem remembering Mallarmé's death; indeed he appears to have had some difficulty forgetting it, to the point where one is tempted to ask: of whom is he really speaking, Mallarmé or himself? (Translations here and throughout this introduction are my own).

3. Francis Ponge, *Proêmes* (Paris: Gallimard, 1948).
4. On this image of one poet speaking the words of another, see Verlaine in *Quinze jours en Hollande*: 'Et je pris ma voix la plus "blanche" pour réciter, psalmodier plutôt, à la manière de Mallarmé lui-même, l'admirable poème . . . coquin ['L'Après-midi d'un faune']! Je crois avoir du moins bien *dit* ces vers impeccables qui savent tout énoncer et tout sous-entendre' ('So I adopted my "blankest" voice in order to recite, or rather intone, in the manner of Mallarmé himself, the admirable and . . . saucy poem ['L'Après-midi d'un faune']! I think I did at least *speak* these impeccable lines, which manage to express everything and insinuate everything') (*Œuvres en prose complètes*, ed. Jacques Borel (Paris: Gallimard-Pléiade, 1972), 389).
5. Henri de Régnier, *Faces et profils* (Paris: Mercure de France, 1931), 74.
6. Compare the photograph of Marcel Duchamp, John Cage, and Teeny Duchamp, in Kate van Orden's essay 'On the Side of Poetry and Chaos: Mallarmean *Hasard* and Twentieth-Century Music' (See Chapter 9).
7. *Poésies*, ed. Bertrand Marchal (Paris: Gallimard, 1992), 47.
8. *Poésies*, 70.
9. *Poésies*, 42.
10. See Jacques Derrida 'Mallarmé', in Marcel Arland et al., *Tableau de la littérature française*, volume III (Paris: Gallimard, 1974), 368–79. I discuss this text at length in my piece 'Mallarmé, by Jacques Derrida' in *Derrida in Contexts* (New York: SUNY, 1998).

11. Compare Mallarmé's description of the effect that the mere sight of a name could have on his psyche: 'Je le reconnais, qui se débat sous le mal d'apparaître: parce que Hamlet extériorise, sur des planches, ce personnage unique d'une tragédie intime et occulte, *son nom même affiché exerce sur moi, sur toi qui le lis, une fascination, parente de l'angoisse*' ('I recognize him, struggling with the difficulty of coming into being: because Hamlet exteriorizes, on the stage, the unique character of an intimate and occult drama, *his name even seen on a poster exerts over me, over you who read it, a fascination bordering on anxiety*') (my emphasis, see 'Hamlet', *Igitur, Divagations, Un coup de dés*, ed. Yves Bonnefoy, (Paris: Gallimard, 1976), 186).

12. Compare 'Les mots anglais', (*Œuvres complètes*, ed. Henri Mondor and G. Jean-Aubry (Paris: Gallimard-Pléiade, 1945), 948 and Michael Temple, *The Name of the Poet* (Exeter: University of Exeter Press, 1995), 67.

13. Quoted in *Stéphane Mallarmé*, ed. Harold Bloom (New York: Chelsea House Publishers, 1987), 61.

14. Compare the coinage of this term in the special issue entitled 'Mallarmé: theorist of our times', *Dalhousie French Review*, 25 (1993).

15. *Correspondance complète 1862–1871* ed. Bertrand Marchal (Paris: Gallimard, 1995) 614–15.

16. *Igitur, Divagations, Un coup de dés*, 257.

17. *Igitur, Divagations, Un coup de dés*, 204 and 257.

18. *Igitur, Divagations, Un coup de dés*, 279.

19. *Correspondance complète 1862–1871*, 588.

20. *Correspondance complète 1862–1871*, 589.

21. *La Révolution du langage poétique* (Paris: Seuil, 1974), 364.

22. 'Le silence de Mallarmé', *Faux pas* (Paris: Gallimard, 1943), 117.

23. *Poésies*, 163. Compare the section on Mallarmé's Wagner in *The Name of the Poet*, 126–38.

24. Strictly speaking, one could argue that Valéry does not portray himself as actually present at Mallarmé's death. In his anecdotal accounts, however, he reprojects the final disappearance so many times that one is forced to recognize it as the distinguishing feature of this set of texts. Compare the following: 'Le jour qui j'attendais ne vint jamais' ('The day I was awaiting never came') (*Écrits divers sur Stéphane Mallarmé*, 25); 'Quand vint l'automne, il n'était plus' ('When autumn came, he was no more') (27); and 'Je ne l'ai plus revu. Ce fut pour moi un coup terrible' ('I never saw him again. It was for me a terrible blow') (71).

25. *Vers de circonstance*, ed. Bertrand Marchal (Paris: Gallimard, 1996), 170.

26. *The death of Stéphane Mallarmé* (Cambridge: Cambridge University Press, 1982), vii.

27. 'On demande des malédictions', *Œuvres complètes*, XI (Paris: Mercure de France, 1963–85), 109.
28. Quoted in *Œuvres complètes de Stéphane Mallarmé*, 1636.
29. 'La catastrophe d'Igitur', *Nouvelle revue française* (November, 1926), 536.
30. *De Stéphane Mallarmé au prophète Ezéchiel* (Paris: Mercure de France, 1902); *Stéphane Mallarmé, un héros* (Paris: Mercure de France, 1899); *Mes souvenirs du symbolisme* (Paris: Nouvelle revue critique, 1925).
31. *Le soleil des morts* (Geneva: Slatkine, 1979). See *Name of the Poet*, 180–1 for a brief discussion of the poet's reaction to this somewhat unflattering portrait.
32. *Poésies*, 62.

Chapter Two

1. All references in the text are to Valéry, *Œuvres*, 2 vols, ed. Jean Hytier, (Paris: Gallimard-Pléiade, 1957, 1960), abbreviated as *Œuvres* I and *Œuvres* II. The Mallarmé articles, first published together as *Écrits divers sur Stéphane Mallarmé* (Paris: Gallimard, 1950), appear in *Œuvres* I in the section 'Études littéraires'. Additional publication details for the articles individually and severally can be found in the notes to this section.
2. The *Cahiers* have several references to Nietzsche's superman and the philosophy of power. See Valéry, *Cahiers*, 2 vols, ed. Judith Robinson (Paris: Gallimard-Pléiade, 1973–74), II, 1693–99, 'Index des noms propres . . .'. Subsequent references to the *Cahiers* are abbreviated to *Cahiers* I and *Cahiers* II, preceded by the year of the particular entry.
3. André Gide–Paul Valéry, *Correspondance 1890–1942* (Paris: Gallimard, 1955), 126.
4. Valéry frequently comments on his dislike of reading and his preference for thinking his own independent thoughts. See, for example, *Cahiers* I, 156: 'Je n'aime pas consulter les livres (sinon exceptionnellement) sur les questions qui me semblent pouvoir être travaillées et traitées par le travail mental isolé, à partir de l'observation personnelle directe.' ('I don't like consulting books (or only exceptionally) on questions which seem to me capable of being thought about and treated by independent mental reflection, based on direct personal observation.')
5. Of all Valéry's different models repeatedly listed in the *Cahiers* Mallarmé is the most oppressive—in part because of the personal connection but mainly because, unlike da Vinci, Wagner, or Poincaré, he works in Valéry's own medium of (poetic) language: 'Rien ne m'a plus désespéré que la musique de Wagner . . . Il m'a désespéré autrement que

Mallarmé—Ce dernier plus directement, car son métier m'était plus intelligible.' ('Nothing caused me more despair than the music of Wagner ... in a different way from Mallarmé—The latter more directly, for I could more readily appreciate his exploitation of his medium.') (1941, *Cahiers* II, 979).

6. See Mallarmé, *Correspondance*, 2 vols, ed. Henri Mondor and Lloyd James Austin (Paris: Gallimard, 1959–85), for example, Mallarmé's first letter to Valéry (25 Oct. 1890), a supportive, rose-tinted reminiscence of youth: 'Quant à des conseils, seule en donne la solitude et je vous l'envie, en me rappellant des heures de province et de jeunesse par là-bas, de votre côté' ('As for advice, that only comes from solitude and I envy you that, remembering the time spent in my youth away from Paris in your part of France') (IV, 153–4), or, later, his commiserations (21 May 1897) over Valéry's entry into the drudgery of a bureaucratic job at the Ministry of War: 'Mon pauvre Valéry! Vous voila réduit à songer à votre retraite, dans trente ans—comme je fis' ('My poor Valéry! You are now reduced—as I was—to thinking about your retirement thirty years hence.') (IX, 193).

7. Mallarmé's pain on the death of his son is movingly revealed in *Pour un Tombeau d'Anatole*, ed. Jean-Pierre Richard (Paris: Seuil, 1961). Richard's introduction provides a sensitive and persuasive analysis of the dynamics of the father/son relationship as explored in the text.

8. Gide, by contrast, despite earlier acquaintance and an intellectually close relationship with Mallarmé, is not, for example, a visitor to Valvins; see his letter to Mallarmé of 19 Jan. 1897: 'A Paris vous n'étiez jamais quand je revenais de voyage et malgré mon désir je n'eusse osé m'aventurer jusqu'à Valvins' ('You were never in Paris when I returned from my travels and though I would have liked to see you, I would not have dared to impose upon you at Valvins') (Mallarmé, *Correspondance*, IX, 49, n.1).

9. Valéry first met his wife, Jeannie Gobillard, cousin of Mallarmé's ward, Julie Manet (daughter of Berthe Morisot and Eugène Manet), at Mallarmé's funeral. See Valéry's 1900 remark announcing his engagement to his friend Gustave Fourment: 'M'unir à ce milieu avait été un des projets de S. Mallarmé—et cela se fait . . .' ('Uniting me with this milieu was one of S. Mallarmé's projects—and now it is coming about . . .') (*Œuvres* I, 26–7). See also his letter of 16 Feb. 1941 to Henri Mondor: 'c'est Madame Mallarmé qui avec Vève complice a eu l'idée de me marier et a fait tout ce qu'il fallait pour que cette idée se réalisât.' ('It was Madame Mallarmé who with Vève as her accomplice, had the idea of getting me married and did everything necessary to bring the idea to fruition.') (*Lettres à quelques-uns* (Paris: Gallimard,

1952), 232). Gide, in contrast, in his letter to Valéry following Mallarmé's death, asks Valéry's advice on how best to send condolences to the family: 'une grande timidité m'avait toujours empêché de parler à Mme ou à Mlle Mallarmé, de sorte qu'à peine si elles me connaissaent.' ('I was always too shy to talk to Mme or Mlle Mallarmé, with the result that they hardly know me.') (*Correspondance Gide–Valéry*, 334).

10. Valéry's letter to Gide, giving the details of Mallarmé's death and funeral and recounting his last visit to Mallarmé at Valvins, gives a clear picture of the personal closeness of the father/son relationship. It also describes a symbolic anointment by Mallarmé of his spiritual successor: 'Je m'étais habitué avec lui à une familiarité absolument filiale sur ses propres indications . . . Il y a six ou sept semaines j'ai passé la journée là-bas à Valvins. Il m'a semblé las—il était tout blanc—et son canot qui hier flottait encore sur sa corde, était, me dit-il, délaissé. Nous allons causer dans sa chambre. Il me montra des brouillons d'*Hérodiade* en train, etc., changea de flanelle devant moi, me donna de l'eau pour les mains et me parfuma ensuite avec son parfum.' ('I had become accustomed, with his encouragement, to behave towards him with the familiarity of a son . . . Six or seven weeks ago, I spent the day out there in Valvins. I thought he seemed tired—he looked drawn and pale—and his boat which was still floating on its mooring yesterday, had, he told me, not been used. We went into his bedroom to talk. He showed me the drafts of *Hérodiade* he was working on, etc., changed his clothes in front of me, gave me water to wash my hands and then perfumed me with his own perfume.') Even here, though Valéry notes the intellectual reservations that separate him from a beloved 'parent' and friend, 'il comprenait toute sorte de pensée, et mes écarts les plus singuliers trouvaient en lui un "précédent" et au besoin un appui—*opinions mises à part*.' ('he understood all kinds of thoughts and my strangest aberrations found in him a "precedent" and if necessary a support—*opinions apart*.') (*Correspondance Gide–Valéry*, 331–2, my emphasis).

11. A range of different aspects of Valéry's relationship with Mallarmé, including different interpretations of the father/son dynamic, are discussed in interesting articles by James R. Lawler, 'Saint Mallarmé', *Yale French Studies*, 44 (1970), 185–98, Carl P. Barbier, 'Valéry et Mallarmé jusqu'en 1898', and James R. Lawler, 'Valéry et Mallarmé: le tigre et la gazelle', both in *Paul Valéry, Amitiés de jeunesse— Influences—Lectures*, Colloque de l'Université d'Édimbourg, novembre 1976 (Paris: Nizet, 1978), 49–83 and 85–103 respectively, and by Judith Robinson, 'Mallarmé, "le père idéal" ', *Littérature* 56 (1984), 104–18.

12. Valéry's irritation with Mallarmé's ideas and methods emerges in some of his letters, see *Correspondance Gide–Valéry*, 104, 168–9, 204, 233.

Gide, amongst others, notes the potentially crippling effect of Mallarmé's influence on the younger generation: 'Imiter Mallarmé, c'est folie . . . Mallarmé, sous ce rapport, fit beaucoup de bien et beaucoup de mal, comme fait toujours tout puissant esprit. Beaucoup de bien, parce qu'il désignait certains sots plagiaires à une risée méritée; beaucoup de mal parce que l'autorité de ce magique esprit, son despotisme involontaire, d'autant plus redoubtable qu'il était plus voilé de douceur, put incliner quelques esprits non négligeables, mais trop flexibles, ou trop jeunes, pas assez formés, les plier en des postures peu sincères, leur faire adopter une syntaxe, une manière d'écrire qui supposait et que nécessitait une méthode, mais qui sans elle n'était plus que manière et que pure affectation.' ('It was madness to imitate Mallarmé . . . Mallarmé, in that connexion, accomplished much that was good, and much that was bad, as powerful minds always do. Much that was good, because he exposed certain stupid plagiarists to justified ridicule; much that was bad because the authority of that magical spirit, his involuntary despotism which was all the more dangerous for the gentleness of its appearance, was able to impose on some not inconsiderable minds, which were too flexible, or too young and insufficiently formed, and to bend them into postures which were not their own, to make them adopt a syntax, a manner of writing which supposed and was necessitated by a particular method, but which, without it, was nothing but mannerism and pure affectation.') ('Stéphane Mallarmé (*In Memoriam*)' in Gide, *Œuvres complètes*, ed. L. Martin-Chauffier, 13 vols (Paris: Gallimard, 1933–39) II, 452).

13. This inability to exercise the killer instinct on the living Mallarmé remains to the end in Valéry's memory of their relationship, for example: 'Mallarmé était finalement obligé de donner—plus ou moins précairement et artificiellement à la Littérature, une *valeur* que je ne pouvais lui accorder, ne pouvant y voir qu'une application particulière. C'est là—le point sur lequel je n'ai pas eu le temps d'en venir à l'interroger —car je n'osais pas encore toucher à ce centre de son être que ma propre raison d'état situait . . . quand il est mort' ('Mallarmé was finally obliged to attribute—more or less precariously and artificially to Literature, a *value* which I was unable to give it, since in my view it was only a particular application. That was the sensitive subject which I did not have time to bring up with him—for I had still not dared to approach this central concern of his being that my own reasons of State situated . . . when he died'). (1938, *Cahiers* I, 156, Valéry's emphasis).

14. Writing to Gide on 26 Sept. 1898, Valéry describes his grief-stricken paralysis at the burial: 'Ensuite, Quillard m'a forcé à venir près de la fosse et à dire adieu au nom des—Jeunes! Et j'ai été absolument

incapable de dire autre chose que des bredouillements confus, j'étranglais et personne n'a compris, pas plus que moi, les quatre sons que j'ai émis.' ('Then Quillard made me come to the graveside to say farewell in the name of—the younger generation! And I was choking and absolutely incapable of uttering anything except some confused mumbling, and nobody, myself included, understood the three or four sounds I made.') (*Correspondance Gide–Valéry*, 333). There is a similar account in his letter to his brother, Jules Valéry (*Œuvres* I, 1743). To Madame Mallarmé on 15 September 1898, Valéry writes: 'Pour moi, je vous avoue sincèrement que je crois avoir moins pleuré mon propre père' ('As for me I can sincerely tell you that I believe I grieved less for my own father'). (Mallarmé, *Correspondance*, X, Appendice X, 318).

15. Valéry's growing impatience with his 'machin sur Mallarmé' ('his Mallarmé thing') (*Correspondance Gide–Valéry*, 286, 287) reflects a fundamental and persistent difficulty in tackling Mallarmé. The last *Cahier* is still reflecting on material 'Pour le Mallarmé' ('For my piece on Mallarmé') (1944–45, *Cahiers* II, 1141–2).

16. To Gide, 9 June 1912, Valéry expresses his reservations about publishing his long-neglected poems from the 1890s just as Mallarmé's *Poésies* are about to be published by Gallimard: 'Quant à moi, c'est-à-dire au recueil ou herbier de choses séchées, j'y songe, gratte les tiroirs, me dégoûte—et c'est tant mieux—car si je me regrettais, quel surcroît, Seigneur! . . . Jusqu'ici, je ne vois pas ce volume; ni sa forme, ni sa substance, ni sa nécessité. Puis paraître à deux minutes de Mallarmé, c'est de trois ou quatre façons épouvantant. Faut-il monter sur un théâtre qui, après tout et en vérité, n'est pas le mien?' 'As for me, that is to say the collection or herbarium of dried specimens, I work on it, turn out my drawers, am sickened by it—and so much the better!—for if I hankered after my past self, my goodness, what an extra burden that would be! . . . I can't yet visualize the volume, neither its form, nor its substance, nor what gives it its inner necessity. And then, appearing two minutes away from Mallarmé is a terrifying prospect from a variety of points of view. Is it wise to take the stage in an arena which after all is truly not my own?') (quoted *Œuvres* I, 36).

17. See, for example, Valéry's exasperation in a letter to Gide, following the publication of *Charmes* in August 1922: 'La presse, à l'envi, me flanque Mallarmé et les ténèbres y adjacentes à la tête. Je crois que j'ai eu tort de faire cet énorme tirage à deux mille (cinq éditions!!) et surtout d'envoyer à tous ces inutiles journaux.' ('The press miss no opportunity to throw Mallarmé and his obscurities in my teeth. I think I was wrong to have that large print-run of two thousand copies (five editions!!)

and above all to send out copies to those useless newspapers.') (*Correspondance Gide–Valéry*, 488).

18. In an unpublished 1923 letter to his wife Valéry writes: 'Écrire sur Mallarmé est pour moi un supplice bizarre' ('Writing about Mallarmé is a strange form of torture for me') (*Œuvres* I, 46).

19. Geneviève Mallarmé-Bonniot died on 25 May 1919.

20. Valéry's election to the Académie française in 1925 is a factor in an increasing self-assertiveness, the public accolade, unthinkable for his predecessor, empowering him to pursue and situate Mallarmé's glory not as a primary phenomenon but as a function of his own.

21. Valéry's writing on Mallarmé is not of course limited to these texts. There are direct references in poems published and unpublished (see especially, Valéry's unfinished memorial poem to Mallarmé, extracts quoted by Carl P. Barbier, op. cit., pp. 80–3), some of which feeds through into the meditation on life and death of *La Jeune Parque* in the correspondence and in the *Cahiers*. Throughout Valéry's work there is also substantial indirect reference, from small examples such as the punning 'emblem for a library': 'Plus élire que lire' (*Mélanges, Œuvres* I, 303), echoing 1.2 of 'Mes bouquins refermés sur le nom de Paphos' ('My books closed to upon the name Paphos') to the celebrated *tour de force* of Valéry's acceptance speech to the Académie française, which contrives never to mention by name Valéry's predecessor Anatole France but to describe him in terms which recall at least as much Mallarmé, to whose *L'Après-midi d'un faune* he had refused a place in the third *Parnasse contemporain* of 1876.

22. A performance of *Un coup de dés* uniting 'the talents of composers, musicians, visual artists, writers' is planned in Philadelphia for 1998, organized by writer and artist Tom Csazar. Valéry, in a letter to his wife of June 1920, reacts in the same way as Bonniot to a request for a preface to a first unpublished version of *L'Après-midi d'un faune* found among the papers of the composer Ernest Chausson: 'A la réflexion il m'est apparu que ce serait une sorte d'impiété . . . Aucune considération ne peut à mes yeux prévaloir contre cette injonction suprême' ('On reflexion it seemed to me like a sort of sacrilege . . . No consideration can prevail, in my eyes, over that last injunction [Mallarmé's instruction to destroy all his papers after his death].') (*Œuvres* I, 43).

23. To Gide, 7 Oct. 1898, Valéry describes Geneviève Mallarmé's summons to Valvins to help deal with Mallarmé's last note requesting the destruction of his papers: 'j'ai été conduit dans la chambre mortuaire et là, sur la table intacte, on m'a donné à déchiffrer un papier tout griffonné la veille de la mort. J'y ai lu l'ordre de ne rien publier d'inédit et de brûler "ce grand monceau demi-séculaire de notes . . . que je

suis seul à comprendre" . . . Ce lambeau était effrayant d'écriture convulsée—et à côté de lui deux fragments presque finis d'*Hérodiade*, le dernier travail.' ('I was taken into the death chamber and there, on the untouched table, I was given a note to decipher, scrawled on the eve of his death. It contained the order to publish none of his unfinished material and to burn "that huge pile of notes dating back over fifty years . . . which I alone can make sense of" . . . This scrap of paper and its convulsive writing were terrifying to see—and alongside it two fragments, almost completed, of *Hérodiade*, on which he was working at the end.') (*Correspondance Gide–Valéry*, 335).

24. The difference of aim emerges clearly in a *Cahiers* note: 'mon "rêve de poète" eût été de composer un discours,—une parole de modulation et de relation internes—dans laquelle le physique, le psychique et les conventions du langage pussent combiner leurs ressources. Avec telles divisions et changements de tons bien définis. / Mais, *au fait, qui* parle dans un poème? Mallarmé voulut que ce fût le Langage lui-même. / Pour moi—ce serait—l'Être *vivant* ET *pensant* (*contraste, ceci*)—et poussant la conscience de soi à la capture de sa sensibilité–développant les propriétés d'icelle dans leurs implexes—résonances, symétries, etc.— sur la *corde* de la *voix*. En somme, le *Langage* issu de la *voix*, plutôt que la *voix* du *Langage*.' ('My dream, as a poet, would have been to compose a discourse—an utterance of modulation and internal connexion–in which the physical, the psychic and the conventions of language could combine their resources. With this or that division and well defined changes of tone. / But *who is it exactly* who speaks in a poem? Mallarmé wanted it to be Language itself. / For me—it would be—the *living* AND *thinking* Being (*note the contrast*) and pushing consciousness of Self to the capture of one's sensibility–developing the properties of the latter in their implexes—resonances, symmetries, etc.—on the *instrument* of the *voice*. In short, *Language* born of *Voice*, rather than the *Voice* of *Language*.') (1939, *Cahiers* I, 293, Valéry's emphases). See J. R. Lawler, 'Saint Mallarmé', op. cit., 195, for Valéry's moving poem on Mallarmé's voice: *Psaume sur une voix: à propos de Stéphane Mallarmé*.

25. Valéry's idea of 'attente' ('attentive waiting'), is most fully and vividly developed in the dialogue, *Eupalinos ou l'Architecte*.

26. Valéry's 24 June 1898 letter to Mallarmé provides an excellent summary of Valéry's ideal existence: 'J'imagine que vous êtes au milieu même d'un massif de travail, d'air en mouvement et de calme. Rien au monde ne vaut ces quelques choses et si j'avais besoin de la notion du sublime, si on me requérait de la préciser, je dirais que je me représente, à ce sujet, simplement la matinée d'un monsieur qui se porte bien et pense.' ('I imagine you in the middle of a massif of work, summery breezes

and calm. There is nothing in the world to equal these things, and if I needed to express my notion of the sublime, if I were asked to provide a precise definition of it, I would say that I see it quite simply as the morning of someone in good health with time to think.') (Mallarmé, *Correspondance*, X, 231, n. 1).

27. Valéry later claimed that Mallarmé saw *Un coup de dés* as moving in an intellectual direction on the path already taken by Valéry: 'Ce que Mallarmé m'a dit en me communiquant *Le coup de dés*, qu'il avait pensait (*sic*), sur ce type, faire *chaque année*, un ouvrage de caractère *plus intellectuel*—que l'expression poétique ordinaire ne l'admettait—me donna à songer qu'il se heurtait de ce côté à une difficulté qui m'était bien connue—(puisque j'avais renoncé depuis 4 ou 5 ans à la poésie— pour cette raison entre autres). / Vient un moment où les thèmes et les mots possibles en poésie française ne suffisent plus à exciter l'esprit doué d'un certain pouvoir d'abstraction—et le problème insoluble se pose. / Je l'ai abordé 20 ans après avec la J[eune] P[arque].' ('What Mallarmé said to me when he showed me *Le coup de dés*, that he had thought of creating each year on that model a work of a more intellectual type—than ordinary poetic expression normally allows–gave me to think that in that respect he had come up against a difficulty well known to me (since I had given up poetry 4 or 5 years earlier– for this reason amongst others. / There comes a moment when the possible words and themes of French poetry are no longer enough to satisfy a mind endowed with a certain ability for abstract thought—and the insoluble problem presents itself. I treated it 20 years later in The Y[oung] F[ate].') (*Cahier* XXIII (1940), (Paris: CNRS, 1960) 152).

28. Valéry's equating of the training of the mind with the athlete's training of the body can be readily studied in *Cahiers*, I, 321–77, under the rubric 'Gladiator'.

29. John Sparrow, *Visible Words. A Study of Inscriptions in and as Books and Works of Art* (Cambridge: Cambridge University Press, 1969), 119–20, discusses an engraving by the sixteenth-century epigrapher Emanuele Tesauro, where Mercury, messenger of the Gods, with his finger on the blank sheet of a book, enjoins the epigraphic Muse to abandon her inscription on stone for that of the printed page. Mallarmé's gesture appears similarly emblematic.

30. 'Et vous, grande âme, espérez-vous un songe / Qui n'aura plus ces couleurs de mensonge / Qu'aux yeux de chair l'onde et l'or font ici? / Chanterez-vous quand serez vaporeuse? / Allez! Tout fuit! Ma présence, est poreuse, / La sainte impatience meurt aussi!' ('And you, great poet, do you seek a dream / Which will no longer have those deceptive colours / Proposed to mortal eye by wave and golden light / Will you still sing

as vaporous shade? / Come! all dissolves; porous is my presence / Sacred impatience is mortal too.') (*Le Cimetière marin*, st. 17 (*Œuvres* I, 150)).

31. The *Cahiers* show the importance of the remark for Valéry: 'Mallarmé me dit hier (14 juillet 98) à Valvins: le blé—c'est comme le 1er coup de cymbale de l'automne sur la terre' ('Yesterday (14 July 1898) at Valvins Mallarmé said to me: the corn is like the first golden stroke of autumn's cymbals across the earth') (1897–98, *Cahiers* II, 1059) and his touching addition following Mallarmé's death: 'C'est la dernière fois que je l'ai vu (9bre 98)' ('It was the last time I saw him (9 Nov. 98)')

32. The other text in this group is *Sorte de préface* (*Œuvres* I, 680–6) written as an introduction to Mallarmé's *Thèmes anglais pour toutes les grammaires. Les mille proverbes, dictons et phrases typiques de l'anglais groupés d'après les règles de la grammaire* (Paris: Gallimard, 1937).

33. The ambivalence of Mallarmé's *Tombeau de Charles Baudelaire* with its final allusion to the poet of *Les Fleurs du Mal* as a 'poison tutélaire / Toujours à respirer si nous en périssons' ('a tutelary poison / Always to be respired even if the outcome is our death') (Mallarmé, *Poésies*, ed. Bertrand Marchal (Paris: Gallimard, 1992), 61), prefigures Valéry's own ambivalent stance vis-à-vis Mallarmé.

34. Valéry repeats here an idea developed in a 1914 letter to Gide: 'J'ai pu me convaincre que le Mallarmé de 186 . . . et le Rimbaud de 69–70 étaient bien peu éloignés. Il y a eu un moment de croisement . . . On peut bien l'expliquer par l'*époque*. Si l'on veut bien oublier que ces rencontres *au contraire* la définissent, l'époque!' ('I have become convinced that the Mallarmé of 186 . . . and the Rimbaud of 69–70 were quite close to each other. There was a moment when their paths crossed . . . That can be explained by the *era*. But only if it is forgotten that it is such meetings that define an era *rather than the other way about*.') (*Correspondance Gide–Valéry*, 437, Valéry's emphasis).

35. In a *Cahiers* entry Valéry recognizes Mallarmé's poem as the precondition of his own: '*À Mallarmé et moi*—je considère, ce matin, dans l'obscur de l'heure et de la clarté particulière de ce moment d'éveil en présence de l'absence de la lumière—les différences de poèmes comme *Hérodiade, L'Après-midi d'un faune* et la *Jeune Parque*. Celle-ci n'aurait pas existé sans ceux-là, bien entendu. Mais c'est là ce qui est intéressant quant aux différences—de conditions.' ('*To Mallarmé and me*—this morning in the darkness of the hour and the peculiar clarity of this moment of awakening in the presence of the absence of light I reflect on the differences between poems such as *Hérodiade, L'Après-midi d'un faune* and *La Jeune Parque*. The latter would not of course have existed without the former. But that is just what is interesting concerning the differences–of conditions.') (1940–41, *Cahiers* I, 297).

36. These letters were first published in 1923 and 1924, see Mallarmé, *Correspondance* I, 127, n. 5 and p. 195, n. 1.
37. There are only two direct allusions to specific texts, a single, brief passing reference to *Hérodiade*, *Les Fleurs*, *Le Cygne* as the first Mallarmé poems to come to Valéry's notice, and quotation of the celebrated 'Je dis UNE FLEUR' ('I say the word FLOWER') as an illustration of the creative process of attentive waiting.
38. Valéry's characterization of these kindred spirits as 'Essences' reveals a crucial point of difference with Mallarmé. Where Mallarmé emphasizes looking beyond the Self to the virtualities of the Poetic Idea, Valéry stresses the Essence constituted by the Self and the unique space it claims as its own.
39. This is one possible intertextual suggestion to add to the various readings of the final stanza of *Le Cimetière marin*.
40. 'Mais Lui, les yeux voilés, étant de ceux qui ne savent attendre et ne peuvent goûter l'ivresse que de soi, se taisait' ('But He, eyes turned away, being one of those who can only accept and savour his own sense of achievement, remained silent') (*Œuvres* I, 644). Valéry's own stance is similarly self-sufficient: 'Je me suis donné ma gloire—Moi seul le pouvais. Ce fut une critique incomparable et incessante de moi-même.' ('My glory was something I gave myself. Only I could do it. It consisted of an unrivalled and incessant critique of myself.') (1903–5, *Cahiers* I, 35).
41. A 1916 *Cahiers* entry draws a clear distinction between the different visions of Villiers and Mallarmé: 'Villiers fut un improvisateur, un homme capable de dire pendant des heures et de donner l'illusion durant toute une nuit—prestidigitateur illusionniste de café. Son antithèse était Mallarmé qui avait l'esprit du calcul le plus élégant, le génie des combinaisons de mots et des mots. La vision conduisait le langage chez Villiers et la parole l'enivrait—Elle était chez Mallarmé l'objet même de l'art, la signification étant presque l'accessoire de cette fonction, la conséquence plutôt que le principe.' ('Villiers was an improviser, a man able to hold forth for hours and fool his audience through an entire night—a pavement conjuror and illusionist. Mallarmé with the exceptional elegance of his logic and his genius for word combinations and individual words was his complete opposite. Villiers's vision directed his language and words intoxicated him. For Mallarmé language was the object of art, meaning being almost accessory, the consequence, rather than a determining principle.') (*Cahiers* II, 1171).
42. This letter can be read in *Œuvres* I, 1746–49 (1748). It was earlier published in *Lettres à quelques-uns*, 93–96 (95).
43. 'Il y a en moi des parties de tyran—au sens antique. À défaut d'autres

êtres je n'ai tyrannisé que des pensées. Mais je suis certain de contenir des atomes d'absolutisme, des éléments de non-discussion.' ('There are within me elements of the tyrant–as defined by the Greeks and Romans. In the absence of other people, my tyranny has been limited to my thought. But I am certain I contain atoms of absolutism, elements which are not up for discussion.') (1920, *Cahiers* I, 87). For a discussion of some intellectual and political aspects of Valéry's Caesarism, see my article, *Caesarism and Valéry* (forthcoming).

44. Mallarmé, *Correspondance*, X, Appendice X, 318–9.

45. Following the publication of *La Jeune Parque*, the same metaphor is used to stage the need for a refusal by the author to be restricted in his self-development by any item of finished work: 'Je suis dans l'état si remarquable de l'éfrit dont enfin le pêcheur ouvrit la bouteille. J'ai dégagé ma fumée, et maintenant je veux décapiter le pêcheur. / L'éfrit c'est mon ouvrage. Et le pêcheur, moi.' ('I am in the remarkable state of the genie whose bottle is finally opened by the fisherman. I have released my puff of smoke and now I want to decapitate the fisherman. The genie is my poem. The fisherman is me.') (1917, *Cahiers* I, 246).

Chapter Three

1. Gordon Millan, *A Throw of the Dice: The Life of Stéphane Mallarmé* (New York: Farrar Straus Giroux, 1994), 3, henceforth abbreviated ML.

2. Roland Barthes, *Le Degré zéro de l'écriture* (Paris: Seuil, 1953). The full context of Barthes's remark reads: 'Mallarmé, finally, crowned this construction of the Literature-Object by the ultimate act of all objectifications, murder: we know that Mallarmé's whole effort concentrated on a destruction of language, of which Literature would be in a way the cadaver' (12). Later in the work, Barthes explicitly attributes 'this hypothesis of a Mallarmé murderer of language' to Maurice Blanchot (108). These and all subsequent translations of French are mine. Quotations from Sartre's works, as well as Mallarmé's, will be presented in French along with my English translations, which, in order to convey the writer's meaning as accurately as possible, will privilege literal over figurative renderings.

3. Cary Wolfe, 'Rethinking Commitment: Ontology, Genre, and Sartre's *Mallarmé*', *Diacritics* (winter 1991), 77. Moreover, Barthes, mirroring Sartre, perceives 'the structure of suicide' in Mallarmé's verse art.

4. H. W. Wardman, *Jean-Paul Sartre: The Evolution of His Thought and Art* (Lewiston, NY: Edwin Mellen Press, 1992), 185.

5. See, for example, *L'Etre et le Néant*, ed. Arlette Elkaïm-Sartre (Paris: Gallimard 'Tel', 1943), 614–20, henceforth abbreviated EN.

6. In his search for the right term to describe the unique products of Sartre's 'biographical discourse' (1), Michael Scriven, *Sartre's Existential Biogaphies* (London: Macmillan, 1984), rather reluctantly settles on 'existential biographies' after considering 'Literary or post-literary biography', 'Critical biography', 'Marxist or neo-Marxist biography' (29). Benjamin Suhl, *Jean-Paul Sartre: The Philosopher as a Literary Critic* (New York: Columbia University Press, 1970), and Joseph Halpern, *Critical Fictions: The Literary Criticism of Jean-Paul Sartre* (New Haven: Yale University Press, 1976) both situate these works in Sartre's literary criticism. Suhl considers them to be demonstrations of Sartre's 'critical existentialist psychoanalysis' (152); Halpern, as his title indicates, sees them as having a literary fictive dimension themselves.

7. Jean-Paul Sartre, *Mallarmé: la lucidité et sa face d'ombre*, ed. Arlette Elkaïm-Sartre (Paris: Gallimard, 1986), henceforth abbreviated SM.

8. See, for example, Elkaïm-Sartre's *présentation* (SM, 9–10) for a succinct, up-to-date account.

9. Although it is generally recognized that Sartre assembled notes on the Mallarmé project between 1948 and 1952, the editor's introduction to the version published in *Obliques* 18–19 (1979) dates the writing of the text to 1952, making it, as Scriven points out (78), marginally posterior to the *Saint Genet* (written between 1948 and 1951).

10. Although the original Gallimard edition of *Poésies* is dated 1945 and Sartre's preface 1952, when it was written, Elkaïm-Sartre gives 1966 as the date for its actual inclusion as the volume's preface. In the 1992 revised edition, it was replaced by one written by Yves Bonnefoy.

11. 'Tel qu'en Lui-même enfin l'éternité le change', Stéphane Mallarmé, 'Le Tombeau d'Edgar Poe', *Œuvres complètes*, ed. Henri Mondor and G. Jean-Aubry (Paris: Gallimard-Pléiade, 1945), 70, hereinafter cited as *Œuvres complètes*.

12. Douglas Collins, *Sartre as Biographer* (Cambridge: Harvard University Press, 1980), 5.

13. This follows Scriven's account, which provides further details (2ff.).

14. Jean-Yves Debreuille, 'De Baudelaire à Ponge: Sartre lecteur des poètes', in *Lectures de Sartre*, ed. Claude Burgelin (Lyon: Presses Universitaires de Lyon, 1986), 276.

15. For an analysis of Sartre's evolving view of commitment, see Rhiannon Goldthorpe, 'Mallarmé: Sartre's Committed Poet', in *Baudelaire, Mallarmé, Valéry: New Essays in Honour of Lloyd Austin*, ed. Malcolm Bowie, Alison Fairlie, and Alison Finch (Cambridge: Cambridge University Press, 1982), 222–41.

16. See Jean-Paul Sartre, 'Autoportrait à soixante-dix ans', *Situations, X* (Paris: Gallimard, 1976), 137–9, henceforth abbreviated SX.

17. Jean-Paul Sartre, 'Sur "L'Idiot de la famille" ' (SX, 106).

18. Consider, further, the case of *Les Mains sales*. How can Sartre, the man, who admitted to being embarrassed by any tenderness or intimacy with other men, be compared to Hoederer, who offers up his life for love and trust of a young man, Hugo, despite the latter's repeated spurning of his mentor's attempts to bring him more intimately into his confidence? Sartre, in this respect, was more like the rejecting, distancing Hugo, even though he stated publicly that Hoederer, not Hugo, was the one he most admired and identified with. (For a detailed discussion of the Hugo–Hoederer relationship, see my article, 'Ethics and Revolution in Sartre's *Les Mains sales*', in *Situating Sartre in Twentieth-Century Thought and Culture*, ed. Jean-François Fourny and Charles D. Minahen [New York and London: St Martin's Press, 1997]).

19. 'Aux noirs vols du Blasphème épars dans le futur', 'Le Tombeau d'Edgar Poe' (*Œuvres complètes*, 70).

20. The subtitle Ernest Sturm gives to his English translation of *Mallarmé: la lucidité et sa face d'ombre: Mallarmé, or the Poet of Nothingness* (University Park: Pennsylvania State University Press, 1988).

21. Henri Mondor, *Vie de Mallarmé* (Paris: Gallimard, 1941), 13.

22. Wallace Fowlie, *Mallarmé* (Chicago: University of Chicago Press, 1970), 105.

23. Bertrand Marchal, *Lecture de Mallarmé* (Paris: Corti, 1985), 264.

24. 'de ce simple fait qu'il peut causer l'ombre en soufflant sur la lumière', *Igitur* (*Œuvres complètes*, 433).

25. Despite the many possible referents proposed in the debate over the word's meaning, I am of the opinion—supported by the poet himself —that the term was selected exclusively for its exotic sound (a rare 'x' rime in French) and appearance. It is a signifier that, having no referent, has no signified. As such, it is open to receive any signified pointing to any referent the reader chooses to assign it within the context of the poem, which, we must remember, was, in its original version, entitled 'Sonnet allégorique de lui-même' ('Sonnet allegorical of itself'). For Mallarmé's own comments regarding the meaning of 'ptyx', see Stéphane Mallarmé, *Œuvres complètes: Poésies*, ed. Carl Paul Barbier and Charles Gordon Millan (Paris: Flammarion, 1983), 221–2.

26. 'Crise de vers', *Variations sur un sujet* (*Œuvres complètes*, 368).

27. 'celui / son ombre puérile / caressée et polie et rendue et lavée', *Un Coup de dés jamais n'abolira le hasard* (*Œuvres complètes*, 464).

28. Scriven points to a transitional phase where a blurring of characters in Sartre's use of the novel and biography is evident (40).

29. In volume 3 of *L'Idiot de la famille* (Paris: Gallimard, 1972), Sartre repeatedly uses the expression 'chevalier du Néant' to describe individuals among the group of atheistic, nihilistic French writers of the second half of the nineteenth century, whose aesthetic culminated, he believes, in the poetry of Mallarmé.

30. What Sartre terms 'l'universel singulier' is made manifest in the literary work. Goldthorpe defines it as 'a synthesis of the subjective and the objective, the individual and the socio-historical; a "totalizing" synthesis which constitutes the "engagement" of the writer, represents his "liberté créatrice" (creative liberty) and sustains his communication with the reader' (223). Wolfe explains the concept as follows: 'For Sartre, from *Being and Nothingness* on, the self is first and foremost to be conceived of as a totality—man is totalized and constituted by his conditions of existence and in his actions recapitulates and retotalizes those conditions, but in singular and individual form' (78).

31. Roland Barthes, *Mythologies* (Paris: Seuil 'Points', 1957), 199–202.

32. Christina Howells, 'Sartre and Negative Theology', *The Modern Language Review* 76:3 (July 1981), 553.

33. 'lui . . . à qui on fait remonter la présentation, en tant qu'explosif, d'un concept trop vierge, à la Société', *La Musique et les lettres* (*Œuvres complètes*, 651).

34. *Les Interviews de Mallarmé*, ed. Dieter Schwarz (Neuchâtel: Ides & Calendes, 1995), 75, henceforth abbreviated IM. Schwarz carefully documents Mallarmé's relationship to the anarchist unrest of 1892–94 (see 70–82).

35. In their annotated bibliography, *Les Écrits de Sartre* (Paris: Gallimard, 1970), Michel Contat and Michel Rybalka cite a 1960 interview in which Sartre states that 'Mallarmé devait être très different de l'image qu'on a donnée de lui. C'est notre plus grand poète. Un passionné, un furieux. Et maître de lui jusqu'à pouvoir se tuer par un simple mouvement de la glotte! . . . Son engagement me paraît aussi total que possible: social autant que poétique' ('Mallarmé had to be very different from the image that has been given of him. He is our greatest poet. A passionate, furious one. And master of himself to the point of being able to kill himself with a simple movement of the glottis! . . . His committment seems to me as total as possible: social as much as poetic') (262). This portrait differs greatly from the one so painstakingly laid out in 'L'Engagement de Mallarmé', and since it is a statement made spontaneously in an interview without any suppporting evidence, it cannot properly be assessed or relied upon. Although Sartre obviously changed his mind about the nature of Mallarmé's *engagement*, he not only persisted in his view of him as suicidal, but here even claims that

Mallarmé physically committed the act by intentionally choking himself. Although the poet did experience a sudden, fatal respiratory contraction, Millan explains that it occurred during a coughing fit brought on by an acute case of tonsillitis (317).

36. Goldthorpe concludes that Mallarmé, to some degree at least, 'changes Sartre' (238).

37. John Gerassi, *Jean-Paul Sartre: Hated Conscience of His Century*, vol. 1 (Chicago: University of Chicago Press, 1989), 3–4.

38. A version of this essay was presented at the Mallarmé Centenary Conference (to celebrate the delivery of 'La Musique et les lettres' by Mallarmé at Pembroke College, Cambridge on 2 March 1894), Pembroke College, University of Cambridge, 5 March 1994.

Chapter Four

1. Stéphane Mallarmé, *Œuvres complètes*, ed. Henri Mondor and G. Jean-Aubry (Paris: Gallimard-Pléiade, 1951), 55–7.

2. *Mallarmé: The Poems*, trans. Keith Bosley (Harmondsworth: Penguin, 1977), 135–9.

3. Jacques Lacan, *Écrits* (Paris: Seuil, 1966), 843–4.

4. *Reading Seminar XI: Lacan's Four Fundamental Concepts of Psychanalysis: the Paris Seminars in English*, ed. Richard Feldstein, Bruce Fink and Maire Jaanus, trans. Bruce Fink (Albany, NY: State University of New York Press, 1995), 271–2.

5. Roman Jakobson, 'Two Aspects of Language', in *Language in Literature*, ed. Krystyna Pomorska and Stephen Rudy (Cambridge, Mass.: Harvard University Press, 1987), 95–119.

6. Jacques Lacan, *Télévision* (Paris: Seuil, 1973), 72.

7. Paul Valéry, *Œuvres* (Paris: Gallimard-Pléiade, 1957), vol. 1, 139. English version by David Paul in Paul Valéry, *Poems* (London: Routledge and Kegan Paul, 1971), 189.

8. Jacques Lacan, *Les Psychoses* (Séminaire VII) (Paris: Seuil, 1981), 207 ff.

9. 'optimism of the signifier', Jean-Pierre Richard, *Paysage de Chateaubriand* (Paris: Seuil, 1967), 162.

10. The three papers are: 'Fonction et champ de la parole et du langage en psychanalyse', 'La chose Freudienne', 'L'instance de la lettre dans l'inconscient ou la raison depuis Freud'.

Chapter Five

1. 'Critique is therefore dangerous and wearisome.' Friedrich von Hardenberg (Novalis), *Die Enzyklopädie*, II Abteilung: Philosophie, frag. 138.
2. Henri Mondor, *Vie de Mallarmé* (Paris: Gallimard, 1941).
3. Jean-Pierre Richard, *L'Univers imaginaire de Mallarmé* (Paris: Editions du Seuil, 1961), 13.
4. Maurice Blanchot, *Faux pas* (Paris: Gallimard, 1943).
5. See 'Pour l'amitié', in Dionys Mascolo, *A la recherche d'un communisme de pensée* (Paris: Fourbis, 1993), 5–16, for an account of the composition of *Faux pas*.
6. For a recent instance of this, see Jacques Rancière, *Mallarmé. La politique de la sirène* (Paris: Hachette, 1996), 10: 'Maurice Blanchot a donné ses titres de noblesse à cette interprétation qui fait de l'écrivain le héros d'une aventure spirituelle' ('Maurice Blanchot has conferred respectability on the interpretation which makes the writer into the hero of a spiritual adventure').
7. *Le Journal des Débats* (16 April 1941), 3.
8. This is a clear reference to Victor Hugo's collection of poems, *Les Voix intérieures*, which appeared in 1837.
9. Blanchot's use of the term *agiter* opens up a significant avenue of thought. Reading his inaugural reflections, in the midst of war, upon a mode of literary *critique* which is at the same time of intellectual standing, it is interesting to recall that philosophy, for Kant, was 'a permanent armed state' (*ein immer bewaffneter Zustand*), and at the same time 'an agitation (*Agitation*) of the mind'. I take these pointers from Jean-François Lyotard, 'Judicieux dans le différend', in *La Faculté de juger*, ed. Jacques Derrida et al. (Paris: Editions de Minuit, 1985), 195–235.
10. Letter to Villiers de l'Isle Adam, 24 September 1867; letter to Henri Cazalis, 14 May 1867.
11. Mallarmé was crowned 'Prince des Poètes' at a banquet on 27 January 1896.
12. 'Le biographe connaît le "génie" et ignore l'homme' ('The biographer knows the "genius" but does not know the man'), *Journal des Débats*, 23 April 1941, 3; 'Le silence de Mallarmé', *Journal des Débats*, 1 April 1942, 3.
13. *Faux pas*, 117–25.
14. Blanchot's development as a critic is marked initially by an effort to disengage his thinking from that of Paul Valéry. In 1946, an article entitled 'Le mythe de Mallarmé', which opens by welcoming Mondor's edition of Mallarmé's complete works in the 'Pléiade' series, proceeds

to an extended critique of the way Valéry's discipleship ultimately obscured Mallarmé's work. (See *La Part du feu* (Paris: Gallimard, 1949), 35–48.)

15. In 1984, Blanchot recalls that, in a letter to Henri Mondor in 1941, Paul Valéry too reflects upon this same theme: 'Comment et d'où naquit cette étrange et inébranlable *certitude* sur laquelle Mallarmé a pu fonder toute sa vie?' ('How and from where did there arise the strange and unshakable *certainty* on which Mallarmé was able to base his entire life?'). See Paul Valéry, letter to Henri Mondor, 16 February 1941, in *Lettres à quelques-uns* (Paris: Gallimard, 1952), 231. See also Maurice Blanchot, 'La parole ascendante', in Vadim Kozovoï, *Hors de la colline* (Paris: Hermann, 1984), 125. At this much later stage, Blanchot distances himself from the notion of *certainty* which both he and Valéry invoke in 1941.

16. 'L'expérience d'*Igitur*', in *L'Espace littéraire* (Paris: Gallimard, 1955; collection 'Idées'), 133–49.

17. Jean-Pierre Richard, *L'Univers imaginaire de Mallarmé*, 14.

18. See Henri Mondor, 'Avant-propos' to Stéphane Mallarmé, *Correspondance 1862–1871*, ed. Henri Mondor and Jean-Pierre Richard (Paris: Gallimard, 1959), 7.

19. See *Le pas au-delà* (Paris: Gallimard, 1973).

20. 'L'absence de livre', in *L'Entretien infini* (Paris: Gallimard, 1969), 628; 'The Absence of the Book', in *The Infinite Conversation*, translated by Susan Hanson (Minneapolis and London: The University of Minnesota Press, 1993), 428.

21. Malcolm Bowie, *Henri Michaux* (Oxford; OUP, 1973), 68–9.

22. Letter to Cazalis, 14 May 1867.

23. Letter to Cazalis, 3 March 1871.

24. This reference to Novalis is by no means adventitious. The *Enzyklopädie* contains a radical post-Kantian definition of critique which, fragmentary in both its form and its *ratio*, significantly prefigures certain twentieth-century developments in thought. See for example frag. 138; 'der genialischer Denker . . . dessen Behauptungen nichts als unzusammenhängende kritische Prinzipien sind' ('the thinker of genius . . . whose affirmations are nothing but unconnected critical principles').

25. 'La poésie de Mallarmé est-elle obscure?', in *Faux pas*, 131. This first appeared in the *Journal des Débats* in February 1942.

Chapter Six

1. 'Montaigne and Transcendence' (1953), in *Critical Writings 1953–1978*, ed. Lindsay Waters (Minneapolis: University of Minnesota Press, 1989), 7. Abbreviated in the text as CW.

2. De Man quotes Mallarmé in 'The Double Aspect of Symbolism' (1954–56?); 'The Temptation of Permanence' (1955); 'Process and Poetry' (1956); 'The Intentional Structure of the Romantic Image' (1960); 'Wordsworth and Hölderlin' (1966); 'Impersonality in the Work of Maurice Blanchot' (1966); 'Ludwig Binswanger and the Sublimation of the Self' (1966); 'Rousseau and the Transcendence of the Self' (1967); 'The Crisis of Contemporary Criticism' (1967) and 'Criticism and Crisis' (1971); 'The Literary Self as Origin: The Work of Georges Poulet' (1969); 'Lyric and Modernity' (1970); 'The Rhetoric of Blindness' (1971); 'Shelley Disfigured' (1979); and three times in *Allegories of Reading* (1979). Many more essays mention Mallarmé—ten at the least.

3. De Man is also influenced by the Mallarmé interpretation of Karlheinz Stierle, one of whose essays he discusses in 'Lyric and Modernity'; see *Blindness and Insight: Essays in the Rhetoric of Contemporary Criticism*, 2nd edn (Minneapolis: University of Minnesota Press, 1983), 174–86. *Blindness and Insight* will be abbreviated in the text as BI. See also Stierle's 'Position and Negation in Mallarmé's "Prose Pour des Esseintes"', *Yale French Studies* 54 (1977), 96–117; the essay was published in an issue on Mallarmé at a time when de Man was still on the editorial board. On de Man, Mallarmé, and Baudelaire, see Ortwin de Graef, *Serenity in Crisis: A Preface to Paul de Man, 1939–1960* (Lincoln and London: University of Nebraska Press, 1993), 89–91, 144–9.

4. In addition, in 1970 the relation between Baudelaire and Mallarmé 'is not the genetic movement of a historical process'. Rather, it 'is more like the uneasy and shifting border line that separates poetic truth from poetic falsehood', the wavering of which measures 'the absolute ambivalence of language' (BI, 184–5).

5. 'Mallarmé, Yeats, and the Post-Romantic Predicament' (doctoral dissertation, Harvard University, May 1960), 20. Abbreviated as PRP.

6. 'Anthropomorphism and Trope in the Lyric', in *The Rhetoric of Romanticism* (New York: Columbia University Press, 1984), 252. Abbreviated as RR.

7. 'The Contemporary Crisis of Romanticism', in *Romanticism and Contemporary Criticism: The Gauss Seminar and Other Papers*, ed. E. S. Burt,

Kevin Newmark, and Andrzej Warminski (Baltimore: The Johns Hopkins University Press, 1993), 10. Abbreviated as RCC.

8. *Mallarmé, or the Poet of Nothingness*, trans. Ernest Sturm (University Park and London: Pennsylvania State University Press, 1988), 136, 144.

9. In 1966, the same year that de Man debates Mallarmé's suicide texts with Blanchot, he writes of de Staël in analogous terms: 'Against the fundamental inconstancy of being, the self is defenseless. It can only let itself be driven toward the abyss of its own destruction, hastening if possible the deliberation of physical time by what will it has left. From this point of view, Madame de Staël's fictions, much more than the ironic *Werther* are an ill-disguised exhortation to suicide. But even in one of her earliest fictions, in the little narrative called *Zulma*, the heroine, a victim of infidelity, is allowed the few minutes necessary to interpret her destiny. This duration granted Zulma, which saves her from nothing and in no way diminishes her pain, nonetheless plays an important part: in this brief narrative, it symbolizes the act of literary creation' (CW, 175). De Staël also composed a defence of suicide.

10. 'Lurid Figures', in *Reading de Man Reading*, ed. Lindsay Waters and Wlad Godzich (Minneapolis: University of Minnesota Press, 1989), 82–104, and 'More Lurid Figures', *Diacritics* 20 (1990), 2–27.

11. ' "A Pathos of Uncertain Agency"; Paul de Man and Narrative', *Journal of Narrative Technique*, 20 (1990), 195–209.

12. Having treated de Man's reading of *Un coup de dés* elsewhere, I focus here on *Hérodiade* and *Igitur*.

13. *Revolution in Poetic Language*, trans. Margaret Waller (New York: Columbia University Press, 1984), 227. See also 231.

14. Translation by M. Temple. *Œuvres complètes*, ed. Henri Mondor and G. Jean-Aubry (Paris: Gallimard-Pléiade, 1945), 74. Abbreviated as *Œuvres complètes*.

15. Kevin Newmark makes a similar point in his comprehensive reading of 'Une dentelle . . . ': 'the figure of the bed . . . becomes infinitely more blasphemous . . . by shading into the uncertain status of the three letters *"l-i-t"* that return to haunt the rhyming words of the second stanza' ('Beneath the Lace: Mallarmé, the State, and the Foundation of Letters', *Yale French Studies* 77 [1990]), 264.

16. Similarly, de Man notes in his dissertation that for Mallarmé ' "ennui" is not the cause of sterility: to the contrary, the one unable to know "ennui" must be called sterile' (PRP, 44–5).)

17. See Newmark 256–7; Barbara Johnson, 'Allegory's Strip-Tease: *The White Waterlily*', in *The Critical Differences: Essays in the Contemporary Rhetoric of Reading* (Baltimore: The Johns Hopkins University Press,

1980) 13–20; and Leo Bersani, *The Death of Stéphane Mallarmé* (Cambridge: Cambridge University Press, 1982), 68–73.

18. 'Shaking Down the Pillars: Lamentation, Purity, and Mallarmé's "Hommage" to Wagner', *PMLA* 111 (1996), 1108–9.
19. See Lacan, *Écrits: A Selection*, trans. Alan Sheridan (New York and London: W. W. Norton, 1977), 55.
20. *The Sublime Object of Ideology* (London: Verso, 1989), 133.
21. *The Four Fundamental Concepts of Psycho-Analysis*, ed. Jacques-Alain Miller, trans. Alan Sheridan (New York and London: W. W. Norton, 1978), 166.
22. *Unfolding Mallarmé: The Development of a Poetic Art* (Oxford: Oxford University Press, 1996), 83.
23. *The Space of Literature*, trans. Ann Smock (Lincoln and London: University of Nebraska Press, 1982), 43. See also Leslie Hill, 'Blanchot and Mallarmé', *MLN* 105 (1990), 889–13.
24. See also BI, 71.
25. *A Rhetoric of Motives* (Berkeley: University of California Press, 1969), 8.
26. 'Far from being a knowledge with a positive and determinate content', de Man writes in 1956, 'the process of becoming is thus essentially the knowledge of a nonknowledge, the knowledge of the persistent indetermination that is historical temporality' (CW, 67).
27. De Man uses this famous line as the epigraph to his dissertation and quotes it in 'Rousseau and the Transcendence of the Self' (RCC, 34) and in 'Lyric and Modernity' (BI, 179). Many other pieces seem to be written under its legend.
28. For Hegel, 'the duty of the member of a Family' is to ensure that 'the individual's ultimate being, too, shall not . . . remain something irrational, but shall be something *done*, and the right of consciousness be asserted in it.' *Phenomenology of Spirit*, trans. A. V. Miller (Oxford: Oxford University Press, 1977), 270.
29. *The Seminar of Jacques Lacan (VII: The Ethics of Psychoanalysis*, trans. Dennis Porter), ed. Jacques-Alain Miller (New York: W. W. Norton, 1988–).
30. This motif appears most notoriously at the end of 'Shelley Disfigured': 'what we have done with the dead Shelley, and with all the other dead bodies that appear in romantic literature . . . is simply to bury them, to bury them in their own texts made into epitaphs and monumental graves' (RR, 121).
31. See Jean Hyppolite, 'The Figure of the Immutable' and 'Unity of Actual Reality and Self-Consciousness', in *Genesis and Structure of Hegel's Phenomenology of Spirit*, trans. Samuel Cherniak and John Heckman (Evanston: Northwestern University Press, 1974), especially 199–206.

32. De Man deals with the 'symmetrical structure' of animation in 'Autobiography as De-Facement', in which the animating poet is de-animated by his use of prosopopoeia (RR, 78). But at no point is the poet *made legible* by his commerce with legends, since legends themselves are not legible.

33. In his note on *Hamlet*, Mallarmé represents a similar suspension as 'l'heure extraordinaire' that 'n'est plus ou pas encore' (*Œuvres complètes*, 299).

34. 'Black and White Myths: Etymology and Dialectics in Mallarmé's "Sonnet en yx" ', *Texas Studies in Literature and Language* 36 (1994), 193.

35. 'Force and Signification', in *Writing and Difference*, trans. Alan Bass (Chicago: University of Chicago Press, 1978), 9. On the passion of writing's difficulty in 'Force and Signification', see Christopher Johnson, *System and Writing in the Philosophy of Jacques Derrida* (Cambridge: Cambridge University Press, 1993), 23–6.

36. De Man quotes the passage in which Baudelaire remarks that '[Guys] seems to be in anguish of not going fast enough, of letting the phantom escape before the synthesis has been extracted from it and recorded' (BI, 158). Guys's drawings parallel Mallarmé's verbal negations of objects—especially their beginning stages, 'pencil-marks that merely designate the place assigned to various objects' (BI, 158). Nothing but the place takes place in them.

37. *Studies in Poetic Discourse*, trans. William Whobrey and Bridget McDonald (Stanford: Stanford University Press, 1986), 59.

38. *Dissemination*, trans. Barbara Johnson (Chicago: University of Chicago Press, 1981), 214–15.

39. 'Reading for Example: "Sense-Certainty" in Hegel's *Phenomenology of Spirit*', in *Readings in Interpretation: Hölderlin, Hegel, Heidegger* (Minneapolis: University of Minnesota Press, 1987), 167.

40. *Mallarmé and the Art of Being Difficult* (Cambridge: Cambridge University Press, 1978). Of course, undecidability can be a mark of tenacity and courage and at the same time of morbidity and awkwardness as well.

41. *Letters from Prison*, volume 1, ed. Frank Rosengarten, trans. Raymond Rosenthal (New York: Columbia University Press, 1994), 299.

Chapter Seven

1. A note on the title-page of the article explains that in fact Derrida's text originally had no title, 'La double séance' being supplied by the review *Tel Quel*.

2. This distinction between the theoretical and the practical will not, naturally enough, survive the deconstructive process, but it is worth pointing out that Derrida's other text on Mallarmé ('Mallarmé', in *Tableau de la littérature française*, Vol. III (Paris: Gallimard, 1974), 369–78) stresses this value of the practical in a context where many other familiar terms are being placed in question: 'nous commençons à entrevoir que quelque chose a été machiné . . . pour déjouer les catégories de l'histoire et des classifications littéraires, de la critique littéraire, des philosophies et herméneutiques de tout genre. Nous commençons à entrevoir que le bouleversement de ces catégories aura aussi été l'effet de ce qui fut, par Mallarmé, écrit.

On ne peut même plus parler ici d'un *événement*, de l'événement d'un tel texte; on ne peut plus interroger son *sens* sauf à retomber en deçà de lui, dans le réseau de valeurs qu'il a *pratiquement* remises en question; celle d'événement (présence, singularité, singularité sans répétition possible, temporalité, historicité)' ('we are beginning to glimpse there has been some machination . . . to outplay the categories of history and of literary classifications, of literary criticism, of philosophies and hermeneutics of all sorts. We are beginning to glimpse that the upsetting of these categories was also the effect of what was, by Mallarmé, written.

We can no longer even speak of an *event* here, the event of such a text; we can no longer interrogate its *meaning* without falling back short of it, into the network of values it has *practically* placed in question; that of event (presence, singularity, singularity without possible repetition, temporality, historicity)') (369: all italics Derrida's); and again at the end, arguing that Mallarmé cannot be contained within the philosophical representation of rhetoric: 'Son texte échappe au contrôle de cette représentation, il en démontre *pratiquement* la non-pertinence.' ('His text escapes the control of this representation, it demonstrates *practically* its non-pertinence.') (378). All translations of passages from Derrida are my own.

3. In *Diderot: Thresholds of Representation* (Columbus: Ohio State University Press, 1986), James Creech takes issue with Derrida's claim in 'La double séance' (216–17, n. 12) that even Diderot does not escape this programme. In a 'postscript' entitled 'Idealism and Reversal: On a note by Jacques Derrida' (172–4), Creech argues that something other than the reversal of Platonism Derrida attributes to Diderot is happening in the latter's texts. This is indubitably the case, but can be presented as *critique* of Derrida only if one fails to note the difference between the moment in Derrida at which an 'official' doctrine is being reconstructed, and the moment at which that official doctrine is shown necessarily to

be untenable on its own terms. It is true that Derrida nowhere produces this second moment with respect to Diderot, nor indeed with respect to many other authors, whom further commentators can then enjoy themselves defending.

4. The *Tableau* text gives a relatively simple example which does not reappear in 'La double séance', from *Les Mots anglais*: 'Lecteur, vous avez sous les yeux ceci, un écrit . . .'.

5. Derrida discusses at some length the very considerable complexities of the text by Paul Margueritte that Mallarmé refers to, and summarizes as follows: 'un mimodrame "a lieu", écriture gestuelle sans livret, une préface est projetée puis écrite *après* l' "événement" pour précéder un livret écrit *après coup*, réfléchissant le mimodrame au lieu de le commander.' ('a mimodrama "takes place", unscripted gestural writing, a preface is projected then written *after* the "event" to precede a script written *after the fact*, reflecting the mimodrama instead of commanding it.') (226).

6. This structure of what it is tempting to call 'reflexivity' is often the source of misapprehension: cf. Descombes's complaints about a similar moment in Foucault, which I discuss in 'Outside Language', *Oxford Literary Review*, Vol. 11 (1989), 189–212. Rodolphe Gasché devastatingly pointed out the error of some 'deconstructive criticism' in identifying deconstruction with reflexivity: cf. 'Deconstruction as Criticism', *Glyph* 6 (1979), 177–216; reprinted in *Inventions of Difference* (Cambridge: Harvard University Press, 1994).

7. I discuss this structure in the context of deixis more generally in 'Index', *Legislations: The Politics of Deconstruction* (London: Verso Books, 1994), 274–95.

8. In 'Psyché: invention de l'autre' (in *Psyché: inventions de l'autre* (Paris: Galilée, 1987), 11–61), Derrida develops a similar argument around Francis Ponge's 'Fable', which begins 'Par le mot *par* commence donc ce texte / Dont la première ligne dit la vérité' ('With the word *with* begins then this text / Whose first line tells the truth'): 'Dans le corps d'un seul vers, sur la même ligne divisée, l'événement d'un énoncé confond deux fonctions absolument hétérogènes, "usage" et "mention", mais aussi hétéro-référence et auto-référence, allégorie et tautégorie.' ('In the body of a single line, on the same divided line, the event of a statement confuses two absolutely heterogeneous functions, "use" and "mention", but also hetero-reference and self-reference, allegory and tautegory.') (23). The undecidability about use and mention Derrida exploits here and elsewhere (cf. for example *De l'esprit* (Paris: Galilée, 1987), 52) can in fact be extended to the seminal Fregean distinction between *Sinn* and *Bedeutung*, as I try to show in a forthcoming work.

The principle of these arguments can be given by Derrida's simple claim in *Limited Inc.* that 'la différance est la référence' ('*Différance* is reference').

9. I use 'official' here to refer to the doctrine most obviously put forward by Plato's text, the reading most obviously encouraged by it. It is axiomatic in deconstructive thinking that such a reading always co-exists more or less uneasily with other textual resources it cannot by definition control.

10. Cf. 248: 'Le Mime *joue* dès lors qu'il ne se règle sur aucune action effective, et ne tend à aucune vraisemblance. Le jeu joue toujours la différence sans référence, ou plutôt sans référent, sans extériorité absolue, c'est-à-dire aussi bien sans dedans.' ('The Mime is *play-acting* from the moment he is no longer governed by any effective action, nor aims at any verisimilitude. The acting always plays upon difference without reference, or rather without referent, without absolute exteriority, i.e. equally without interiority.')

11. See also 'Le théâtre de la cruanté et la clôture de la representation'; *L'écriture et la différence* (Paris: Seuil, 1967).

12. Compare 239: 'Le référent étant levé, la référence demeurant' ('The referent being lifted, the reference remaining').

13. To this extent, all the remarks about ghosts in 'La double séance' anticipate the 'hauntology' developed much later by Derrida in *Spectres de Marx* (Paris: Galilée, 1993).

14. This involves Derrida's acceptance of a famous Hegelian argument from the *Greater Logic*. Absolute difference collapses back into absolute identity. Cf. G. W. F. Hegel, *The Science of Logic*, Book II, Section I, Chapter 2, and Derrida's comments in *Positions* (Paris: Minuit, 1972), 59–60 and note 6, and at the end of 'Violence et Métaphysique', in *L'écriture et la différence*, 227, n. 1.

15. Cf. the remarks in *Positions* on a 'strategy without finality'. It is important not to read this concept of strategy as leading to a political voluntarism, where readings would be dictated by desired political outcomes determined in advance of the reading. This was the mistake which inspired a certain sort of 'left' deconstruction, as recommended and variously practised by Tony Bennett and Terry Eagleton among others.

16. Cf. 282: 'S'il y a un système textuel, un thème n'existe pas' ('If there is a textual system, a theme does not exist').

17. 'Excès irréductible du syntaxique sur le sémantique' ('Irreducible excess of the syntactic over the semantic') (250), 'excès de la syntaxe sur le sens' ('excess of syntax over meaning') (261). Syntax here refers to the fact that meaning is not to be understood as atomically specifiable, but,

in the wake of the Saussurean view of language and differences-without-positive-terms, as relational or 'lateral'. It would be interesting to compare this notion of syntax to the notion of 'grammar' developed by Wittgenstein.

18. Cf. 204, 291, 293, 312.

19. Cf. the discussion of 'entre', leading to 'On n'est même plus autorisé à dire que "entre" soit un élément purement syntaxique. Outre sa fonction syntaxique, par la re-marque de son vide sémantique, il se met à signifier.* Son vide sémantique *signifie*, mais l'espacement et l'articulation; il a pour sens la possibilité de la syntaxe et il ordonne le jeu du sens. *Ni purement syntaxique, ni purement sémantique*, il marque l'ouverture articulée de cette opposition.' {*Derrida's note: 'Dès lors, le syncatégorème "entre" a pour contenu de sens un quasi-vide sémantique, il signifie la relation d'espacement, l'articulation, l'intervalle, etc. Il peut se laisser nominaliser, devenir un quasi-catégorème, recevoir un article défini, voire la marque du pluriel. Nous avons dit les "entre(s)" et ce pluriel est en quelque sorte "premier". L' "entre" n'existe pas.'} ('We are no longer even justified in saying that "between" is a purely syntactic element. Apart from its syntactic function, by the re-mark of its semantic emptiness, it begins to signify.* Its semantic emptiness *signifies*, but it signifies spacing and articulation; its meaning is the possibility of syntax and it orders the play of meaning. *Neither purely syntactic, nor purely semantic*, it marks the articulated opening of that opposition. {*Derrida's note: 'Given this, the syncategoreme "between" has as its meaning-content a semantic quasi-emptiness, it signifies the relation of spacing, articulation, the interval, etc. It can allow itself to be nominalized, become a quasi-categoreme, receive a definite article, or even the mark of the plural. We said "between(s)" and this plural is in some sense "first". The "between" does not exist'}) (251–2 and n. 27).

20. Cf. 267 ff. on the letter *i*.

21. Cf. for example the very prudent progression in *La voix et le phénomène* from a reasonably traditional use of 'commentaire' and 'interprétation' to a reading '*A travers* le texte de Husserl, c'est-à-dire dans une lecture qui ne peut être simplement ni celle du commentaire ni celle de l'interprétation' (Paris: PUF, 1967), 98 ('*Through* Husserl's text, i.e. in a reading which cannot simply be a question of commentary nor one of interpretation'). On the concept of analysis, see especially 'Résistances' (in *Résistances: de la psychanalyse* (Paris: Galilée, 1996), 13–53, and especially 41ff. on the complex relation of deconstruction to analysis: let us say provisionally that deconstruction is the *hyperbolic exasperation* of analysis).

Chapter Eight

1. 'Littérature potentielle' in Raymond Queneau, *Bâtons, Chiffres et Lettres* (Paris: Gallimard, 1950; édition revue et augmentée, Idées / Gallimard, 1965), 340. Translated in *Oulipo: A Primer of Potential Literature*, ed. and trans. Warren F. Motte Jr. (Lincoln & London: University of Nebraska Press, 1986), 62. Motte cites this in his introduction to the book, stating that '[Mallarmé] occupies a privileged position in the Oulipian laboratory'.

2. cf. Noël Arnaud's remarks: 'Academe, in the Oulipo's first decade, blissfully ignored Raymond Queneau and the Grands Rhétoriqueurs, considering them alike to be mere entertainers. It had just begun—in France at least—its infatuation with surrealism and psychoanalysis.' (*Oulipo: A Primer*, p.xii). Noël Arnaud's foreword wittily summarizes the history of the group and its intellectual co-ordinates past and present. A more impassioned and confrontational polemic may be found in Jacques Roubaud's 'What Have They Done to Us? The Theory Monster and the Writer' in *Ideas From France: the Legacy of French Theory*, ICA Documents (London: Free Association Books, 1989).

3. The history and membership of the Oulipo is well documented. *Oulipo: A Primer* (cited above), is a useful collection of texts translated into English. The primary French sources are *La Littérature potentielle: Créations, re-créations, récréations* (Paris: Gallimard, 1973), *Atlas le littérature potentielle* (Paris: Gallimard, 1981), and Jacques Bens, *OuLiPo 1960–1963* (Paris: Christian Bourgois Éditeur, 1980). Atlas Press is due to publish a major anthology in 1998.

4. Marjorie Perloff, *Radical Artifice: Writing Poetry in the Age of Media* (Chicago: University of Chicago Press, 1991), 137–8. There are of course more sceptical views, for example that of Serge Gavronsky who, in his introduction to *Towards A New Poetics: Contemporary Writing in France* (Berkeley: University of California Press, 1994) sees the Oulipo as 'a marginal experiment, the last formalist hurrah, as it were'. (page 45, n. 1). The group is still active, comprising to date at least thirty members, and has published forty pamphlets in the series *La Bibliothèque Oulipienne* since 1992.

5. Perloff, *Radical Artifice*, 139.

6. cited by Jean Lescure, 'Petite histoire de l'Oulipo' in *La Littérature potentielle*, p. 33. Translated in Motte, *Oulipo: A Primer*, p. 38.

7. ibid. p. 34.

8. Queneau was briefly involved with the Surrealists, but was one of many expelled by André Breton: an experience which much later led to the

Oulipo's strict policy against excommunication. For an account of the affair, see Mark Polizzotti, *Revolution of the Mind: The Life of André Breton* (London: Bloomsbury, 1995) 313, 327.

9. See Georges Perec, 'Histoire du lipogramme' in *La Littérature potentielle*, 73–89. Translated in *Oulipo: A Primer*, 97–108.

10. Alfred Jarry, *Gestes et opinions du docteur Faustroll, pataphysicien* (Paris: Fasquelle, 1955), 16–18. Furthermore, chapter 19, on the Island of 'Ptyx', is a prose poem dedicated to the older writer.

11. Ross Chambers, 'An Address in the Country: Mallarmé and the Kinds of Literary Context', *French Forum*, 11 (1986), 199–215; Jacques Roubaud, *La vieillesse d'Alexandre: essai sur quelques états récents du vers français* (Paris: François Maspero, 1978), Chapter 2: 'Crise de vers' 37–59; in addition, Roubaud has written specifically on *Un coup de dés* (an article to which I have unfortunately been unable to refer—it is cited in Graham Robb, *Unlocking Mallarmé* (New Haven: Yale University Press), 241 n. 13).

12. Harry Mathews, *A Mid-Season Sky: Poems 1954–1991* (Manchester: Carcanet Press, 1992), 70.

13. Harry Mathews, 'Abanika, traditore?' tr. Marie Chaix, *L'Arc*, 76 (1979) 73–6; revised tr. as 'Le dialecte de la tribu' by Martin Winckler in *Cuisine de pays* (Paris: P.O.L., 1990); 'The Dialect of the Tribe' in Mathews, *Country Cooking and Other Stories* (Providence, RI: Burning Deck, 1980), 39–51. Quotation taken from pp. 44–5.

14. Stéphane Mallarmé, *Œuvres complètes*, ed. Henri Mondor and G. Jean-Aubry (Paris: Gallimard-Pléiade, 1945), 385. Title hereafter cited as *Œuvres complètes*. Translation taken from *Mallarmé*, edited with an introduction and prose translations by Anthony Hartley (Harmondsworth: Penguin, 1965), 201.

15. Quoted in: *Stéphane Mallarmé, Selected Letters of Stéphane Mallarmé*, ed. and tr. Rosemary Lloyd (Chicago: University of Chicago Press, 1988), xi and 39.

16. See David Bellos, *Georges Perec: A Life in Words* (London: Harvill, 1993) 381–4.

17. Michael Temple, *The Name of the Poet* (Exeter: University of Exeter Press, 1995).

18. Georges Perec, *Beaux Présents, Belles Absentes* (Paris: Seuil, 1994), 7.

19. Cited in Henri Mondor, *Vie de Mallarmé* (Paris: Gallimard, 1941), 507. The source is given as Maurice Guillemot, *Villégiatures d'artistes* (Paris: Flammarion, 1898).

20. *Œuvres complètes*, 385. Translation from Hartley, *Mallarmé*, 202.

21. *Œuvres complètes*, 455. Translation from Hartley, *Mallarmé*, 209.

22. *Œuvres complètes*, 663. Translated by Bradford Cook in *Mallarmé:*

Selected Prose Poems, Essays, and Letters. (Baltimore: Johns Hopkins Press, 1956), 15.

23. *Œuvres complètes*, 380. Translation in Cook, *Mallarmé*, 26.

24. Jacques Scherer, *Le 'Livre' de Mallarmé: premières recherches sur des documents inédits* (Paris: Gallimard, 1957), especially the section 'Grandeur et servitude de l'analyse combinatoire', 85–90.

25. Bens, *OuLiPo 1960–1963*, 194.

26. ibid., p. 234.

27. See, for example, the discussion of Roussel in Alastair Brotchie and Andrew Thomson (eds), *Atlas Anthology 4—Raymond Roussel: Life Death and Works* (London, Atlas Press, 1987), and the essays in the English translation of Roussel's *How I Wrote Certain of My Books*, ed. Trevor Winkfield (repr. Boston, MA: Exact Change, 1995).

28. 'Crise de vers', in *Œuvres complètes*, 364. Translation from Hartley, *Mallarmé*, 167.

29. 'Crise de vers', in *Œuvres complètes*, 363. Translation from Cook, *Mallarmé*, 37.

30. 'Crise de vers', in *Œuvres complètes*, 363. Translation from Hartley, *Mallarmé*, 165.

31. See Temple, *The Name of the Poet*, cited above, and Graham Robb, *Unlocking Mallarmé* (New Haven and London: Yale U.P., 1996), 14–31, especially the discussion of one the 'Loisirs de la Poste', which finds 'a hidden word, a double etymological pun, an anagram and an allusion to a synonym' in a twenty-eight syllable 'address' (p. 20).

32. Malcolm Bowie, *Mallarmé and the Art of Being Difficult* (Cambridge: C.U.P., 1978), 66. /see also n. 77, pp. 170–71 for his examples of such criticism. Bowie's discussion of 'Prose' is a useful complement to the work of Clive Scott mentioned below (n. 41).

33. ibid., 68.

34. Georges Perec, 'Histoire du lipogramme' in *La Littérature potentielle*, 75. Translated in *Oulipo: A Primer*, 98–9.

35. *Œuvres complètes*, 139. Translated in Marian Zwerling Sugano, *The Poetics of the Occasion: Mallarmé and the Poetry of Circumstance* (Stanford: Stanford U.P., 1992), 176. Marian Zwerling Sugano also makes the link with the Oulipo and permutational poetics, see *The Poetics of the Occasion*, 255 n. 8.

36. Bens, *OuLiPo 1960–1963*, p. 29. The occasion was the third of the Oulipian monthly meetings on January 13th 1961. Queneau's demonstration is included in the essay 'Littérature potentielle' (see n. 1 above).

37. Raymond Queneau, 'Littérature potentielle', 335–6. Prose translation in Motte, *Oulipo: A Primer*, p. 59, verse translation by M. Temple.

38. The mesostic uses the letters of an author's name to select portions of text from a work, so that the name is spelled out vertically on the page when the fragments are presented. The length of fragment, however, is left to Cage's discretion: the conflation of applied rule and creative decision produces a new text from a source text which is part programmed, part chosen. See Marjorie Perloff, *Radical Artifice*, 150.
39. Graham Robb, *Unlocking Mallarmé*, 64.
40. Stéphane Mallarmé, *Correspondance 1862–1892* ed. Henri Mondor and Lloyd James Austin, 9 vols. (Paris: Gallimard, 1959–1983), I:278. *Translation from Selected Letters of Stéphane Mallarmé*, 86–7.
41. Queneau, 'Littérature potentielle', 337, translated in Motte, *Oulipo: A Primer*, 60. The question of rhyme has been addressed with great insight and scrupulous attention in the work of Clive Scott, e.g. *French Verse-Art: A Study* (1980), or *The Riches of Rhyme* (1988), among others.
42. *La Littérature potentielle*, 181–5. The title of the section, 'La Redondance Chez Phane Armé' inadvertently prefigures the syllabic fragmentations of the name which pervades Mallarmé's texts as discussed in Michael Temple's study *The Name of the Poet*.
43. Raymond Queneau, 'Littérature potentielle', 339–40, translated in Motte, *Oulipo: A Primer*, 62.
44. Allen Thiher, *Raymond Queneau* (Boston: Twayne, 1985), 63–4.
45. Harry Mathews, 'Vanishing Point' in *Immeasurable Distances: The Collected Essays* (Venice, CA: Lapis Press, 1991), 227.
46. *Atlas de littérature potentielle*, p. 286.
47. Harry Mathews, 'L'Algorithme de Mathews', in *Atlas de littérature potentielle*, 97.
48. ibid. p. 99.
49. ibid. p. 99.
50. Bens, *OuLiPo 1960–1963*, 208–11
51. Bens, *OuLiPo 1960–1963*, 158.

Chapter Nine

1. Mallarmé, 'Richard Wagner, rêverie d'un poète français', from *Divagations*, in Yves Bonnefoy (ed.), *Igitur, Divagations, Un coup de dés* (Paris: Gallimard-Poésie, 1976), 169, hereinafter cited as *Divigations*; trans. in Bojan Bujic, ed., *Music in European Thought, 1851–1912* (Cambridge: Cambridge University Press, 1988), 243. For early French essays championing Wagner, see Hector Berlioz, 'Concerts de Richard Wagner, la musique de l'avenir', *Journal des débats* (9 February, 1860), and Charles Baudelaire, 'Richard Wagner et *Tannhäuser* à Paris', *Revue européenne* (1 April, 1861); both essays reprinted in translation in Bujic,

Music in European Thought. For an excellent recent appraisal of Baudelaire's admiration of Wagner see Philippe Lacoue-Labarthe, *Musica Ficta (Figures of Wagner)* (Stanford: Stanford University Press, 1994), 1–40. This paper elaborates upon ideas broached in an earlier work entitled 'Modern Poetics of Chance: Boulez, Mallarmé, Cage'. That paper was presented at the conference 'Mallarmé: Music, Arts, and Letters' held at Indiana University, September, 1994 and is published in the proceedings, *Yearbook of Comparative and General Literature*, 42 (1994), 70–82. Thanks go to Carlo Caballero, Mary Shaw, and Michael Temple for innumerable comments and insights offered on earlier drafts of this paper, to Laura Kuhn for making the John Cage Trust available to me at odd hours and answering biographical questions about Cage, to M.C. Richards for a phone interview about Cage, and to Mary Davis, Tracy Fernandez, and Leslie Ross for helpful exchanges along the way.

2. Mallarmé, 'Richard Wagner' in *Divagations*, 174.
3. Trans. in Bujic, *Music in European Thought*, 245.
4. Two important recent studies have influenced my reading of Mallarmé's Wagner essay in the emphasis they place on Mallarmé's conception of theatre: Lacoue-Labarthe, *Musica Ficta*, 41–84 and Mary Lewis Shaw, *Performance in the Texts of Mallarmé: The Passage from Art to Ritual* (University Park, PA: The Pennsylvania State University Press, 1993).
5. Théodore de Wyzéwa, 'La musique descriptive', *Revue wagnérienne* 1 (1885), 77; translation from Bujic, *Music in European Thought*, 249–50.
6. Charles Baudelaire, 'Correspondances', in *Les fleurs du mal*, ed. Claude Pichois (Paris: Gallimard, 1972), 38.
7. Mallarmé, 'Richard Wagner, rêverie d'un poëte français', *Revue wagnérienne*, 1 (1885), 195–200 and *Divagations*, 168–76; trans. in Bujic, *Music in European Thought*, 242–6.
8. Mallarmé, 'Quant au livre', in *Divagations*, 270.
9. This discussion has benefited from Carlo Caballero, 'Mallarmé and the Idea of Pure Music', paper read at the 110th Convention of the Modern Language Association, San Diego, California, 27 December 1994. I greatly appreciate his generosity in sharing it with me.
10. Victor Cousin, *Histoire des derniers systèmes de la philosophie moderne sur les idées du vrai, du beau, et du bien* (Paris: Didier, 1846), 196–204. I thank Carlo Caballero for pointing me toward Cousin.
11. Mallarmé, 'Crise de vers' in *Divagations*, 250.
12. 'le vers libre et le poëme en prose. Leur réunion s'accomplit sous une influence, je sais, étrangère, celle de la Musique entendue au concert; on en retrouve plusieurs moyens m'ayant semblé appartenir aux Lettres, je les reprends', ('free verse and the prose poem. Their coming together

has come about under the influence—foreign, I know—of Music heard in the concert hall. One finds [in music] several methods which seem to me to have belonged to Letters, so I am taking them back,') Mallarmé, Preface to *Un coup de dés*, in *Œuvres complètes*, ed. Henri Mondor and G. Jean-Aubry (Paris: Gallimard-Pléiade, 1945), 456. Hereinafter cited as *Œuvres complètes*.

13. *Œuvres complètes*, 456.
14. *Œuvres complètes*, 455.
15. Kathleen Henderson Staudt, 'The Poetics of "Black on White": Stéphane Mallarmé's "Un coup de dés"' in *Ineffability: Naming the Unnamable from Dante to Beckett*, ed. Peter S. Hawkins and Anne Howland Schotter (New York: AMS Press, 1984), 151.
16. Mallarmé in a letter to Gustave Kahn, *Correspondance*, eds Henri Mondor and Lloyd James Austin, 11 vols. (Paris: Gallimard, 1959–85), vol. 9, 276.
17. See *Collected Poems: Stéphane Mallarmé*, trans. by Henry Weinfield (Berkeley and Los Angeles: University of California Press, 1994), 176, 179. Hereafter cited as Weinfield.
18. Weinfield, 179.
19. Mallarmé, 'Crayonné au théâtre', in *Divagations*, 179.
20. Shaw, *Performance in the Texts of Mallarmé*, 182.
21. Shaw, 183.
22. Shaw, 183.
23. On avant-garde performance and its roots in Futurism, Dada, and Surrealism, see Shaw, 243–58.
24. Mallarmé, *Œuvres complètes*, 477; trans. Weinfield, 144.
25. See, most importantly, Boulez, 'Sonate que me veux-tu?' and 'Construire une improvisation' in *Points de repère*, ed. Jean-Jacques Nattiez (Paris: Seuil, 1981), in English in *Orientations: Collected Writings*, ed. Jean-Jacques Nattiez, trans. Martin Cooper (Cambridge, Mass.: Harvard University Press, 1986); 'Aléa' originally published in *La nouvelle revue française* 59 (1957), 839–57 and reprinted in *Relevés d'apprenti* (Paris: Seuil, 1966), in English in *Notes of an Apprenticeship*, trans. Herbert Weinstock (New York: Knopf, 1968); and *Par volonté et par hasard* (Paris: Seuil, 1975), in English under the title *Conversations with Célestin Deliège*, trans. anon. (London: Eulenburg, 1976). Publications on the subject of Boulez and Mallarmé are numerous; for a recent and fairly comprehensive bibliography see Mary Breatnach, *Boulez and Mallarmé: A Study in Poetic Influence* (Aldershot: Scolar Press, 1996). The influence of Mallarmé on Boulez is also reviewed in Peter F. Stacey, *Boulez and the Modern Concept* (Lincoln: University of Nebraska Press, 1987), 77–106.

26. Boulez's scores are published by Universal Editions, London. Other pieces nominally influenced by Mallarmé's conception of mobile form in the notes for *Le Livre* include *Livre pour quatuor* (1948–49) and *Structures, deuxième livre* (1956–61).

27. *Relevés d'apprenti*, 181.

28. Boulez, 'Aléa', *La nouvelle revue française*, 840–1; trans. Weinstock in *Notes of an Apprenticeship*, 36–7.

29. Boulez is helped in this regard by the closing chapter of Mary Breatnach's book. See Breatnach, 'From Beethoven and Wagner to Boulez' in *Boulez and Mallarmé*, 141–5. On Boulez's synthesis of tendencies within the Franco-Russian and Austro-German traditions that reach back to Wagner, Mahler, Schoenberg, and Stravinsky, see David Gable, 'Boulez's Two Cultures: The Post-War European Synthesis and Tradition', *Journal of the American Musicological Society* 43 (1990), 426–56.

30. Boulez, 'Aléa', *La nouvelle revue française*, 839–40; trans. from *Notes of an Apprenticeship*, 35.

31. For definitions of 'indeterminate', 'aleatoric', and 'chance', see John Cage, 'Composition as Process: Indeterminacy', in *Silence* (Middletown, CT: Wesleyan University Press, 1961), 35–40. For a recent interpretation of this essay see James Pritchett, *The Music of John Cage* (Cambridge: Cambridge University Press, 1993), 107–9.

32. Mallarmé, *Correspondance*, vol. 1, 137; trans. Weinfield, 169.

33. Pierre Boulez in a letter to John Cage of August, 1951, *Pierre Boulez, John Cage, correspondance et documents*, ed. Jean-Jacques Nattiez (Winterthur: Amadeus Verlag, 1990), 163; trans. from Boulez, *Orientations*, 141.

34. Cage, *Pierre Boulez, John Cage, correspondance*, 163; trans., *Orientations*, 141–2.

35. David Gable, 'Ramifying Connections: An Interview with Pierre Boulez', *The Journal of Musicology*, 4 (1985–86), 112.

36. The course of their relationship is reviewed by Jean-Jacques Nattiez in *Pierre Boulez, John Cage, correspondance*, 13–37.

37. Cage, *For the Birds: John Cage in Conversation with Daniel Charles* (Boston: Marion Boyars Press, 1981), 180–1.

38. Cage, *Pierre Boulez, John Cage, correspondance*, 151.

39. Boulez, 'Aléa', *La nouvelle revue française*, 839; trans. from *Notes of an Apprenticeship*, 35.

40. Cage's interaction with these sources is intelligently reviewed in David W. Patterson, 'Appraising the Catchwords, c. 1942–1959: John Cage's Asian-Derived Rhetoric and the Historical Reference of Black Mountain College', Ph.D. diss., Columbia University, 1996.

41. Jonathan Scott Lee discusses Mallarmé's influence on the chance aesthetics of Cage in 'Mimêsis and Beyond: Mallarmé, Boulez, and Cage' in *Writings about John Cage*, ed. Richard Kostelanetz (Ann Arbor: University of Michigan Press, 1993), 180–212. Another important article that compares the aesthetics of Cage and Mallarmé and consistently observes disjunctions between them is Gerald L. Bruns, 'Poethics: John Cage and Stanley Cavell at the Crossroads of Ethical Theory' in *John Cage: Composed in America*, eds Marjorie Perloff and Charles Junkerman (Chicago: University of Chicago Press, 1994), 213–15, 219.

42. Cage, *Pierre Boulez, John Cage, correspondance*, 154. David Tudor, a pianist and life-long friend of Cage's, premiered Boulez's piano sonatas in America. He studied Artaud in preparation to play Boulez's *Deuxième Sonate pour piano* and would go on to read Mallarmé as he prepared his rendition of the *Troisième Sonate*.

43. Cage, 211.

44. Cage, 215. Boulez's gift may have been a 'thank you' for the copy of Ezra Pound's *Cantos* that Cage had given him in 1950.

45. Scherer, *Le 'Livre' de Mallarmé: Premières recherches sur des documents inédits* (Paris: Gallimard, 1957). Catalogued as part of Cage's library at the John Cage Trust.

46. Cage, *For the Birds*, 180–1; Boulez, *Orientations*, 147. It is important to note that Cage seems to have taken Scherer's edition of the notes for *Le livre* as a finished posthumous edition of *Le livre*, conferring upon it the status of a completed work that it does not carry in literary circles. Perhaps the notes for *Le livre* impressed Cage as something similar to Duchamp's *Green Box*.

47. See van Orden, 'Modern Poetics of Chance', 76–9. As for other settings of *Un coup de dés*, Ronald Surak has recently composed a setting which Mary Shaw kindly brought to my attention.

48. John Cage, *Roaratorio, An Irish Circus on Finnegans Wake*, a book on the production ed. Klaus Schöning (Königstein: Athenäum Verlag, 1982), 85. The score to ____, ____ *Circus on* ____: *means for translating a book into a performance without actors, a performance which is both literary and musical or one or the other* has been published by Edition Peters for Henmar Press, 1979.

49. Cage, *Roaratorio*, 85.

50. Bernard Weinberg, *The Limits of Symbolism: Studies of Five Modern French Poets* (Chicago: University of Chicago Press, 1966), 427.

51. Cage, *Roaratorio*, 79.

52. See James McCalla, 'Sea-Changes: Boulez's *Improvisations sur Mallarmé*', *The Journal of Musicology* 6 (1988), 83–106.

53. Jean-Yves Booseur, *John Cage, suivi d'entretiens avec Daniel Caux et Jean-Yves Bosseur* (Paris: Minerve, 1993), 158.

54. Cage, '26 Statements Re Duchamp', in *A Year from Monday* (Middletown, CT: Wesleyan University Press, 1967), 70–2.

55. *Un coup de dés* was a fundamental text for Duchamp, a poem he thought could explain cubism to uninitiated viewers, for example, and one he referred to sometimes playfully in his own work. See Calvin Tomkins, *Duchamp: A Biography* (New York: Henry Holt and Co., 1996), 160, 209.

56. Duchamp cited in Tomkins, *Duchamp*, 368. I gloss Tomkin's text in my argument.

57. Tomkins, *Duchamp*, 369.

58. Tomkins, *Duchamp*, 396.

59. Tomkins, *Duchamp*, 396.

60. Cited in Tomkins, *Duchamp*, 132.

61. Duchamp, *Catalogue raisonné*, ed. Jean Clair (Paris: Musée National d'Art Moderne, 1977), 60–1.

62. Reproduced in the documentary monograph *John Cage*, ed. Richard Kostelanetz (New York: Praeger Publishers, 1970), between pages 78–9.

63. Richard Kostelanetz *John Cage (ex) plain (ed)* (New York: Schirmer Books, 1996), 105–6. Kostelanetz overemphasizes the notational discontinuity of the work but correctly observes its 'noncentered activity'.

64. Mallarmé, 'Quant au livre' in *Divagations*, 267. On Duchamp and chess see Tomkins, *Duchamp*, 210 ff.

65. *Music for Marcel Duchamp* was background music for Duchamp's appearance in Hans Richter's surrealist film *Dreams that Money Can Buy* (1948), a brief piece for prepared piano employing eight pitches in additive phrase structures reminiscent of the *Sonatas and Interludes for Prepared Piano* (1946–48). *Sculptures Musicales* is a conceptual piece based on the description for a musical sculpture Duchamp included in *Green Box*, which reads (in Cage's translation) 'Sounds lasting and leaving from different points and forming a sounding sculpture which lasts.' Cage's score includes some very non-prescriptive parameters for how to construct the sculpture which recall those Duchamp included on the second version of *Erratum musical*. Cage's *Song Books (Solos for Voice 3–92)*, 2 vols. (New York: Henmar Press, 1970) include several references to Duchamp: No. 23 is a version of *Reunion*; No. 65 employs Duchamp's profile as a melodic contour and the text 'La mariée mise à nu par ses célibataires même', as does No. 70; and No. 91 employs part of the '36 Mesostics Re and not Re Duchamp' as its text. Cage's non-musical compositions referring to Duchamp include the verbal

compositions '26 Statements Re Duchamp' in *A Year from Monday*; '36 Mesostics Re and not Re Duchamp', in *M, Writings '67–'72* (Middletown, CT: Wesleyan University Press, 1973); and 'James Joyce, Marcel Duchamp, Erik Satie: An Alphabet', in *X, Writings '79– '82* (Middletown, CT: Wesleyan University Press, 1990); and the visual works *Chess Pieces* (1944) and *Not Wanting to Say Anything about Marcel* (1969). In its reliance on a dictionary and chance operations, and the fact that here the musician makes a visual piece for an artist who composed a musical one, *Not Wanting to Say Anything about Marcel* strikes me as Cage's response to *Erratum musical*, one version of which he owned. Marjorie Perloff unfortunately misses this connection in her article ' "A duchamp unto my self": "Writing through" Marcel', in *John Cage: Composed in America*, 106–9. Kostelanetz also discusses the piece in his monograph, *John Cage (ex) plain (ed)*, 105–9. For a discussion of *Reunion*, see the recent study of Cage's performance art by William Fetterman, *John Cage's Theatre Pieces: Notations and Performances* (Amsterdam: Hardwood Academic Publishers, 1996), 90–93.

66. Cage, *Silence*.
67. On the open work, see Thomas DeLio, *Circumscribing the Open Universe* (Lanham, MD: University Press of America, 1984).
68. Mallarmé, *Œuvres complètes*, 456.
69. Pousseur, *Coups de dés en echos* (Milan: Edizioni Suvini Zerboni, 1993).
70. Cage, *Silence*, 8.
71. Mallarmé, *Œuvres complètes*, 455.
72. *Œuvres complètes*, 460.
73. Weinfield, 128.
74. Mallarmé, *Œuvres complètes*, 466–7.
75. Weinfield, 134.

Chapter Ten

1. Mallarmé, 'Prose' in *Œuvres complètes*, ed. Henri Mondor and G. Jean-Aubry (Paris: Gallimard-Pléiade, 1945), 55-6. Translation taken from *Mallarmé* ed. and trans. A. Hartley (Harmondsworth: Penguin, 1965), 62. These lines are also cited as the epigraph, and provide the pretext for the title of Kristeva's 'Mémoire' in *L'Infini*, 1 (1983), translated as 'My Memory's Hyperbole', *New York Literary Forum* (1984), 12–13.
2. *Révolution du langage poétique* (Paris: Gallimard, 1974); translated by M. Waller as *Revolution in Poetic Language* (New York: Columbia University Press, 1984).
3. Kristeva, 'Polylogue' in *Polylogue* (Paris: Seuil, 1976), 176; 'The Novel

as Polylogue', in *Desire in Language: A Semiotic Approach to Literature and Art*, trans. T. Gora, A. Jardine, L. S. Roudiez (Oxford: Blackwell, 1980), 162.

4. *Polylogue*, 176; *Desire in Language*, 162.

5. Kristeva's dynamic model corresponds point for point to Bataille's theorization of the erotic and of transgression in *L'érotisme* (Paris: Minuit, 1957); *Eroticism* (London: Marion Boyars, 1987). See my *The Time of Theory* (Oxford: Oxford University Press, 1996) for a discussion of Kristeva's debts to Bataille.

6. Cf. Kristeva, 'Le sujèt en procès' in *Polylogue*; 'The Subject in Process' in *The Tel Quel Reader*, ed. and trans. P. ffrench and R.-F. Lack (London: Routledge, 1998).

7. The thematics of the 'traversée' are introduced in Sollers's 'Dante et la traversée de l'écriture', in *Logiques* (Paris: Seuil, 1967); 'Dante and the Traversal of Writing' in *Writing and the Experience of Limits* trans. D. Hayman, P. Barnard (New York: Columbia University Press, 1983). These thematics are pursued in Kristeva's *La traversée des signes* (Paris: Seuil, 1978).

8. Cf. Kristeva, *Révolution du langage poétique* (Paris: Seuil, 1974), 210 and *passim*. The English translation of this book includes only the first of three sections, excluding 'Le dispositif sémiotique du texte' and 'L'état et le mystère'. Translations from the French of these missing sections are therefore my own.

9. This and the following two citations from Mallarmé, *Œuvres complètes*, 474–5; *Mallarmé*, trans. and ed. A. Hartley, 230–3.

10. Ibid.

11. Ibid.

12. Kristeva, *Séméiotiké* (Paris: Seuil, 1969), 206; translation my own.

13. *Séméiotiké*, 212.

14. Kristeva, *Le temps sensible: Proust et l'expérience littéraire* (Paris: Gallimard, 1994), 360–2 and 399–429.

15. *Le temps sensible*, 354; translation my own.

16. *Le temps sensible*, 262.

17. *Le temps sensible*, 262.

18. Kristeva, *Révolution du langage poétique*, 373; Revolution in Poetic Language, 373.

19. *Révolution du langage poétique*, 64; *Revolution in Poetic Language*, 64.

20. *Révolution du langage poétique*, 65; *Revolution in Poetic Language*, 65.

21. J.-P. Richard, *L'univers imaginaire de Mallarmé* (Paris: Seuil, 1963).

22. Kristeva, *Révolution du langage poétique*, 189–97; *Revolution in Poetic Language*, 217–26.

23. Kristeva, *Histoires d'amour* (Paris: Denoël, 1983), 128–31; *Tales of Love*,

trans. L. S. Roudiez (New York: Columbia University Press, 1987), 135.

24. *Histoires d'amour*, 130; *Tales of Love*, 135.
25. Mallarmé, *Œuvres complètes*, 283–4 / *Mallarmé: Selected Prose Poems, Essays and Letters*, trans. and ed. B. Cook (Baltimore: The Johns Hopkins University Press, 1956), 6.
26. Ibid.
27. Kristeva, *Histoires d'amour*, 130; *Tales of Love*, 135.
28. *Histoires d'amour*, 130; *Tales of Love*, 136.
29. *Histoires d'amour*, 130; *Tales of Love*, 134.
30. Kristeva, *Pouvoirs de l'horreur* (Paris: Seuil, 1980), 158; *Powers of Horror* (New York: Columbia University Press, 1982), 134.
31. *Pouvoirs de l'horreur*, 158; *Powers of Horror*, 134.
32. See my article, 'The Corpse of Theory: Excavation of an Encounter: Blanchot / Bataille', in *Parallax*, 4 (Spring 1997).
33. J. Paulhan, *Les fleurs de Tarbes ou la Terreur dans les Lettres* (Paris: Gallimard, 1941).
34. Kristeva, 'Poésie et négativité' in *Séméiotikè*, 185–216.
35. 'Poésie et négativité', 187; translation my own.
36. 'Poésie et négativité', 199.
37. 'Poésie et négativité', 197.
38. 'Poésie et négativité', 207.
39. 'Poésie et négativité', 298.
40. 'Poésie et négativité', 190.
41. 'Poésie et négativité', 189.
42. See Suzanne Guerlac's, 'The Sublime in Theory', in *Modern Language Notes*, 106 (1991) and her excellent book *The Impersonal Sublime* (Stanford, CA: Stanford University Press, 1990) for a discussion of Kristeva's theories in relation to the notion of the sublime.
43. For more extensive histoires of *Tel Quel* group and of Kristeva's involvement see my *The Time of Theory*, and *The Tel Quel Reader*, ed. and trans. P. ffrench and R. F. Lack.
44. Kristeva, 'Mémoire' in *L'Infini* 1 (1983); 'My Memory's Hyperbole' in *New York Literary Forum* (1984).
45. P. Sollers, 'Littérature et totalité' in *Logiques* (Paris: Seuil, 'Collection Tel Quel', (1968); originally in *Tel Quel* (26 (Summer 1966); 'Literature and Totality' in *Writing and the Experience of Limits*.
46. Sollers, 'Littérature et totalité', 67; 'Literature and Totality', 63.
47. 'Littérature et totalité', 68; 'Literature and Totality', 64.
48. 'Littérature et totalité', 69; 'Literature and Totaltiy', 65.
49. 'Literature and Totality', 66; 'C'est que la littérature, Mallarmé le

découvre, est beaucoup plus que la littérature' ('Littérature et totalité', 70).

50. 'Littérature et totalité', 72; 'Literature and Totality', 67.
51. 'Littérature et totalité', 78; 'Literature and Totality', 75.
52. 'Littérature et totalité', 86; 'Literature and Totality', 83.
53. 'Littérature et totalité', 86; 'Literature and Totality', 84.
54. 'Littérature et totalité', 86.
55. Kristeva, *Révolution du langage poetique*, 209–93. This book analyses Mallarmé and Lautréamont, whose works are analysed in parallel. In a similar manner, Kristeva read Artaud and Bataille together two years earlier at a *Tel Quel* colloquium.
56. *Révolution du langage poetique*, 276–9.
57. Cited in *Révolution du langage poetique*, 239.
58. Cf. R. Barthes, *S/Z* (Paris: Seuil, 'Collection Tel Quel', 1970), 15 / *S/Z* trans. R. Miller (Oxford: Blackwell, 1970), 13–14.
59. Cf. Derrida, *La dissémination* (Paris: Seuil, 'Collection Tel Quel', 1972); *Dissemination* trans. B. Johnson (Chicago: University of Chicago Press, 1981), *passim* but especially 'La double séance'; 'The Double Session', on Mallarmé and Plato, given as a paper at *Tel Quel*'s 'Group for Theoretical Studies'.
60. Cited in *Révolution du langage poétique*, 225.
61. *Révolution du langage poetique*, 236 and 240 onwards.
62. *Révolution du langage poetique*, 239.
63. Mallarmé, 'Autobiographie' in *Œuvres complètes*, 663; *Mallarmé: Selected Prose Poems, Essays and Letters*, 16.
64. Cf. G. Genette, *Mimologiques* (Paris: Seuil, 1976); *Mimologics* trans. T. E. Morgan (Lincoln: University of Nebraska Press, 1995); R. G. Cohn, 'Mallarmé contre Genette' in *Tel Quel* 69 (Spring 1977).
65. Mallarmé, *Œuvres complètes*, 663; *Mallarmé: Selected Prose Poems, Essays and Letters*, 16–17.
66. Mallarmé, 'Le mystère dans les lettres', *Œuvres complètes* 368; *Mallarmé: Selected Prose Poems, Essays and Letters*, 33.

Chapter Eleven

1. Jérôme Thélot, 'Le Premier Poème', *Sud*, 15 (1985; Colloque 'Yves Bonnefoy', Cerisy-la Salle), 143–53. Galway Kinnell's translation of 'Je te voyais courir sur des terraces' is from Bonnefoy, *On the Motion and Immobility of Douve* (Newcastle upon Tyne: Bloodaxe, 1992).
2. Yves Bonnefoy, *Le Nuage rouge* (Paris: Mercure de France, 1992), 195. Unless otherwise indicated, all translations are my own.
3. Yves Bonnefoy, *L'Improbable et autres essais* (Paris: Gallimard, 1992),

263: 'On ne s'étonne d'y [in *La Chanson de Roland*] voir apparaître ce vers décasyllabe si "objectif", lui dont les quatre pieds initiaux engagent si fermement la conscience dans la stabilité du savoir, cependant que sa deuxième partie, dans son rythme ternaire infus, consent au temps humain par un acte de sympathie, mais pour le reprendre dans l'éternel' ('We are not surprised to encounter [in *La Chanson de Roland*] the intensely "objective" decasyllabic line, whose four initial syllables install consciousness so firmly in the stability of knowledge, while its second part, with its innate ternary rhythm, admits human time by an act of sympathy, but only to re-absorb it into the eternal'). Hereinafter cited as *L'Improbable*.

4. In Thélot, *Poétique d'Yves Bonnefoy* (Geneva: Droz, 1983), 256, Bonnefoy says that his remarks about the decasyllable 'concernent le 4/6 comme il existe dans la tradition poétique–et en effet je veux, personnellement, autre chose, que dit 6/4' ('concern the 4/6 as it exists in the verse tradition–and in fact I, personally, want something other, which is expressed by 6/4'). Hereinafter cited as *Poétique d'Yves Bonnefoy*.

5. As Benoît de Cornulier, *Art poëtique: Notions et problèmes de métrique* (Lyon: Presses Universitaires de Lyon, 1995), 22, puts it: 'Ce qui est métrique n'est donc pas *un* vers, mais *des* vers, par équivalence mutuelle; et ce qu'on appelle le *mètre* d'un vers singulier consiste moins en la conformité de cette expression singulière avec une norme abstraite qu'en un rapport réciproque d'*équivalence contextuelle en nombre syllabique* entre plusieurs suites verbales voisines disjointes' ('What is metrical is not the single verse-line, but a sequence of lines, by virtue of their mutual equivalence; and what is called the 'metre' of an isolated line consists less in the fact that this isolated set of words conforms to an abstract norm than in a reciprocal relationship of *contextual syllabic equivalence* between several adjacent but separate verbal strings').

6. Mallarmé, *Œuvres complètes*, ed. Henri Mondor and G. Jean-Aubry (Paris: Gallimard-Pléiade, 1945), 362: 'Les fidèles à l'alexandrin, notre hexamètre, desserrent intérieurement ce mécanisme rigide et puéril de sa mesure; l'oreille, affranchie d'un compteur factice, connaît une jouissance à discerner, seule, toutes les combinaisons possibles, entre eux, de douze timbres' ('Those faithful to the alexandrine, our hexameter, loosen this rigid and puerile mechanism's measure from within; the ear, set free from this artificial meter, experiences pleasure in discerning, on its own, all the possible combinational permutations of twelve notes'). Hereinafter cited as *Œuvres complètes*.

7. Clive Scott, 'Mallarmé's Mercurial E', *Forum for Modern Language Studies*, 34 (1998), 43–55.

8. Mallarmé, *Correspondance complète 1862–1871 suivie de Lettres sur la poésie 1872–1898 avec des lettres inédites*, ed. Bertrand Marchal, pref. Yves Bonnefoy (Paris: Gallimard, 1995), 636. Hereinafter cited as *Correspondance*.

9. Jean-Pol Madou, 'La Poétique d'Yves Bonnefoy: Un défi au "nihilisme" mallarméen', in *Yves Bonnefoy: Poésie, art et pensée*, ed. Yves-Alain Favre (Pau: Université de Pau, 1983), 33, expresses the burden of these last lines thus: 'L'évidence chez Bonnefoy, c'est le soleil de la mort que toute chose porte en son sein, la fulgurance de la foudre qui scelle de ses lettres de feu la vérité d'un paysage, la rupture d'une artère d'où gicle le sang' ('Evidence, in Bonnefoy's work, is the sun of death which everything carries within it, the dazzling brightness of the lightning which seals the truth of a landscape with its fiery letters, the rupture of an artery from which the blood spurts').

10. Bonnefoy, *L'Improbable*, 127, describes the significance of Rimbaud's exploitation of the *impair*, this 'blessure inguérissable' ('incurable wound'), thus: 'Il a permis une lutte et, au-delà, une entente, don't l'e muet est la cheville secrète' ('He made a conflict [with the *vers pair*] possible, and beyond that conflict, a new understanding, whose secret linchpin is the mute e').

11. Paul Valéry, *Œuvres*, ed. Jean Hytier, 2 vols (Paris: Gallimard-Pléiade: 1957, 1960), I, 623.

12. Bonnefoy, *Le Nuage rouge*, 201.

13. Marceline Desbordes-Valmore, *Poésies*, ed. Yves Bonnefoy (Paris: Gallimard-Poésie, 1983), 27.

14. Roland Barthes, *Le Plaisir du texte* (Paris: *Éditions du Seuil*, 1973), 105.

15. Cartier-Bresson defines the 'decisive moment' as follows: 'We work in unison with movement as though it were a presentiment of the way in which life itself unfolds. But inside movement there is one moment at which the elements in motion are in balance. Photography must seize upon this moment and hold immobile the equilibrium of it' ('The Decisive Moment' in *The Art of Photography 1839–1989*, ed. Mike Weaver (London: Royal Academy of Arts, 1989), 266).

16. Bonnefoy, 'Foreword', in *Henri Cartier-Bresson Photographer*, ed. Robert Delpire (London: Thames and Hudson, 1980), 5. Hereinafter cited as *Henri Cartier-Bresson*.

17. Bonnefoy, *Entretiens sur la poésie (1972–1990)* (Paris: Mercure de France, 1990), 136. Hereinafter cited as *Entretiens*.

18. Desbordes-Valmore, *Poésies*, 18.

19. Bonnefoy, *Entretiens*, 244. Elsewhere, Bonnefoy connects this transformation of the common into the proper with the preservation of 'l'épaisseur d'être' of place: 'Le langage est bien au travail, qui différencie

le lieu, mais c'est par des noms, des noms propres qui en préservent l'épaisseur d'être, non par les mots conceptuels, qui défont l'unité du monde' ('Language is indeed at work, differentiating the place, but it is by names, by proper nouns which preserve the density of its being, not by concepts, which unravel the world's unity') (*La Vérité de parole*, 52).

20. Roland Barthes, 'Proust et les noms', in *To Honor Roman Jakobson: Essays on the Occasion of his Seventieth Birthday*, 2 vols (The Hague: Mouton, 1967), I, 152–3.

21. Mallarmé, *Vers de circonstance avec des inédits*, ed. Bertrand Marchal, pref. Yves Bonnefoy (Paris: Gallimard-Poésie, 1996), 35–6. Hereinafter cited as *Vers de circonstance*.

22. Richard Pevear's translation of 'Une pierre' is from Bonnefoy, *Poems 1959–1975* (New York: Vintage, 1985). Jean Starobinski's commentary cited below is from his preface to Bonnefoy, *Poèmes* (Paris: Gallimard-Poésie, 1982), 7–8.

23. Frédéric Deloffre, 'Versification traditionnelle et versification libérée d'après un recueil d'Yves Bonnefoy', in *Le Vers Français au 20ᵉ siècle*, ed. Monique Parent (Paris: Klincksieck, 1967), 43–64.

24. Bonnefoy, 'On the Translation of Form in Poetry', *World Literature*, 53 (1979), 379.

25. William Shakespeare, *Hamlet, Le Roi Lear*, trans. and pref. Yves Bonnefoy (Paris: Gallimard, 1978), 8. Hereinafter cited as *Hamlet, Le Roi Lear*.

26. W. B. Yeats, *Quarante-cinq poèmes suivis de La Résurrection*, trans. and pref. Yves Bonnefoy (Paris: Gallimard-Poésie, 1993), 17.

27. Others have argued that Bonnefoy's admiration for Mallarmé is unmistakable, and that the two poets have much in common, as is evidenced in a shared thematics and lexicon (see R. A. York, 'Bonnefoy and Mallarmé: Aspects of Intertextuality', *Romanic Review*, 71 (1980), 307–18, and Brigitta Coenen-Mennemeier, 'Räume und Figuren bei Mallarmé und Bonnefoy', in *Heinrich Lausberg zum Gedenken: Akten eines wissenschaftlichen Kolloquiums*, ed. Wolfgang Babilas (Münster: Nodus Publikationen, 1995), 159–68).

Index to Works by Stéphane Mallarmé

Index of Names

Lacoue-Labarthe, Philippe, 259n
Lautréamont, Comte de (pseud. of
  Isidore Ducasse), 183, 186, 267n
Léautaud, Paul, 26
Lee, Jonathan Scott, 262
Lefébure, Eugène, 205
Le Lionnais, François, 144, 145,
  149
Linnaeus, Carolus (Carl von
  Linné), 73

Madou, Jean-Pol, 269n
Mallarmé, Anatole (son), 25
Mallarmé, Elizabeth Félicie
  (mother), 49, 54
Mallarmé, Geneviève (daughter),
  5, 49, 232n, 235n
Mallarmé, Marie (wife), 5, 49,
  232n, 234n
Manet, Eugène (brother of
  Édouard Manet), 34, 231n
Manet, Julie (daughter of
  Eugène), 231n
Marchal, Bertrand, 55, 56
Margueritte, Paul, 133, 142, 252n
Marinetti, Filippo Tommaso, 166
Mathews, Harry, 146, 147, 151,
  157–8
Mauclair, Camille, 21
Mendès, Catulle, 25
Michaux, Henri, 101
Millan, Gordon, 54, 244n
Miller, Paul Allen, 121
Minahen, Charles D., 1, 9, 22,
  227n
Mockel, Albert, 21
Molière (Jean-Baptiste Poquelin),
  155
Mondor, Henri, 17, 54, 81,
  86–101, 206, 245n
Morisot, Berthe, 231n
Motte Jr., Warren F., 255n

Newmark, Kevin, 248n
Nietzsche, Friedrich Wilhelm, 65,
  124–5, 230n
Novalis (pseud. of Friedrich von
  Hardenberg), 81, 106, 245n,
  246n

Oulipo, 20, 143–159, 255n
Ovid, 123

Paulhan, Jean, 188
Pearson, Roger, 113
Peirce, Charles S., 215
Perec, Georges, 147, 151, 153,
  264n
Perloff, Marjorie, 144–5, 147,
  264n
Plato, 71, 113, 126–9, 132–6,
  141–2, 189, 251n, 253n, 267n
Poe, Edgar Allan, 37, 55, 119,
  146, 189
Poincaré, Raymond, 230n
Ponge, Francis, 2, 228n, 252n
Poulet, Georges, 97
Pound, Ezra, 154, 262n
Pousseur, Henri, 178–9
Proust, Marcel, 184–5

Queneau, Raymond, 144, 152,
  153–6, 158, 159, 255n

Rabelais, François, 152
Racine, Jean, 155, 122
Ray, Man, 166
Régnier, Henri de, 3, 54, 64
Renard, Jules, 207
Renoir, Auguste, 5
Richard, Jean-Pierre, 79, 81, 97,
  138, 143, 159, 186, 206, 231n
Richter, Hans, 263n
Rimbaud, Arthur, 2, 13, 35, 65–6,
  103, 188, 226, 238n, 269n